R PATROL
LONG RANGE
DESERT GROUP

R PATROL
LONG RANGE
DESERT GROUP

BRENDAN O'CARROLL

Pen & Sword
MILITARY

First published in Great Britain in 2024 by
PEN & SWORD MILITARY
An imprint of
Pen & Sword Books Ltd
Yorkshire – Philadelphia

Copyright © Brendan O'Carroll, 2024

ISBN 978-1-03610-974-5

The right of Brendan O'Carroll to be identified as author of this work has been asserted by him in accordance with the Copyright, Designs and Patents Act 1988.

A CIP catalogue record for this book is available from the British Library.

All rights reserved. No part of this book may be reproduced or transmitted in any form or by any means, electronic or mechanical including photocopying, recording or by any information storage and retrieval system, without permission from the Publisher in writing.

Typeset by Concept, Huddersfield, West Yorkshire, HD4 5JL
Printed and bound in England by CPI Group (UK) Ltd, Croydon CR0 4YY

Pen & Sword Books Limited incorporates the imprints of Atlas, Archaeology, Aviation, Discovery, Family History, Fiction, History, Maritime, Military, Military Classics, Politics, Select, Transport, True Crime, Air World, Frontline Publishing, Leo Cooper, Remember When, Seaforth Publishing, The Praetorian Press, Wharncliffe Local History, Wharncliffe Transport, Wharncliffe True Crime and White Owl.

For a complete list of Pen & Sword titles please contact
PEN & SWORD BOOKS LIMITED
47 Church Street, Barnsley, South Yorkshire, S70 2AS, England
E-mail: enquiries@pen-and-sword.co.uk
Website: www.pen-and-sword.co.uk
or
PEN AND SWORD BOOKS
1950 Lawrence Rd, Havertown, PA 19083, USA
E-mail: Uspen-and-sword@casematepublishers.com
Website: www.penandswordbooks.com

Contents

Acknowledgements vi
Introduction vii

1. The Long Range Patrol: Formation 1
2. One Man's Story 21
3. First Missions 35
4. The Long Range Desert Group 55
5. Libyan Taxi Service 71
6. With the SAS 89
7. Supporting the Eighth Army 105
8. With the Free French at Zouar 119
9. Road Watch 141
10. Air Attack 165
11. Ground Actions 185
12. On Leave 207
13. R Patrol Gunner/Medical Orderly 221
14. Buster Gibb Remembers 233
15. The Aftermath 255

Appendix I: The LRP Lament 277
Appendix II: R Patrol Truck names and Officers 278
Appendix III: A Selection of Images from Trooper Frank McKeown's
        Photo Album 279

Bibliography 291
Index 293

Acknowledgements

To my wife Margaret for her ongoing support and encouragement in the writing of these historical accounts, and also undertaking the onerous job of proof-reading; a big task that she did with great skill and patience. Thank you for all you do to make these books possible.

To my wonderful children Diana Hofmann, Michelle Subritzky and Patrick O'Carroll for their continued loving support and technical expertise with my projects.

Huge thanks to Nicholas Hofmann for his technical skills in restoring the quality of some of the original photos, several of which were in poor condition. Most of these were taken by LRDG men with their personal cameras, so many of the images are not of the same quality as those taken by official photographers.

My sincere thanks to Bruce Hammond for his kindness in providing images from his father Bill Hammond's photo albums and allowing me access to some of his father's LRDG artifacts to photograph. To Dennis and Alex Gibb and the Gibb family for access to the LRDG photo albums of their father, Buster Gibb. Also, to Duncan McKeown for kindly supplying images from his father Frank McKeown's album that appear in Appendix III of this work. Finally, to Fiona and Liana Ashenden for contributing photos and artifacts from their father/grandfather Ron Davies.

My gratitude once again to the family members of the late LRDG veterans for their permission to publish personal wartime photos and stories: Leighton Burne, Wayne Burnnand, Ian Chard, Warren Davis, Heather Dodunski, Brian Ellis, Jason and Nik Magerkorth, Myles and Maxine Gedye, Jann Keightley, Richard Lawson, Filani Macassey, Dave Mackay, Dana Pratt, Max Saunders, Roger Steele, Rosemary Steele and Charlie Waetford.

I also wish to acknowledge others for their contribution in supplying photographs, information and sources that helped to make this work possible. They are Bob Amos-Jones, Roberto Chiarvetto, Charlie Down, Paul Farmer, Kuno Gross, David Harrison, Andre Hofmann, Glen Hunter, Imperial War Museum (London), Phillip James, Mike Leet, Brent Nunn, Dave McCann, Ethan O'Carroll and Margot O'Carroll, Geoff Oldham, Jonathan Pittaway, Ronan Reid, Ian Scown, Isabelle Subritzky, Emily Subritzky, the late Jack Valenti of the LRDG Preservation Society and Simon Willis.

Brendan O'Carroll
2024

Introduction

Since 2000 I have published eight Long Range Desert Group-related books, mostly focused on the activities of the New Zealand patrols (W, T and R) within the unit. Half of those works dealt directly with some specific individuals and the activities of T Patrol; for example *The Barce Raid*, *Bearded Brigands*, *Incident at Jebel Sherif* and *Fighting with the LRDG*. This is only because these stories were readily accessible for publication. My other books served more as a general LRDG overview; a photographic reference work.

To complete my study of the New Zealanders in the LRDG, this volume will tell the story of R Patrol, which received much less attention in my previous books. It will not be a comprehensive examination of the history of the patrol, but an insightful overview of its formation, selected missions and activities as told mostly in the words of the participants themselves. This is by way of wartime operational reports, diaries, personal letters and interviews conducted with the author and other post-war researchers. This provides a human touch to the story, examining the thoughts and observations of those who were part of the patrol. It is also representative of similar experiences of all those who served, including the British and Southern Rhodesian troops who made up the LRDG.

This narrative is further enhanced by 288 images, including maps and artwork. Most photographs are from personal cameras and sourced from the albums of veterans, so the quality of some of the images is not as sharp as those taken by official photographers. Nonetheless, they still help to illustrate the study.

Within its ranks R Patrol had some very distinguished members who played a significant part in the LRDG tale. New Zealander Lieutenant D.G. (Don) Steele was one of the founding officers of the unit when it was initially known as the Long Range Patrol and was their first R Patrol commander. He was later promoted to major and became the Commanding Officer of A (NZ) Squadron LRDG based at Siwa. His work also included coordinating LRDG/SAS combined operations. Steele was awarded the Order of the British Empire in recognition of his services while in command at Siwa and later at Jalo. His post-war recollections provide a wonderfully descriptive insight into the formation of the unit and the early days of the patrols. Another who joined at the same time was Gunner Claude 'Bluey' Grimsey, a British-born New Zealander who was an artistic and well-educated man who kept a very comprehensive record of the early operations. He also designed both the LRP and LRDG scorpion badges.

Others were both British-born New Zealanders, Captains C.B.H. (Dick) Croucher and L.H. (Tony) Browne. Together they were navigators and joined as lance corporals and eventually rose to the rank of captain. They served with great distinction in the Group until the end of the war. Croucher received a Mention in Despatches and Browne was decorated with a Military Cross, Distinguished Conduct Medal and a Mention in Despatches, plus a civil Order of the British Empire. Their post-war recollections and official reports tell a fascinating story.

One most notable R Patrol leader was a British officer, Captain J.R. (Jake) Easonsmith, who replaced Don Steele as R Patrol commander. He was considered by his peers as the most successful patrol commander in the LRDG and the one for whom the New Zealanders had the greatest respect. A selection of his extraordinary R Patrol missions is described via his Operation Reports. He was awarded the Military Cross in November 1941 for gallantry in action. Later, following promotion to major, he went on to lead T and G Patrols on the famous Barce Raid in September 1942, for which he received the Distinguished Conduct Medal. A year later he was promoted to lieutenant colonel and became Commanding Officer LRDG. He was killed in action in the battle for Leros in the Aegean Dodecanese Islands on 16 November 1943.

Also recorded are the accounts of R Patrol officers Lieutenant J.R. Talbot and Second Lieutenant K.F. McLaughlin, whose close encounters with the enemy are also described, as are the Operation Reports written by Military Medal winners Sergeants L.A. Willcox and C. Waetford in the absence of their captured officers.

Furthermore, to gain a detailed perspective from an NCO's viewpoint, there are the most vividly written observations and stories as told to the author by Alfred Duncan 'Buster' Gibb. He served in both W and R Patrols. During the 1990s he wrote comprehensive letters to the author and on other occasions had animated conversations about his LRDG experiences. This delivers a fascinating personal insight into the everyday life of an LRDG man. He articulated their activities, misdeeds and the daily challenges he faced as an NCO, helping his men to manage the extremes of desert life and warfare behind enemy lines.

W and R Patrol veteran Alf Saunders also shared his recollections with the author. He served alongside Buster as a trooper, and his remembrances provided another view into the early days of the LRDG.

In the main these stories will describe personal recollections of R Patrol members, the formation of the unit, the early missions of the Long Range Patrol (LRP), the vehicles, supplies, weapons and equipment, also the formation of the Long Range Desert Group, serving as a 'Taxi Service' for behind-the-line missions carrying agents, Commandos, military observers, rescuing downed airmen and escaped PoWs. Chapters are also devoted to working with the SAS, supporting the Eighth Army and undertaking the Road Watch. Furthermore, there are dramatic accounts of air attacks and ground actions against enemy convoys and engagements with armoured cars.

The concluding chapters reflect on the troops enjoying leave, the story of being a gunner and medical orderly including an overview of the wellbeing and conditions of the men in the Group. Veteran Buster Gibb describes a vivid selection of reminiscences, and finally to complete the work, I have included some after the desert war and post-war comment.

Chapter One

The Long Range Patrol: Formation

The Long Range Desert Group had its beginnings in July 1940, when Major Ralph Bagnold conceived the unit. He was a British Army signals officer, geographer, and desert explorer. Following the Italian entry into the war in June 1940, Egypt was now considered under threat, as Libya had been an Italian colony since the 1920s. Consequently, the British Middle East GHQ needed urgent intelligence as to the enemy activity in southern Libya close to the Egyptian border.

Bagnold, who along with a small group of fellow explorers ventured into Libya in the 1920s and 30s, where they acquired considerable knowledge of desert travel, navigation, and survival techniques. Armed with these abilities, he offered his services to General Sir Archibald Wavell, Commander-in-Chief Middle East, to lead a patrol far behind the lines to try to establish the Italian dispositions and intentions. With southern Libya well beyond the range of aerial observation, he immediately authorized Bagnold's plans for an overland reconnaissance unit to be formed, with six weeks to recruit and prepare the force. This officially became the No. 1 Long Range Patrol Unit, also known as the LRP.

Bagnold recorded that the desert was a greater danger than any human enemy as failure in that environment might mean death to all those taking part. Therefore he first concluded that men with desert knowledge were needed. With that in mind, he travelled to Palestine to speak to the Australian Corps Commander, General T.A. Blamey about releasing some of his troops to serve in the LRP, preferably Australians from Queensland who were accustomed to a hot environment. However, Blamey refused, not wanting his soldiers under British command. Subsequently Bagnold turned to the New Zealanders who had not yet been deployed and were still based at their training camp at Maadi. On 1 July, Bagnold arranged with General H.M. Wilson and Brigadier E. Puttick to commit NZ troops to the LRP, the first of which arrived in Cairo on 7 July. Its first volunteers answered a call specifying men 'who do not mind a hard life, scanty food, little water, lots of discomfort, and possess stamina and initiative.'

These men had been training in Egypt since their arrival in early 1940 and were available for attachment. Major Bagnold selected the New Zealanders, describing them as 'tougher and more weather beaten, a sturdy basis of sheep farmers, leavened by technicians, property owners and professional men including a few Māori. Also shrewd, dry humoured and curious of every new thing.' The selection of New Zealanders for the task was more curious because they had less experience of desert conditions than any of the other troops available at the time, but under Bagnold's watchful eye they adapted very quickly to the rigours of desert life and warfare. Five officers and eighty-five other ranks from the Second New Zealand Expeditionary Force (2NZEF) were seconded for special patrols' duty. The detachment included eighteen administrative and technical personnel. Consequently for the first six months of its operations the LRP was manned almost entirely by specially selected members from the 2NZEF.

Major Bagnold was the commanding officer who oversaw three patrols. The two fighting patrols were T and W commanded by the pre-war desert explorer Captain P.A. (Pat) Clayton and Captain E.C. (Teddy) Mitford (1st Royal Tank Regiment), respectively; also R Patrol, which was initially intended to carry supplies. It was led by a New Zealander, Second Lieutenant D.G. (Don) Steele, 27th (NZ) MG Battalion 2NZEF. The 'Kiwis' were not expected to command fighting patrols until they gained more experience in the desert. Lieutenant L.B. (Bruce) Ballantyne was the adjutant and quartermaster, while Lieutenant F.B. (Frank) Edmundson was the medical officer. They were both New Zealanders. Lieutenant W.B. (Bill) Kennedy Shaw, who joined from the Colonial Service in Palestine, was the intelligence officer.

The vehicles in the three patrols bore Māori names beginning with the letters W, T and R. Trooper Clarke Waetford was the only Māori in the unit at the time, and Lieutenant J.H. (Jim) Sutherland asked him if he could help with giving the individual vehicles Māori names. His preference was that R Patrol started with 'Roto', the T Patrol with 'Te' and W Patrol with 'Wai'. The trucks were also numbered: for example, W Patrol displayed a white letter and number in a black painted rectangle, 'W2', T Patrol in a black diamond, and R Patrol in a black circle. These were painted on either side of the bonnet. This tactical insignia style was discontinued with the introduction of the Ford trucks in early 1941. The first patrols consisted of twenty-seven to thirty-two men travelling in eleven desert-adapted Chevrolet WA trucks. They were led by a commander's pilot vehicle, a Ford 01 V8 15cwt. Furthermore, each patrol included a wireless truck and a fitter's truck that carried tools and spare parts to enable repairs to be done beyond the range of assistance.

A headquarters' unit oversaw the patrols. In addition there was a Heavy Section (logistical support trucks) under Lieutenant C.A. Holliman. These were employed to transport supplies to bases and to establish forward hidden dumps, which helped to extend the range of operations to great distances.

Second Lieutenant Don Steele was the first commander of R Patrol. In 1949 he recorded his LRDG service recollections for the New Zealand War History Branch archive. His account of the formation of the Long Range Patrol provides an interesting personal perspective on the beginnings of the unit:

> I think it was early July that I first heard of the formation of No. 1 LRP. I remember that we had just come in from an early morning shoot and were having breakfast when the C.O. (Lt. Col. Ingles) came out to our camp off the Suez Road and told me to go at once back to Maadi (2NZEF base) and see

the adjutant. I was scared stiff, and wondering what I had done or left undone, until he mentioned that he had detailed me to go on some special job which he thought would suit me very well. Something to do with a desert exploration party, he thought. I fairly ate up the miles into Cairo on an old motorcycle. Never was a morning so fresh and fair.

Back at camp I was told that a party of men had already left, and I was to join them in the old horse lines at Abbassia. My job, to see that they got a fair deal from the Tommies. When I arrived, I found the men sitting about, outside an old stable. They looked pleased with themselves. From what I had heard from the Divisional Cavalry men who had already been there a few days, it sounded a good show. Presently, the old hands (Div Cav) stirred into sudden activity. A car rolled up and out sprang a little man who, with a slight stammer, began to scold everyone in sight. Meanwhile screaming, 'Where's Ballantyne?' and poking about among a heap of equipment. On the arrival of Lieutenant Ballantyne, the blast transferred to him, finishing with 'Who are these people? Haven't I told you we can't have all sorts of people hanging about here!' On learning that 'these people' were the new recruits from the 27th (MG) Bn. Major Bagnold immediately became his usual charming self, and the men were welcomed to the unit.

The New Zealand officers present were all strangers to me, but in the days to come we were to get to know each other very well. It would be hard to find a better team. Lieutenant Ballantyne was, among other jobs, adjutant; Lieutenants J.H. (Jim) Sunderland and R.B. (Ralph) McQueen, general duties; Lieutenant F.B. (Frank) Edmundson was the medical officer and I was supposed to be in charge of gunnery.

None of us knew much about our work. I was lucky, however, as I was able to find a few men who knew something about the Lewis gun, and we were able to start classes right away. Classes in stripping etc. on guns always impress COs, especially if they are ignorant of the subject themselves, so I was set. Not so poor Bruce Ballantyne, Jim Sutherland and Ralph McQueen. They were in the most unenviable position of having no set tasks. It was a case of 'Do this, do that, get this fixed, see Brig. so and so at Middle East Forces (ME), awful old fool, and tell him what you want', and so on, till they were nearly in tears. But one could not help loving the 'Old Man'. Bagnold (Baggers to the troops) was a character. Charming, quick-tempered, tireless and shrewd as could be, he was the driving force that made the LRDG possible. He worked himself to a shadow and carried everyone else along in spite of themselves. One could only give of one's best to Baggers.

One of their chief consolations would be something like this: after days or perhaps even weeks of trying to get some part or piece of equipment from an unyielding RAOC 'wallah', or some such person, and having stood torrents of scathing comment from Bagnold, he would say, 'I will get you an authority.' Then later, 'Take this to that b-bloody fool at ME.' Oh, they found that good! (The b-bloody fool was usually a Brig., sometimes even a

Maj. Gen. The authority from perhaps the GOC in C himself.) And when they knew we had the blessing of the most high, how nice they were!

Apart from training, the first weeks at Abbassia were spent in getting everything ready for the work ahead. The trucks, many of which were taken over from the Egyptian Army, had to be modified to suit our special requirements, and new vehicles obtained from the agents in Alexandria. This was very pleasant as few of us had been to Alex. and we could usually have a day or so there. The modifications consisted of taking cabs, windscreens and doors from the trucks and adding extra leaves to the springs, sealing off the overflow pipes on the radiators and coupling up condenser cans. Gun mountings and boxes for equipment were fixed to the sides. The Bagnold Sun Compass was mounted above the dashboard between the two seats. After the first training run seats themselves were stuffed with old rags etc. to make them less springy. All this sounds very simple but the difficulty of getting the innumerable bits and pieces made, and remade slightly differently, nearly drove the unfortunates responsible crazy.

The one thing above all else that made us the envy of the ME Forces was our ration scale. For this we must thank the efforts of Lieutenant Frank Edmundson, our medical officer. He was given the task of working out a scale of rations suitable for the proposed operations. Told to make up a ration which would keep the men fit and well over a long period with no fresh food, gruelling conditions of heat and water shortage along with the risk of boredom, he did a great job. Though I think I did once hear someone say, 'What, pineapple again!'

One of the greatest items in the issue was the rum ration. Time and time again this proved its worth. At the end of a long day pushing and hauling, unloading and carrying equipment to get trucks through soft sand, it was found that the men could not eat. However, after a tot of rum, they were new men in no time. Ready for their food and willing and able to do the numerous maintenance jobs necessary in the patrol. Bagnold on his pre-war desert trips had found the tonic effect of rum. He demanded it for the LRDG, and we got it, though it was not on general issue to the army.

While all these odd jobs were going on in the horse lines the organisation of the unit was being worked out. Remember nothing on these lines had been done before and immortalised in any training pamphlet. This all came out of the head, mainly Bagnold's. There had been Light Car Patrols in the 1914–18 war, but no one knew any details. Captain Mitford had been with us from the start and had been a tower of strength. He also understood Bagnold and could often turn his wrath. That helped a lot. It was generally thought that Mitford would command one of the patrols. Then Captain Pat Clayton arrived, and it was thought he would command the second patrol. Lieutenant Bill Kennedy Shaw, a very quiet man, arrived and began to teach the navigators their duties. Everybody could see that he was to be marked down as the intelligence officer. Lance Corporal Dick Croucher, 27th (NZ) MG Bn assisted Shaw in teaching Astro navigation as he had a mate's ticket in the Merchant Marine. And so it all came about.

The unit was divided into three patrols originally X, Y and Z. X and Y, the two fighting patrols, were to be commanded by Clayton and Mitford and Z was to be a supply patrol under myself. It had been decided earlier that the trucks would be given names. Māori names it was thought, as the crews were New Zealanders. I wanted to name my own after a lake at home and I thought that all my trucks would be named *Roto* something also. The name of the patrol changed as a matter of course from Z to R. Similarly, all the X trucks were given a name beginning with T, the Y trucks' names beginning with W. And so X and Y patrols became T and W.

As soon as the patrols received their trucks, we were able to get away to some patches of real sand not far from home and try out our skill, or lack of it, in driving. The mysteries of sand mats and sand channels were very soon mastered, and we were almost ready to go out into the real desert. Speedometers had to be checked on measured kilometres and the patrol navigators practised in the use of the sun compass. The trucks were packed first this way, then that, until finally we found out just how to fit in all the hundred and one things we had to carry.

With such activity going on, speculation was rife as to our first trip into enemy territory. All the time we had been in barracks we had had the idea of security drummed into us and everyone was warned that any breach would mean instant return to the old unit. The men quickly learned how it could affect their own personal safety and, I think, became the most security minded men in the ME. Later, experience proved to us how true this was and I believe a great measure of our success was due to this one factor.

Early in August a small party under Clayton left Cairo shrouded in secrecy. Where they were going and what they intended to do we did not know. But this was it, the real thing. While they were away and with almost as much hush, hush, we also left. But we went only as far as the Qantania and Rammak dunes in the desert, a few miles west of Cairo. It was a training run, but we loved it. This was the real desert. Not a tree or a shrub, not even an Arab selling oranges for miles and miles and miles. The trucks got stuck and were dug and pushed out. The navigators got themselves lost or not, according to their ability. We formed column and every other formation so dear to the Armoured Regiments. In fact, we tried to squeeze in every experience we were ever likely to meet when we got out on patrol.

R Patrol was to be a supply patrol, and as such could muck along in the sand till it got experience or lost itself in the desert. By good fortune, just before setting out on our first patrol General Wavell inspected the unit. R Patrol was the first to be gone over. And he did go over us. He climbed over every truck and was horrified to find that our armament was only one Lewis gun and one Boys anti-tank rifle. The other patrols had plenty, but we were only a supply patrol. The RAOC could not supply. Wavell turned to the

Brig. ROAC and said, 'You have plenty of guns in store, see that they get them!' We did, that day.

While we were away, the heavy transport under Shaw laid dumps of petrol along the route we would be following when we left for enemy territory. We had taken extra petrol with us to be dumped at the end of our outward run and the Marmon-Herrington heavy trucks, having gone out fully laden, were to ferry it on when they had disposed of their own load. Theirs was a thankless task. A mention should be made of Staff Sergeant Archie McLeod who loved the Marmon-Herrington 6-ton trucks and was our best fitter. Many of the modifications made to the trucks and other equipment were due largely to his inventive genius.

By early September all was ready and we lost no time in getting away on our first patrol. All three patrols were more or less together for the first day and night. Next morning after travelling a few miles we parted, W and HQ going SW, while T and R continued on in a westerly direction headed for the fleshpots of Siwa where we arrived a couple of days later.

On arrival we camped in the sand just out of fly range to the east and south of the village. There we filled, soldered and cased our tinned water supplies (in empty four-gallon petrol tins and cases, supplied by the Shell Co. with the caps loose), and picked up a supply of petrol which had been sent down from Matruh.

And then the fun began. Oh, not the enemy. Just the sand. One hundred miles of hell. The sand was soft, we were still very green, and it was hot, so very hot, but we made it. And having made our first crossing of the Great Sand Sea, we felt that we were indeed desert mariners.

However, on Friday 13 September, my truck was almost put out of action, but not by the enemy. While running down the western side of the Sand Sea my truck caught fire. At the time the whole patrol was heavily laden with extra stores to form a new dump roaring along at 90kph. This was their top speed and so none were able to tell me about the fire. It was not till Private Spotswood who was with me felt the flames licking his neck that we were aware of the trouble. This gives some idea of the speeds attainable on good going.

Steele did not mention in his writing the cause of the fire. He had been smoking a pipe and the wind had blown the glowing tobacco ball from his pipe into the scrim camouflage net packed in the back. The wind and the speed caused the tobacco to glow and set fire to the dry scrim. His vehicle was the Ford V8 15cwt command car *Rotoma* and was going faster than the heavier-laden Chevrolet WA trucks travelling behind. The fire was not noticed by Steele and Private R.O. Spotswood due to their speed, so a following Chevrolet crew led by Corporal A.D. (Buster) Gibb saw the danger and drove at full speed to get alongside the Ford and fired a Lewis gun to get their attention. It worked, and Spotswood turned around and saw the flames. They stopped along with the rest of the column and quickly threw out the stores and munitions, including mines, before the superficial scrim fire engulfed the vehicle's contents. Had it gone unnoticed for a longer time the Ford may have exploded. Private Eric Harcourt, who was in the back of Gibb's truck, recalled witnessing the event:

> We were racing across an area known as Pebble Plain. It was about 50 miles across, dead flat, and coated with black pebbles about an inch in circumference. Good fast going! Looking over the others in front I thought I saw white smoke coming from Steele's Ford 15cwt. He had petrol and mines for a load. The petrol was Egyptian and the tin containers we knew as flimsies were very thin and leaked all the time. I realised in a flash what had happened. Someone in the truck had been smoking and thrown away the butt, but we later found out it was probably the burning tobacco from the skipper's pipe. The wind had caught it and blown it on to the scrim camouflage net we used at the time, and it caught on fire. But with our heavily laden Chev truck we couldn't catch up with the speeding Ford. Then I had a bright idea. I called Bill Hammond our gunner, and asked if he had any tracer in his Lewis gun magazine. 'One in five,' he replied. I told him to fire two or three bursts over the skipper's truck to let him know his net is on fire. Bill swung his Lewis gun around and let go about five bursts. I watched the red of the tracers go over Steele's truck and the next moment saw a cloud of dust as they braked, and they both jumped out and pulled the net away. We then caught up and, without thinking about the risk of explosion, helped them haul out the burning scrim and the charred boxes of grenades, mines and ammunition. The mine boxes had burnt through and the mines were red hot, but luckily, they and the fuel tins had not exploded.
>
> When we all pulled up by them Steele wanted to know who had fired the tracer. Bill admitted he acted on orders, so Steele and Spotty shook our hands and that was that.

Navigation skills were essential for the future success of the patrols. Lance Corporal C.H.B. (Dick) Croucher was a navigator with R Patrol. Before the war he had served in the Merchant Marine and was already familiar with navigation as a ship's mate. He helped Lieutenant Kennedy Shaw in teaching navigation skills to the troops. When General Freyberg threatened to withdraw his New Zealanders from the Group, Bagnold, being short of navigators, offered Croucher an immediate commission provided he transferred to the British army. He agreed, though much to the upset of General Freyberg, and received an immediate promotion from lance corporal to a second lieutenant with the Royal Tank Corps and rejoined the LRDG.

Croucher took command of R2 Patrol for a time which included a trip to the Free French at Zouar in Chad. There he endeavoured to instruct the French officers in Astro navigation and the use of the sun compass, but was hampered by his inability to translate the technical terms into French.

He then spent some time in GHQ Cairo issuing navigation equipment and instructing officers and NCOs from the Eighth Army in Astro navigation which he said was a dead loss, because at that time there was no earthly chance of them ever getting hold of a theodolite!

Bagnold wrote a brief overview of navigation in a document titled *Notes on the Long Range Desert Patrols 11/2/1941* as follows:

Dead Reckoning Navigation

The so-called navigation practised in the Army, which has never operated far from mapped landmarks, consists in setting a predetermined course and keeping to it. This breeds a reluctance to alter course and a consequent tendency to drive straight through areas of bad going instead of avoiding them by detour. In dune areas and in rocky country it is impossible to keep a straight course for any appreciable distance. Moreover, the object of cross-country navigation is to know at all times one's actual position on the map, rather than to travel by some previously specified route. Hence it is far better that the leader be free to pick his own way as he goes along, and that the navigator be given the subordinate role of noting down compass and mileage readings and of plotting on the map the possibly winding course taken by the leader.

This method needs a compass which (a) indicates directly and continuously the bearing on which the vehicle is travelling, no matter what that bearing may be, and (b) can be read by the eye alone, without having to be set by hand whenever a reading is taken.

Some magnetic aero compasses conform to these requirements, but up to now the difficulty of compensating this against the errors introduced by the vehicle, its moving steel parts, spare springs, weapons etc. renders their accuracy far too uncertain for long journeys over unknown country.

The sun compass, of the direct reading type used by the Egyptian Army (made to Lieutenant Colonel Bagnold's design by Messrs. E.R. Watts and Co. of London) has been found to be extremely accurate and reliable. It gives the true bearing, is deadbeat, and once set up on the vehicle is influenced only by personal errors in reading it and in estimating the time of day. (For accurate work it is necessary to keep local solar time correct to two minutes.)

The errors in dead-reckoning with speedometer and sun compass to be expected with an experienced navigator are of the order of 3% in distance and 1.5 degrees in bearing.

Astronomical Position Finding

Since dead-reckoning errors are liable to accumulate from day to day, it is necessary on long journeys to take astronomical fixes of the position of each night's camp. This needs a small theodolite, a wireless time signal receiver, a pair of reliable watches, Air Almanac, mathematical tables etc. Bubble sextants have been tried out in lieu of theodolites, but they are not at present robust enough to withstand the rough treatment to which they are exposed when carried by truck cross-country.

Each patrol has two navigators who hold the rank of corporal or lance corporal.

(**Left**) Major Ralph Bagnold, the founder of the Long Range Desert Group. He was a British army signals officer, geographer and desert explorer. (**Right**) Major D.G. (Don) Steele, R Patrol's first commander with the Long Range Patrol. Promoted in August 1941, he became Commanding Officer A (NZ) Squadron LRDG. Steele was later awarded the OBE in recognition of his services working with the SAS planning operations while in command at Siwa and later Jalo.

The first two New Zealand patrol commanders, Abbassia barracks, Cairo, 1940. Lieutenant L.B. Ballantyne (left), T Patrol, and Lieutenant D.G. Steele (right), R Patrol. They are driving in the R Patrol Ford 01 15cwt V8 command car.

Corporal C.H. (Dick) Croucher of R Patrol, 1940. He was with the Merchant Marine before the war and helped teach navigation to the LRP. Croucher rose through the ranks to a patrol commander and by the end of the war was the LRDG adjutant and Intelligence officer. He stands in front of a Chevrolet WA with a captured Italian vehicle plate attached to its grille.

The Onward badge of the Second New Zealand Expeditionary Force (2NZEF). These were commonly worn on NZ LRDG headdress before the introduction of the LRDG badge in 1942.

An NZ Divisional Cavalry greetings card from Egypt, 1940. A large contingent of the LRP recruits came from that regiment.

A simple map of Libya from the Cairo-based *Parade* magazine dated 8 March 1941.

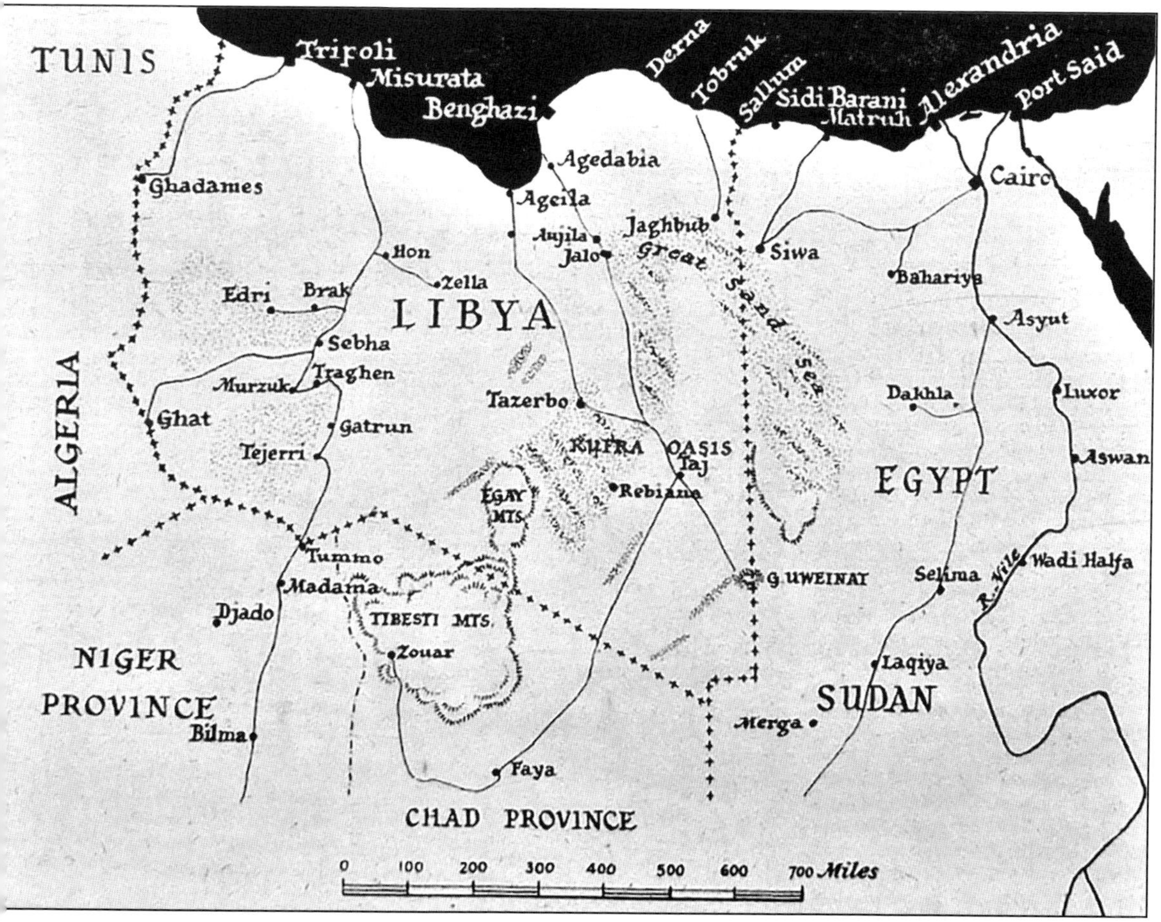

Maaleesh, George - We're not allowed to say just where we are going...
(Prize winning sketch - R.E. Tretheway)

(**Left**) A cartoon appearing in the *NZEF Times* newspaper reinforcing the importance of security, an essential aspect while operating with the LRP.

(**Opposite**) A Ford V8 cresting a large sand dune is about to slide down. Another waits on the ridge.

(**Below**) Illustrations taken from a military manual showing two views of the .55 Boys anti-tank rifle. These were designed not to disable a tank but to create casualties to those inside. The LRDG always endeavoured to avoid encounters with armoured vehicles. The weapon was carried for about a year, but rarely used in action and generally considered of little use by the troops.

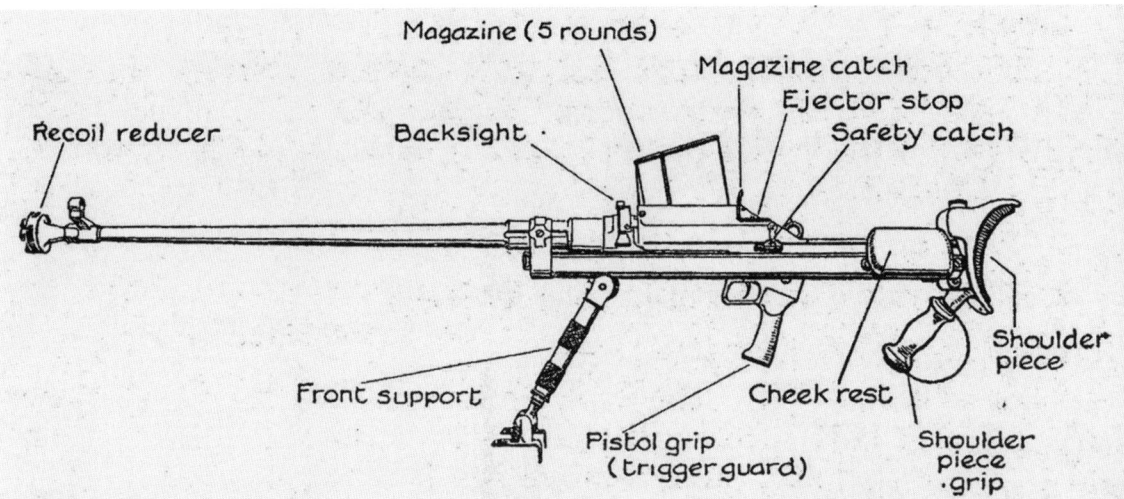

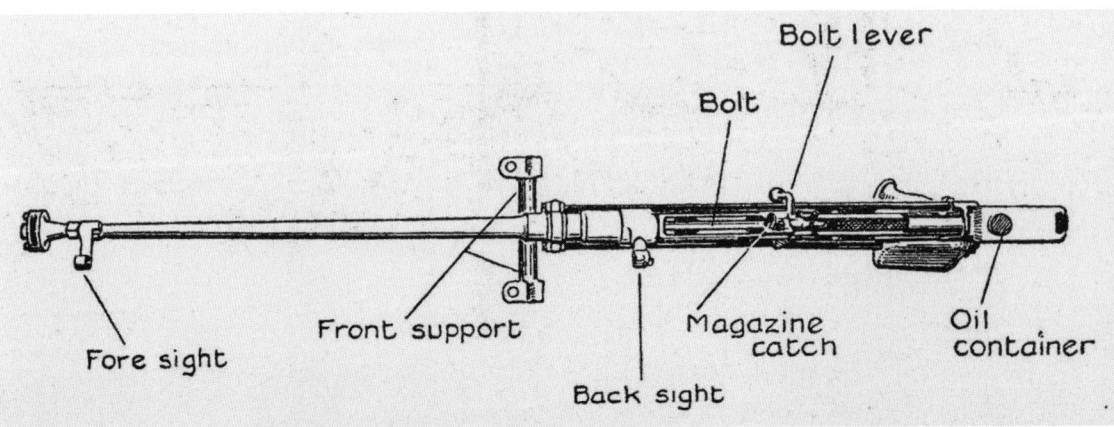

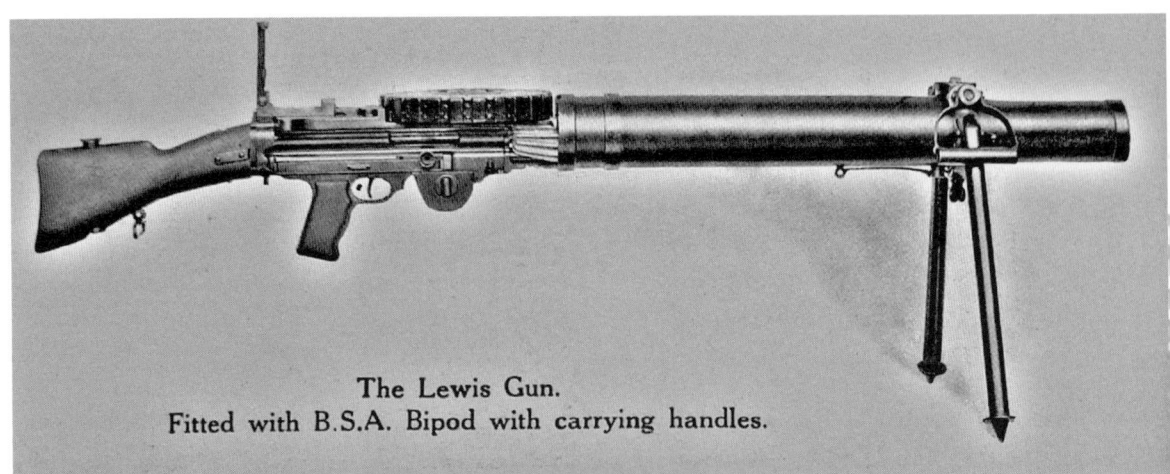

The Lewis Gun.
Fitted with B.S.A. Bipod with carrying handles.

The Lee-Enfield Rifle.

(**Above**) The R Patrol crew here are dressed for extreme cold. The rolled-up sand mats on each side of the vehicle were employed to ease the front wheels through soft sand. The lights and windscreens were covered with cloth to prevent reflection.

(**Opposite, above**) The .303 Lewis gun with its 47-round magazine was a mainstay weapon with the early patrols. Some were still being used through to late 1942, when more effective machine guns like the Vickers K became available.

(**Opposite, centre**) A Lee Enfield Mk III .303 service rifle. These were fitted into rack clips close to the driver and passenger for ready use.

(**Opposite, below**) A .303 Vickers Mk 1, belt-fed, water-cooled heavy machine gun. These guns were usually mounted on trucks but, if necessary, could be used on the ground employing the tripod.

A painted Tiki displayed on front of an R Patrol truck. The trooper is unidentified.

(**Opposite, above**) R Patrol Chevrolet WA *Rotoiti*; the driver is Private E. Harcourt. Note the Māori Tiki on the bonnet. T Patrol displayed a Kiwi.

(**Opposite, below**) An original Māori greenstone (jade) Tiki. It symbolized the connection between man and nature, between heaven and earth, and represented creation and life itself. On R Patrol trucks it was painted green with a red tongue and red-ringed eyes. In addition, it was occasionally displayed as personalized art on New Zealand military vehicles in general. When worn around the neck it is described as a Hei Tiki, as displayed by Trooper L. Donaldson. It was a common talisman worn by New Zealand soldiers.

Lieutenant D.G. Steele's Ford *Rotoma* being cleaned out following an accidental fire.

Steele's Ford stuck in the sand. It flies the R Patrol green pennant with a white letter. Note the aero compass below the driver's seat and the EY grenade-launching rifle next to the pith helmet. A SMLE .303 rifle is also clipped to the side.

A driver's view looking across the bonnet into the desert. The Lewis gun is mounted on the side ready for action.

A Chevrolet WA camouflaged with scrim hessian fabric. This was later replaced with netting as the scrim stood out in the landscape. The Lewis gun is at the ready in case of an air attack. The men relax with their reading. Left: Trooper M.E. Hammond, Private E. Harcourt and Private M. Allen (RAMC medical orderly).

Lance Corporal J.W. Eyles, R Patrol navigator, attending to his theodolite.

Chevrolet WA trucks lined up at Abbassia barracks ready to receive stores in preparation for a mission.

Lance Corporal C.G. (Curly) Ball of R Patrol. He stands in front of W Patrol trucks *Waikaha* and *Waitere* parked in the Abbassia barracks, Cairo 1940.

Chapter Two

One Man's Story

Gunner C.O. (Bluey) Grimsey was serving with the 34th A/T Battery of the 7th Anti-Tank NZ Artillery Regiment when he joined the LRP on its formation in July 1940. He wrote a detailed wartime account which gave a vivid personal insight into the beginnings of the unit and his experiences as a recruit who joined without knowing what he was being seconded to:

> It was approaching our third month in Egypt after we arrived from New Zealand, and although Italy had long since declared war so far we had seen no action and we began to wonder how many more months we would have to go on doing fatigues, digging gun pits, cleaning equipment, morning route marches, monotonous gun drills and the hundred and one other jobs that go to fill in a day's work for the average soldier. Jobs which often just seemed invented to keep us busy with no interesting objective ahead.
>
> The sergeants had all filed out and I was just beginning to make headway with the heap of dirty crockery when a bombardier came into the kitchen and yelled, 'Report to the orderly room at once, you are going out on a stunt!' This might mean anything, from a couple of days desert manoeuvring to a fully equipped mimic battle lasting perhaps two weeks or more, certainly nothing to get very excited about, except perhaps the prospect of getting away from the humdrum of petty fatigues and monotonous drills.
>
> Imagine my surprise then, when on reporting to the orderly room I was told to pack up all of my gear, hand in my rifle to the quartermaster store and report to HQ pay office, as I was leaving the battery for an indefinite period. Four of us who had been selected for this stunt were told, 'You chaps have been picked out and are expected to stand up to hard work and pretty tough conditions. You may not see the old battery again. Good luck and keep up the good name of the battery.' That was all before we loaded our gear into the waiting truck and set out for we knew not where!
>
> I don't know what thoughts my three companions had on the matter, but at least I pictured our being sent away out into the 'blue' (the desert), somewhere where beneath a merciless sun we would be digging slit trenches – those impromptu little funk holes which have proved so invaluable in the war during air attacks – or gun pits, with poor food and little water.
>
> What was our surprise then, when we finally drew into the barrack square of the Royal Horse Artillery in Abbassia and eventually found ourselves comfortably ensconced with some eighty other New Zealanders in a large

Royal Horse Artillery barrack room. All questions as to how long we would be there or to where we were going were met with the same evasive answers. We learned only that we now belonged to the Long Range Patrol (LRP); well anyway, it sounded rather adventurous.

Next day we four were introduced to our new gun, a 37mm calibre and much lighter than the anti-tank 2-pounder with which we had been training previously and which we learned was to be mounted and fired from the truck, much the same as a gun is fired from the deck of a ship – in fact, as will be seen later, our whole show was not unlike a land navy or 'desert fleet' as we sometimes called it.

Each patrol consisted of eleven trucks and was divided into four troops, A, B, C and D. A included the troop commander and wireless truck; B, C and D each contained three trucks heavily armed with Lewis, Vickers or Boys anti-tank rifle, as the case may be. In addition, service rifles and revolvers were carried as personal defensive weapons.

Our group contained three such patrols, W, T and R, in all numbering thirty-three vehicles. Besides these we had two huge supply lorries (Marmon-Herringtons), together with an accompanying wireless truck, making a grand total of thirty-six vehicles. Each patrol was entirely self-supporting and carried supplies of water, benzine and food for six weeks' desert travel; also, each individual truck carried food and water to sustain a crew of three for a fortnight.

Bearing these facts in mind, one can realize what a formidable fleet we were, our combined fire power being greater than anything hitherto accomplished in modern desert warfare. Of our largest gun, the 37mm Bofors we had one to each patrol, these being a formidable weapon against the heavier carriers and tanks which we might have to engage. These guns have a muzzle velocity of 2,625ft per second, an effective range of 5,000 yards and power to pierce 2-inch armour plating at that range, were indeed a weapon with which to reckon. Imagine then the consternation of the enemy on discovering a gun of this type with a 365-degrees traverse mounted on a truck able to fly across the desert at 50 miles per hour.

The whole show, which I understand was the inspiration of our OC, Major Bagnold, was formed primarily for long-range patrolling of the vast desert areas, it being possible to travel for six weeks or more and cover anything up to 3,000 miles during that time. All our trucks were fitted with special sand-track tyres and steel sand trays, these being steel ramps which are placed under the back wheels of the vehicle when bogged in loose sand. Also, sand mats. These mats proved of invaluable assistance, being constructed of strong canvas between which were sewn bamboo rods at equal distance. The mat, itself some 2 feet wide by 30 feet long, was placed underneath the front wheels of the truck, enabling it, once it had climbed onto the steel tray behind, to travel and gain speed over loose sand.

Another ingenious device invented by Bagnold was the condenser cans on each truck. These cans, placed on the running board and connected to the top of the radiator by means of a tube, collected and condensed the steam from the radiator when hot, the water from there being again drawn back to the radiator when the vehicle was stopped and allowed to cool by means of the resulting vacuum thus brought about in the radiator. This, I need hardly add, was of tremendous importance in a country like this where water is not only of great scarcity, but the carrying of it materially reduced our capacity to carry other things almost as important, such as food and ammunition.

Weeks were spent under the able and patient guidance of our OC, Major Bagnold, who for years had made long and successful expeditions into the desert and, in truth, knew desert travel as perhaps few men indeed ever will. So that is a brief description of what was to later become known as the Long Range Desert Group.

Gone were those tedious route marches, gone also were those monotonous parades and rifle and foot drill. In their stead came the job of dismantling and cleaning equipment, new equipment which we learnt to prize as our own personal property. Drivers too were busy on their trucks, tightening a screw here and there, grinding in a valve there, getting everything ticking over like clockwork. Everyone was taking a personal pride in their new 'show'. Our trucks, all newly painted and camouflaged, looked an impressive sight indeed. Each troop had a coloured sign: A had green, B black, C yellow and D red. A square for W Patrol, a diamond for T and a circle for R painted on either side of the bonnet. The leading truck of each troop flew the troop colour flag.

Will we ever forget that first practice manoeuvre in the desert after a month's intensive preparation! I think not. We all thought we knew, the most of us having been there eight months, but we were soon to learn that even so, we knew little about the desert proper. The morning we set out in full strength through the streets of Cairo, waving to the girls who seem to be always sitting up on those funny little balconies just to be waved at, we were full of confidence. The natives, or 'wogs' as we termed them, driving their motley herds of black sheep with huge tails plus goats grinned and waved too, and the leader of a heavily laden train would salute and yell, 'Hello Mr New Zealand!' Or the driver of those funny little flat-topped carts laden with black veiled females would curse and stick out his tongue as he frantically pulled off the road to save his human cargo and diminutive donkey.

Pyramids loomed ahead like some colossal, ethereal, geometrical figures. Through the Indian camp, then situated within the shadow of the Pyramids, and up on to the high ground overlooking the desert proper, we climbed and halted to receive our orders. Three patrols, W, T and R, were to travel independently in open or anti-aircraft formation, there being a fifteen-minute interval and ten to fifteen kilometres distance between each patrol. W Patrol set off first and soon we were spreading across good firm sand at 45–60 kilometres per hour. Topping a rise, we were able to look back and see the other two patrols dotted like ants in the far distance with little puffs of white sand dust rising behind each truck.

Away out in the open plain country, where the sand is clean, level and the view unbroken by dunes or hills, this fast travel produced an unusual sensation; one seemed to be flying as it were with no indication of speed. Also, it is in that flat country that one saw those fascinating mirages. Trucks seemed to be travelling through lakes of water or at times skimming a few inches off the ground, their reflection showing as clearly as on the glassy surface of a lake. Again, little hills would appear on the horizon, seemingly floating in mid-air as if suspended by invisible skyhooks, gradually descending to join with the sand as we approached.

Later on, we struck softer sand, when the trucks lost speed, necessitating a change down to third and sometimes even second gear; then that sickening, 'Judder … judder … judder …!' stop. We would get out, scoop away the loose sand from the front of the back wheels, place our sand trays, roll out our mats in front of the front wheels, and push while the driver endeavoured to gain speed to carry us on to the firmer sand. We had lots of this at first until we learnt to charge at the soft spots at full speed and crash our gear lever through just at the right second. Experience and working in the terrific heat soon taught us the knack.

We stopped for half an hour at eleven o'clock, received an issue of chocolate, refuelled and checked our tyre pressures which on account of the heat tended to increase rapidly; we had to keep tyre pressure down in the loose sand in spite of the 12-inch tread of our special sand-track tyres.

That night we struck our first real sand dune. Just before sundown it loomed ahead like a low fleecy cloud on the horizon. Closer it resembled a giant yellow curling tidal wave some 40 feet high and stretching due north and south, rising sheer off the flat gravel and sand. We camped under the dune, lit a fire and cooked tea, a weary but a happy crowd. After our last cup of tea and rum issue we sat around the fire and yarned for a while before rolling out our blankets beneath the stars and going to sleep.

Up at daybreak, our OC decided to give us our first lesson in surmounting sand dunes, although I must admit the dune in question looked an impossible obstacle. First, we were taught to walk over the sand to judge its texture; if the sand remained firm beneath our tread, it could be surmounted by the truck driven properly. On the other hand, if one's feet sank in sand as loose as sugar, one had to look for another place to direct the driver. Few of us, I think, will forget the first truck to go over. Some of us were with our trucks waiting for our turn; others were getting a better view from the crest of the dune. The first truck, making a wide circle and going back about a quarter of a mile, came tearing at the dune at about 50 miles per hour; sheer momentum took it nearly to the top, when failure overtook the driver. He waited there just that split second too long to change gear. There was a crashing of gears and the truck stopped within a few feet of the summit. Again and again he tried and at about the fourth attempt went sailing over in third gear, to go slithering down the slope on the other side.

Soon we were all at it and gaining confidence at every attempt. Later in the day we had become so efficient that we were sent off in troops to try out our skill. One truck, taking the dune where the sand was particularly firm and the angle of slope not so great, sped up to 40 or 50 miles per hour, leapt the crest and, flying into the air, crashed on its nose some 30 feet down from where it took off, shooting the driver and his passenger out on to the sand, smashing the front axle and crumpling the radiator like so much tinfoil. Fortunately, no one was seriously injured. Before the day was ended two other trucks met a similar fate, although all the men escaped without broken bones. Fitters worked all night and the following day, putting in new axles, changing wheels and made the lorries serviceable to continue the journey, which apart from this first gruelling venture was most successful.

Gunner C.O. 'Bluey' Grimsey, R Patrol, studying a sun compass. He is wearing the New Zealand 'lemon squeezer' felt hat which displays the LRDG badge designed by Grimsey.

A Chevrolet WA gun truck mounting a 37mm Bofors anti-tank gun. Grimsey served as a gunner on this vehicle.

The sleeping arrangements of R Patrol members alongside their truck R4 *Rotowai*. Private E.T. Russell is resting against an unrolled sand mat which served both as an effective windbreak and a headboard. Two men slept while one kept watch. Each man had two hours on, four hours off. The trucks are usually dispersed, and each crew is responsible for protection of its own vehicle.

R Patrol truck *Rotowaro*. It was unusual to see the canvas hood in place which indicates it may be travelling in friendly territory. Behind the lines it would have restricted the aerial view looking out for hostile aircraft.

Radio truck *Rotowhero* heads the patrol into the desert. In the Chevrolet WA the No. 11 radio was housed in the back compartment of the vehicle. The wireless operator Signalman A. Pressick mans the .55 Boys anti-tank rifle.

A Chevrolet WA stuck in the sand. A good view of the rear framing which the troops referred to as the 'pig pen'. The vehicle mounts a Boys anti-tank gun and a Lewis machine gun.

A patrol spread out to avoid the soft sand, although some are already stuck and employing their sand mats and trays to extract themselves.

The crew of *Rotomahana* view the remains of petrified trees in the desert.

R Patrol men pose beside a bogged truck. Note that most of them are wearing overalls on this occasion. At that time it was unusual to see two Lewis guns mounted on a truck.

R Patrol members alongside a Chevrolet WA patrol truck. Front left, Tpr. R.J. Landon-Lane; third from left, SQMS. D. Barrett; Capt. F.B. Edmundson the LRDG medical officer, Capt. D.G. Steele, Cpl. A.D. Gibb. Middle: left, Tpr. M.E. Hammond, Pte. A.D. Cosgrove; third left, Cpl. C.G. Ball; fifth left, Pte. F.R. Brown, Pte. E. Harcourt, L/Cpl. R.A. Tinker. All others unidentified.

A Bofors gun truck sweeps over a large sand dune with a vast desert vista in the background.

A truck about to proceed into some rocky landscape on the road to Chad.

Gunner Bluey Grimsey stands on a spectacular sand dune, 1940.

A 2in mortar, a number of which were carried by all patrols. Trooper I.H. McInnes won the Military Medal for his effective mortar-shooting against the Italian fort at Murzuk, setting the tower on fire.

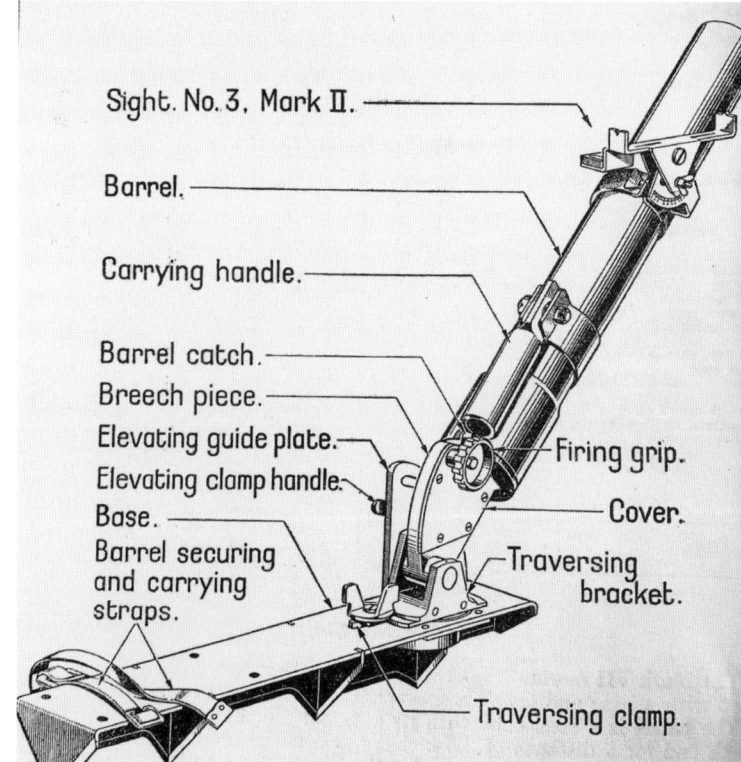

A diagram of a 2in mortar taken from a military manual.

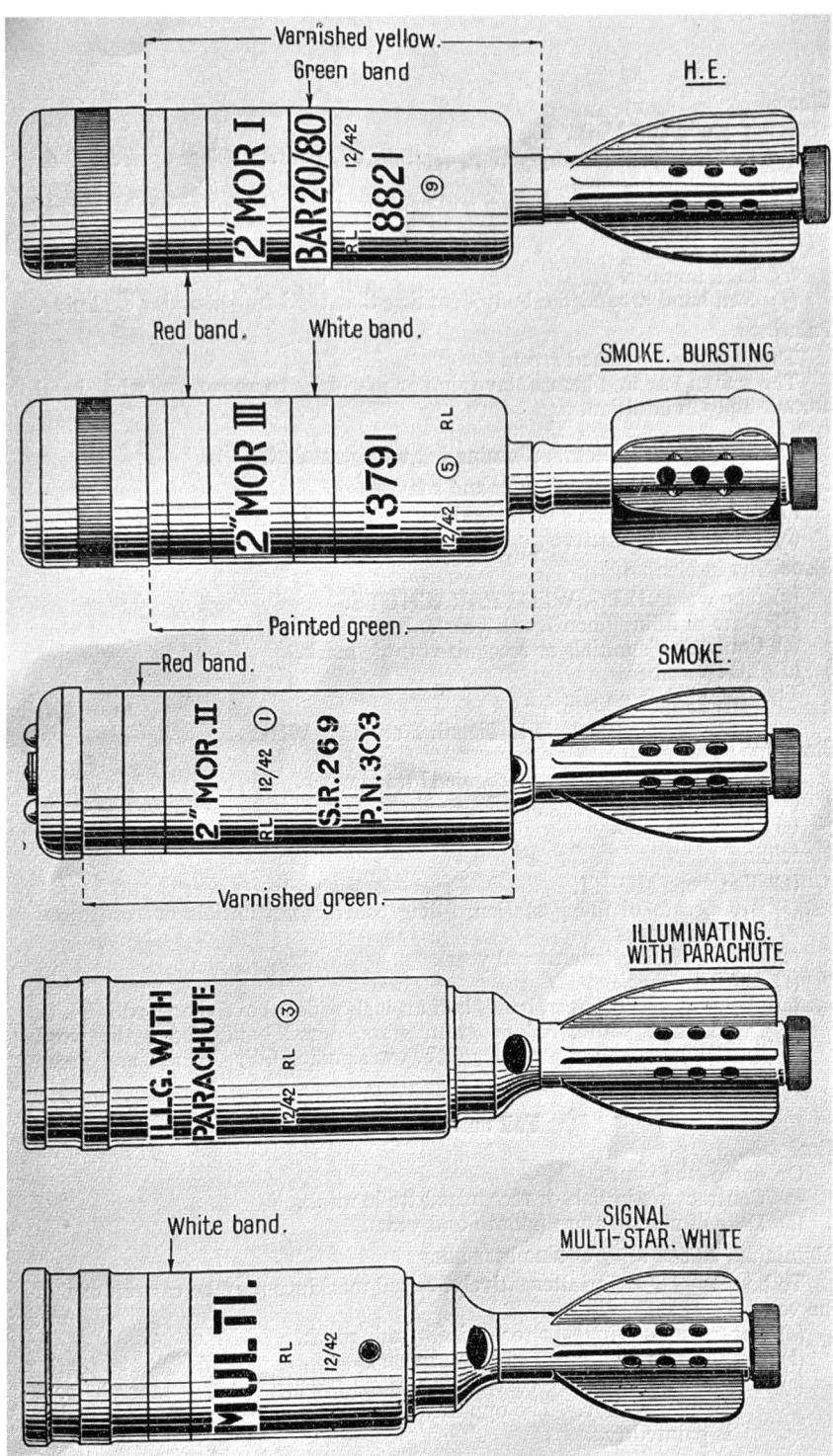

The variety of mortar bombs that could be fired by the 2in mortar.

Lieutenant Steele rests by his Ford V8 as he settles in for the night.

Chapter Three

First Missions

Towards the end of October, R and T Patrols made simultaneous sorties into southern and northern Libya. While undertaking such an operation on 31 October 1940, Captain D.G. Steele's R Patrol found an enemy bomb dump buried in the sand. They dug up seventy-five 18kg bombs and 640 2kg bombs along with ten 44-gallon drums of petrol, all of which were destroyed. Later that same day they burned an unguarded Savoia-Marchetti SM.79 bomber and 160 drums of fuel. Gunner Bluey Grimsey was with R Patrol during this discovery and its aftermath. He recorded events from the time he left Cairo until the mission was completed:

> On 24 October 1940, we set out ostensibly to lay minefields in enemy territory and to continue the reconnaissance work which we had begun a month earlier. That Thursday night we camped out 80 kilometres from the Pyramids, having started off late in the afternoon. I shall always remember the next Friday morning as I had occasion to be severely reprimanded by our skipper, Captain Steele. It happened this way. I had volunteered to get up early and assist with cooking the breakfast, my sergeant, McGregor, giving me his watch and telling me to call him at 4.30am. I went one better and got up at 4.15 and so quickly did we execute our chores that we had breakfast ready before 5.30am. Unhappily it did not get sufficiently light to proceed on our journey until 6.00am, and stumping around in the dark, cold morning in the dawn quite unnecessarily was not at all to our skipper's liking, nor to the men's either for that matter. However, we did not make the same mistake again.
>
> The next day, that is Friday October 25, we made good going over the rather bad gravel-sand country and we camped at Gard el Rammak, the second dune belt which stretches away to the northern horizon like some arrested tidal wave that has been turned into a pillar of sand. On Sunday we reached Ain Dalla oasis some 600km south-west of Cairo. This was our first watering place and one which we use for a halfway stop across Egypt to take on water and where we also have supplies in the form of benzine and food secreted in the rocks a few miles from the oasis. For a stranger to hear us talk of Ain Dalla, it might be assumed there was some sort of civilisation there. I can assure you, however, it consists entirely of a small hill of sand, some seven date palms bearing very small fruit, hardly edible, and a few sharp-thorned bushes. There was running water which some thoughtful person had seen fit to control and divert into a 6-inch pipe which the water

had washed in the sand, and which was now surrounded by benzine boxes in place of the porcelain of a modern bath.

We stayed at Dalla that night and the greater part of Sunday, doing general maintenance on the trucks and refilling with water and benzine, setting out again late in the afternoon. On Monday 28 we arrived at Pottery Hill. It was so named because at its base there can be found some huge earthenware water jars, left there no doubt some thousands of years ago, possibly by camel traders fleeing from invading Bedouins. So far, I have not learned their history. They are beautifully shaped, like a huge egg with a small, moulded neck, and some show signs that at one time they also had either a handle or a spout, which in every case had been broken off, no doubt by a thoughtless vandal. To me it is most distressing the way some amateur collectors and souvenir hunters wreak wanton destruction on such art treasures. I shall never forget an officer, happily he was not one of our own officers, proudly exhibiting a piece of rock painting he had chipped off a cave. Probably some work of art executed many years before Christ. If everyone followed this useless practice, soon there would be no trace of the knowledge such art had brought us down through the centuries.

We set out on our course on Tuesday. It was a beautifully cool morning, yet not too cold. Now the sand had changed from ochre to deep gold, like ripe corn, merging to purple haze on the far distant horizon where black and gold sand hills diffused with purple blue haze caught the first rays of the morning sun. The golden sand strewn with black rocks, our trucks sank deep beneath the golden crust, revealing patches of pink and purple sand dust. This very fine dust would sometimes bring us to a stop, and we would then have to get to work with our sand trays and mats to climb through to where the crust was firmer and where our tyre tread would again be perfectly imprinted in the firm granules.

On Wednesday, 30 October, we arrived at Uweinat where our real work would begin. The place is a huge rock formation denuded of all vegetation, rising as it were sheer out of the desert. As yet we knew little of what lay within that natural fortress, although we had been there before and we knew there were landing grounds for Italian planes, also that there was water in the hills and some sort of garrison there. Tracks in the sand told us that heavy transport had recently passed by, doubtlessly bringing supplies of food, ammunition and petrol.

We reconnoitred Uweinat that night and then, striking north-west, tried rather unsuccessfully in the failing light to span the intervening belt of sand dunes, and so camped the night in the cover of the dunes. To the upset of my mates, I foolishly put salt instead of sugar in the first brew of tea. Despite attempts to drink the salty tea, with our thirst having been made acute already by a particularly hot day, I soon had a second billy of water boiling. Water, our most precious necessity, was strictly rationed when we were away from any oasis and except on extreme occasions one bottle per day was the normal ration apart from morning and evening tea and a drink of lime juice a day. I have known a man to offer half a week's pay (50 piastres or 10 shillings) for an extra bottle of water from one of his mates while in Libya and be refused.

On Thursday, after a hurried breakfast of porridge and curried fish, we set out at 0630 hrs on our patrolling duties, looking for fresh tracks and suitable places to lay our mines. We had little real success until just before noon whilst coasting along in 'air' formation, when our skipper in front gave the halt signal and we all stopped. Still in scattered formation, we watched him dismount and proceed to investigate two innocent-looking petrol drums and then start to dig round in the sand with his hands. We, in our Bofors gun truck, were immediately behind Captain Steele, and soon saw him run back to his truck for his shovel which he used to excavate a box from beneath the slight mound near the drums, then another and another. Opening one, we found it neatly packed with bombs wrapped like eggs, their detonators and firing mechanisms similarly packed in separate compartments. Soon the squad had unearthed a whole dump of aerial bombs of various calibres, along with 44 gallons of aero petrol.

While a few trucks kept a lookout from a distance, the cases of bombs were all excavated and placed atop of the petrol, with detonators exposed in such a position that they could be made a target for the Vickers guns. One was mounted on the skipper's Ford, the idea being to ignite and blow up the dump with tracer fire from a safe distance. We retreated some 800 yards. Captain Steele sent a burst of fire toward the exposed boxes. Woomph! Flame belched 400 feet skyward, followed by dense black smoke. We turned tail and made for the hills. Some of the bombs which were falling all around, filled with TNT, might explode too near to be healthy, so we took no chances. As we sped to the rocks, I watched the black smoke curling 1,000 feet into the still hot air. There was another explosion and a colossal mushroom of flame seethed skyward, sending out rockets of flame.

After lunch we again struck south towards where we knew there should be a landing ground. Away in the distance could be seen dancing mirages, so common that time of day on the flat country. Huge lakes appeared and floating islands apparently suspended by invisible sky hooks gradually came down to connect with the earth as we approached. Then there was another strange mirage, not unlike a spout of water reflecting the rays of the sun. We all gazed at this and wondered what our skipper proposed to do. As we approached, it slowly took shape as some shiny object reflecting the sun. Soon we could see it was some type of aircraft on the ground. We stopped within a thousand yards and Captain Steele sent a burst from the Vickers gun in the direction of the plane. There was no movement or sign of life, so we cautiously advanced. We had come across a Savoia (Savoia-Marchetti SM.79) Italian plane of the heavy bomber type, quite modern, but with a damaged undercarriage and probably awaiting repairs, those responsible little dreaming that enemy troops would make it necessary for them to put a guard on the machine so many hundreds of miles from enemy territory.

We fired Verey lights into the petrol tanks and the plane became a hot, molten mess. After searching the landing ground, we found four 44-gallon drums of aero petrol which we promptly fired by sending tracer shells into them. In less than an hour we had rendered useless about 15,000 British pounds worth of enemy material. Altogether that day we reckoned we had inflicted 30,000 pounds worth of damage to the enemy. Although it was reported shots had been fired from the hills while we were destroying the landing ground, there were no casualties.

That evening we carefully laid land mines along the transport routes, the tracks of which we could plainly see in the sand. Having refilled some tins of water we found in the Italian landing ground, we set course north-west and camped for the night some 80 kilometres from the scene of operations.

On Friday 1 November, while having a break after crossing some rough country, someone yelled, 'Look, there's a plane!' Like lightning, we ran to our vehicles and made for the low hills covered with loose rocks which we considered would give us some protection. We got there without a hitch, and no sooner had we done so than three enemy planes appeared, two heavy machines and a smaller one of the Ghibli type.

At first, they circled overhead at 1,000 to 1,500 feet and some of us thought we were so well concealed by our natural camouflage of the rock, but such was evidently not the case as for the second time they circled and descended to 1,000 feet. The first big plane let loose a stick of bombs which fell all around the trucks without hitting one. Captain Steele fired a burst from his Vickers gun which immediately had the desired result of making the plane climb higher. Perceiving that they intended to bomb us at a fairly high altitude and having regard for our natural camouflage, our only hope was to lie quite still away from our trucks and wait for the worst, knowing that a movement would only reveal our positions and realising that our fire would have little effect at such range. Four times they circled, each plane dropping many small anti-personnel bombs while we lay flat, still availing ourselves of such cover as the rocks would allow.

Little bits of rock and splinters came ricocheting and whining all around us and for the best part of an hour we lay there helpless as the minutes dragged by. Then another plane passed, unloading its deathly hail and another's engines grew louder as it approached to attack. At last, they circled for the last time, still keeping high and headed back towards Uweinat. One by one, we came out from behind our rocks and breathed a sigh of relief when we realised no one had been hit. By a miracle our trucks also were intact, although I am sure the enemy must have thought they had destroyed them, with such a shower of dust and smoke that the bombs had put up all around them. Apart from puncturing a few of our water tins and embedding pieces of shrapnel in our tyres, we were able to proceed, which we did at a hot pace. After two hours of fast going, we stopped for lunch and tried rather unsuccessfully to contact our Vickers Valentia troop carrier plane which we knew was to meet us a few miles from here in what was known as the Gilf.

This plane had been sent from Cairo with Major Mitford and Dr. Edmundson, ostensibly to take back any prisoners we may have taken and to attend to casualties we may have received. We were anxious to prevent it being attacked by hostile aircraft against which such a plane would have little chance. Having tried in vain to get signals through our transmission, we decided to proceed towards the Gilf and the appointed rendezvous.

We had no sooner arrived at the spot when, at 2.30pm we spied the Valentia high up over the Gilf, and firing our Verey light signals, to which they replied, the pilot brought her gently down. How reassuring it was to see the good old red, white and blue on the wings after our last encounter with aircraft.

I shall always remember that afternoon of Friday, November 1, when our trucks disgorged their human cargoes of unwashed, unshaven men, and we went forward to the crew and personnel of the troop carrier. Pilot Officer Farr, who accompanied us on one of our former trips in the desert to pick suitable landing grounds, was piloting the machine for Dr. Edmundson and Major Mitford and had brought some of us mail from our base at Abbassia. How it would have done the hearts of our friends and relatives good to see us out there in the middle of the desert reading their letters.

Then the crew, comprising some six men of the RAF, including a wireless operator, mechanic, gunner and co-pilot, presented us with some sweet limes, our first fresh fruit for over a week, and a benzine tin full of dates and other little luxuries.

We stayed there the following two days, doing little jobs around our trucks and getting fuel from one of our dumps in the Gilf for the Valentia. On the morning of November 4, the plane took off. No sooner had it disappeared from sight than we spotted an Italian plane, no doubt patrolling the area so as to again pick up our tracks. However, it passed harmlessly by on the horizon. We all hoped our plane had escaped its notice.

Alf Saunders of W and R patrol recalled an incident when they were training in the use of the EY (Extra Yoke) grenade-launcher. This grenade cup was fitted to the .303 SMLE No. 1 Mk III service rifle which discharged a No. 36M grenade set to a six-second fuse. These were carried in some of the LRDG vehicles and used with great effect on several actions. The lesson was being conducted by Lieutenant Jim Sutherland, who was demonstrating a live firing exercise in front of about twelve men who formed a circle around him. He first fused a grenade and placed it in the rifle cup, then inserted the special blank firing cartridge into the rifle breech.

With the rifle prepared, he accidentally slammed its butt hard onto the ground. The resulting jar caused the weapon to fire, sending the grenade discharging vertically above the heads of the men. Someone shouted 'Run!' and the group dived for cover behind the nearest sand hummock they could find. The bomb came down and exploded on the spot where the troops had just been standing, showering the sheltering men in sand with metal fragments whistling close by.

Fortunately no one was hurt, and as the men scrambled to their feet they started to chuckle at the sight of the lieutenant's ashen face as he realized how close he had come to wiping out half of his patrol. Alf Saunders shouted without thinking, 'Whose side are you on? The Germans?' He got no reply. In jest, the men ensured it took Jim Sutherland a long time to live that one down. Still, the LRDG proficiency in using this weapon against the enemy was to be well proven.

In January 1941, R Patrol under Captain Steele was given another assignment. They were put under the command of the G.O.C. British troops in Egypt and were tasked with assisting Australian forces who were laying a siege against the Italian garrison in the Giarabub oasis and fort. The 6th Australian Cavalry Regiment watched the northern approaches to the town while R Patrol observed the tracks to the west to prevent any supplies reaching the garrison or the enemy escaping. The Giarabub garrison had a limited supply of ammunition, so on occasion R Patrol would tease the fort into firing at them. The patrol would drive up to an escarpment overlooking the enemy position and blaze away with all their weapons. The Italians would answer with big barrages of mortar and artillery fire. In the meantime, the patrol had quickly withdrawn out of range as the Italians wasted their valuable munitions. For two months the patrol engaged in this watch assignment until it was relieved by T Patrol on 2 March. The Italians were supplied from the air and the siege lasted until 22 March when the Australians successfully stormed the fort.

However, R Patrol enjoyed some raiding while keeping watch. For the troops, the siege had been generally a tiresome task, but veteran Alf Saunders recalled one particular highlight. While the patrol was carrying out a reconnaissance of the approaches to Giarabub oasis, they captured an Italian supply convoy, in which among other general goods, they found several large kegs of cognac. Since they had to report their intelligence-gathering and actions to the Australian Brigade HQ, they decided to also deliver a couple of kegs as a gift to cheer up the troops. The cognac was presented and immediately consumed by the officers and men, even using hats and helmets as drinking vessels. However, in a very short time in the hot sun, they soon became very intoxicated. At this point the Kiwis quietly withdrew before things got too out of hand. The Australians had planned an attack the next day, but due to the troops not being in top condition, it was postponed until the following day.

A.D. 'Buster' Gibb was in the same patrol and recalled the incident with the Italian convoy in an interview with the author in 1998:

> The RAF advised us of a large convoy they had shot up and directed us to it. When we got there the Italians had fled, leaving everything behind and escaped to Giarabub. The convoy was overseen by the Italian Saharan

Tractor Company which consisted of eight big D4 American tractors, each pulling three ten-ton trailer loads with a multitude of supplies. They were escorted by a couple of small Fiat trucks with machine guns in the back. Anything considered useful we gathered, such as tea and sugar and some large sacks of macaroni, plus several barrels of cognac. Having recovered what we wanted we then set fire to the whole convoy that had dispersed around the desert. We then took to the tractors with big hammers to make them worthless.

During the siege we also took the opportunity to mine any roads or tracks we thought the Italians might use to supply the fort at Giarabub. Across one track we laid six mines. Sometime later we visited the area again and found a large Lancia truck immobilised there. It had hit a mine with the front right wheel which had blown off with a part going through the sump. The vehicle evidently continued on, and the left dual was blown with the second mine. Evidence showed it carried on just past the row of mines and some unfortunate jumped off the rear of the truck on to a third mine because there were pieces of him everywhere. Being the scavengers they were, some of our chaps saw immediately that the truck could be mobilised. All it needed was to take the right-hand dual and place it on the front and it could be towed away.

Several months later we came back to the convoy area and made our headquarters there. We would patrol from that area going out in small patrols of three trucks at a time. Those not patrolling spent their spare time restoring the tractors. By scavenging parts from two they managed in time to restore six. They had auxiliary motors that you started to fire the main motor. But we only had one set of plugs which we put in one tractor, start it up, take the plugs out and go to the next one and start it up, and then we would have them all going and be haring around, playing with these tractors just for fun. Only Kiwis would do that! There was also one little Fiat truck that was not damaged. I wanted to take it back to Cairo to drive around in. It had a machine gun on a tripod mounted in the back that would not have been of much good as it had a large wine barrel restricting the full use of the gun. I guess they weren't expecting an attack.

We contacted Cairo and managed to get a spare sump for the Lancia. We had taken one of the duals off, the dual off the other side and put it on the front and made a single wheel on the back. A supply of diesel fuel was also acquired from Cairo and fun and games were enjoyed by all. Unfortunately, some wide-awake character in HQ wondered why we wanted a quantity of diesel when our trucks ran on petrol and set investigations in train. It was not long after that the tractors and the Lancia and Fiat were taken off us. I am sure they found a use for them somewhere else.

Truck *Rotokawa* parked alongside the water pipe at Ain Dalla. They are filling 2-gallon water tins.

R Patrol men resting by Pottery Hill, so named because of the many ancient pots strewn about. From left: Lance Corporal J.I. Schaab, Private F.R. Brown, Corporal C.G. Ball and Trooper L.A. Willcox, Trooper A.M. Saunders. In front: Trooper G.H. Nelson.

A patrol gathered for a halt in the desert to trade with Arabs.

R Patrol men show off a dump of aircraft bombs and fuel that they found buried in the sand.

Captain Steele (left) examines the munitions dump they found before destroying it.

An aircraft recognition profile of a Savoia-Marchetti SM.79 Italian bomber. R Patrol located one of these on the ground and destroyed it.

An aircraft recognition profile of a Caproni Ghibli light bomber. The LRDG often encountered this aircraft in ground-to-air actions.

An RAF Vickers Valentia troop carrier. In October 1940, in conjunction with the LRP in support, this obsolete aircraft flew eight missions on mapping and reconnaissance work.

(**Above**) Trooper A.M. Saunders stands in front of a Ford V8 command car. The trooper on the left is unidentified.

(**Opposite, above**) A wartime map showing the locations of Giarabub and Siwa.

(**Opposite, below**) These Australian troops look pleased with their food rations. During the siege of Giarabub the Italian food supplies were strictly rationed and supplied by air as ground convoys were intercepted by the LRDG or shot up by the RAF.

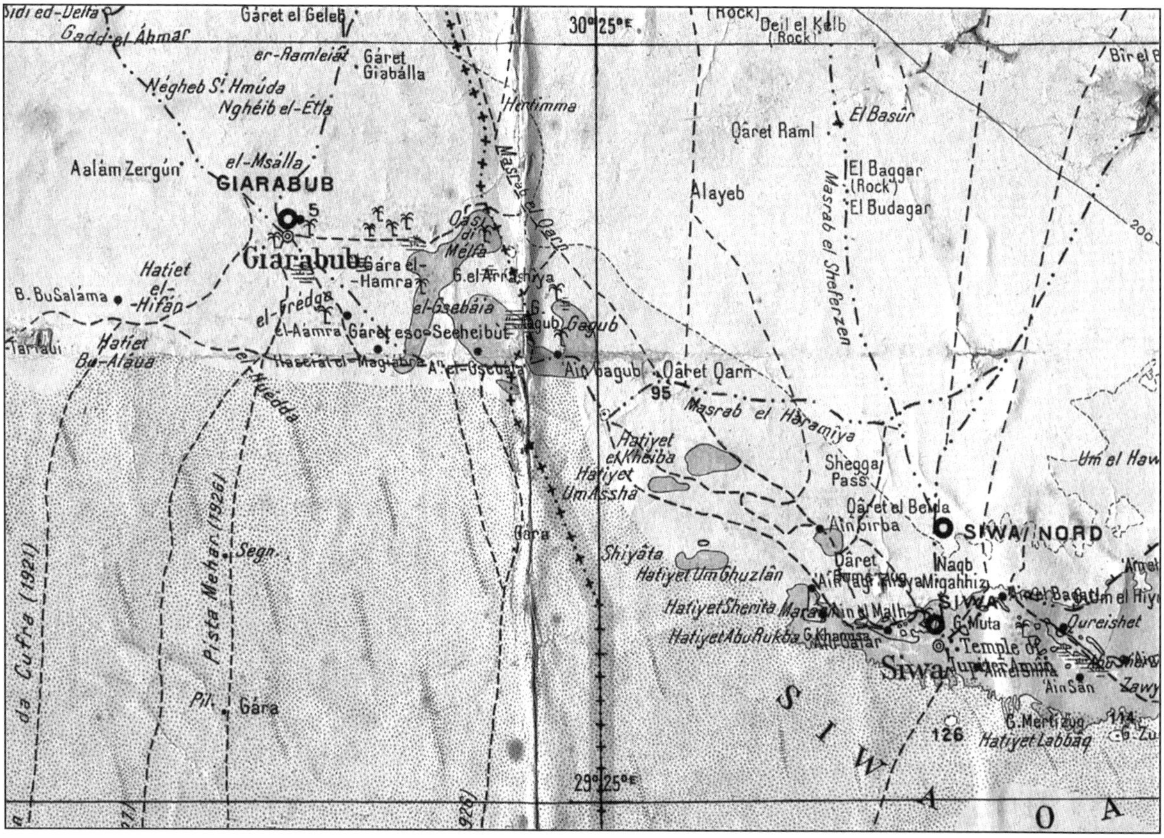
Gadd el Áhmar
Gáret el Geleb
er-Ramleiát
Gáret Giabálla
Négheb S.t Hmúda
Nghéib el-Étla
Hertimma
Aalám Zergún
el-Msálla
GIARABUB
Giarabub
Hatíet el-Hifán
B. BuSaláma
Gára el-Hamra
el-Grédga
el-Aámra
Hatíet Bu-Aláua
Masrab el Qach
30° 25' E
Qâret Raml
El Basûr
El Baggar (Rock)
El Budagar
Alayeb
Masrab el Sheferzen
Ain Gagub
Qâret Qarn
95
Masrab el Haramiya
Hatiyet el Kheiba
Hatiyet Um Assha
Shegga Pass
Qâret el Beida
SIWA NORD
Shiyâta
Hatiyet Um Ghuzlân
Hatiyet Sherita Marag
Hatiyet AbuRukba
Ain el Malh
SIWA
G. Muta
Temple of Jupiter Amon
Siwa
Qureishet
G. Mertizug
126
Hatiyet Labbaq
Um el Haw
Gára
Segn.
Pista Mehar (1926)
da Cufra (1921)
Pil. Gára
29° 25' E
SIWA OA
200

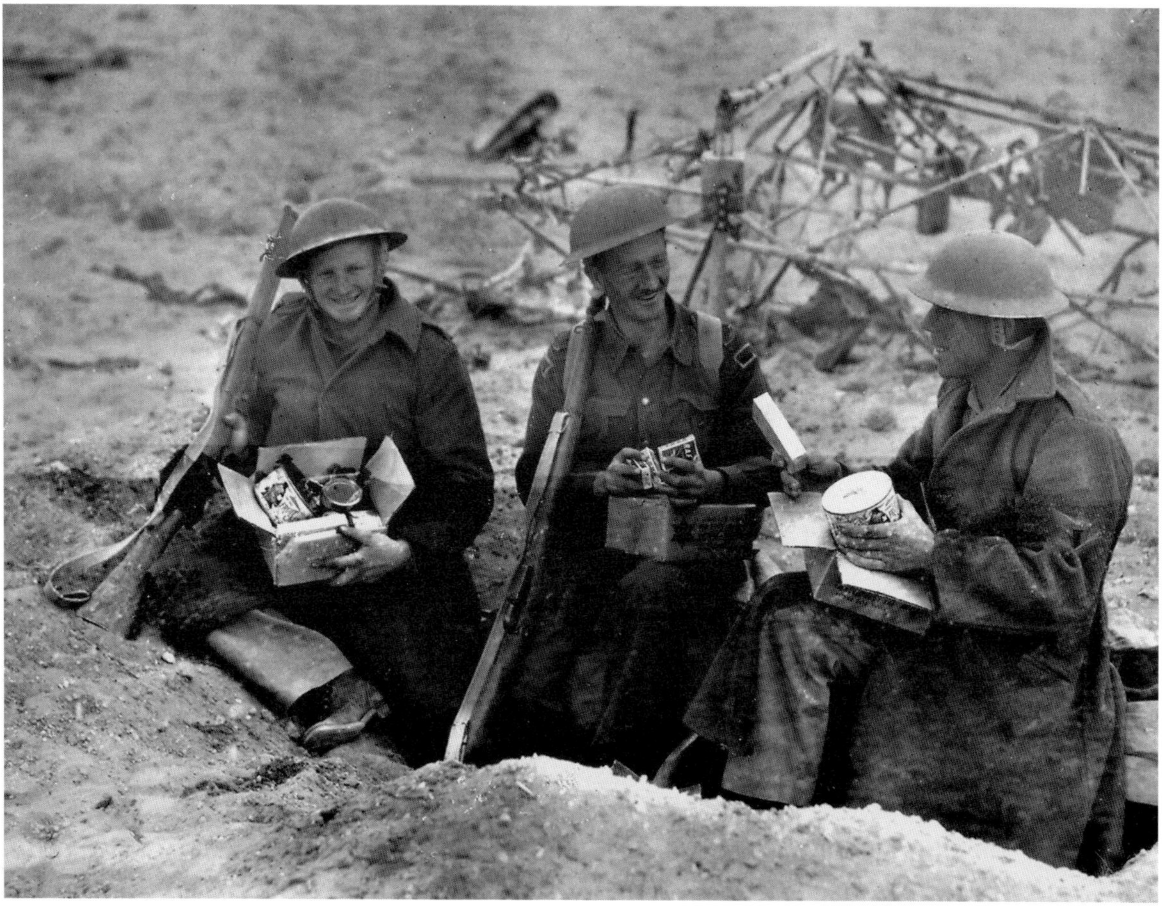

R Patrol pose at the perimeter of Giarabub before the Australian troops successfully attacked the enemy position. Centre, behind the barrel of captured brandy, are Captain D.G. Steele and Lieutenant J.H. Sunderland. Extreme right: Gunner C.O. Grimsey. Sitting left downwards are Trooper M.E. Hammond, Private E. Harcourt, Trooper L.A. Willcox, Trooper A.M. Saunders and Private M. Allen with rum jar.

Italian gunners beside their 105mm field piece. The fort at Giarabub was well supported with artillery. The LRDG used to fire at these positions and then quickly withdraw to entice the artillery to waste their limited ammunition on return fire.

An abandoned Italian *Cannone da 105/28* field artillery piece. The trooper holds a 105mm projectile.

A *Cannone da 152/37* heavy artillery piece left on the road by the Italians.

The LRDG capture a convoy that was on its way to supply Giarabub.

Rummaging through intercepted supplies, they look for anything useful that could be carried away by the patrol. The Italians fled in their faster vehicles when the LRDG appeared on the horizon.

As the patrol drove away it left behind black pillars of smoke as the enemy supplies on the loaded trailers burned.

Mines had been laid on the approaches to Giarabub fort and this Lancia truck was damaged and abandoned. R patrol members, left: Sergeant P. McGregor, Trooper L.A. Willcox and Sergeant A.D. (Buster) Gibb. Behind the truck were found the remains of an Italian soldier who had stepped on a mine.

The recovered damaged Lancia truck being towed by two patrol vehicles. It was later made serviceable again.

A trooper examines one of the two convoy Fiat 508 *Militare* escort vehicles. This one mounted a defensive Fiat-Revelli M1914/35 machine gun in the back.

The DH4 convoy tractors of the Italian Saharan Tractor Company lined up after being captured and reused for recreation by the LRDG for a short time.

Fiat OC1 tractors were used by the Italians to haul smaller loads.

Chapter Four

The Long Range Desert Group

In November 1940, the LRP was disestablished. A new formation known as the Long Range Desert Group was created. In December, under the command of Captain M.D.D. Crichton-Stuart, recruits from the Coldstream and Scots Guards regiments joined the unit as the G (Guards) Patrol. They took over the vehicles and equipment of W Patrol which was now disbanded. Its members either returned to their parent units or reinforced R or T Patrol. On 31 January 1941, a second new patrol was formed known as S (South Rhodesian) Patrol under the command of Captain C.A. Holliman. The third patrol – Y (Yeomanry) – was introduced on 25 February 1941 under the command of Captain P.J.D. McCraith.

At this time Bluey Grimsey wrote a poem titled the *LRP Lament* marking the end of the unit as it transformed into the LRDG (see Appendix I).

In January 1941, Bagnold wrote of his desired criteria for appointing new recruits for the LRDG. As per his *Notes on Long Range Desert Patrols*:

Other Ranks

In selecting men for this work, they should be specially picked. They should be resourceful, alert, intelligent and possessed of a sense of responsibility, and emphasis should be laid on these qualities rather than on mere 'toughness'. The Long Range Patrol is a complicated technical mechanism in which a breakdown might spell disaster even though no enemy is encountered.

Training

The only real training is gained during a long desert journey. Given (a) previous experience in the handling of their weapons, (b) good fitters and mechanics, (c) a nucleus of men with previous experience of the desert, a patrol composed of the right type of man can be made ready to operate against the enemy in his own desert territory after a journey of 1,000 miles across unmapped trackless country.

Don Steele also wrote of the new structure of the LRDG in his post-war recollections:

At this time control of the LRP, which should have been passed to the New Zealanders, was lost to them, owing to the short-sighted policy of 2NZEF. No reinforcements were available and some of the men already with us were forced to return to their parent units. W Patrol was split up among R and T Patrols to bring them up to strength. General Freyberg said to me, 'I cannot have my division split up into all these little forces, you cannot have any more men, and all of you will have to return very soon.' However, very soon after this we got a good write-up in the local Egyptian press about some of our earlier actions and that changed everything. From then on we never had to worry about getting any men we wanted and what is more we could pick and choose. But it was too late, new patrols were made up from the Guards, the Yeomanry and the Rhodesians. Mitford who commanded W Patrol was promoted and given the new A Squadron. Lieutenant J.H. Sutherland went to R Patrol as 2I/C, Lieutenant L.B. Ballantyne to T Patrol as 2I/C and Lieutenant R.B. McQueen went to Group HQ.

When G, Y and S Patrols were trained in desert work the unit was divided into A and B Squadrons and Group HQ. A Squadron was originally made up of G and Y Patrols, B Squadron of R, S and T Patrols. While Group HQ was made up of Signal, Repair and Heavy Transport sections, Group HQ also acted as B Squadron HQ:

> On the relief of the original A Squadron in October 1941 at Siwa by R Patrol, there was a general regrouping of patrols. In what we called the coastal belt it had been found that the full patrols were too conspicuous and owing to the short journeys, too uneconomical. Patrols had therefore been split in two. R Patrol became R1 and R2 Patrols. We were joined later by T1 and T2, and still later by S1, S2, G1, G2 and Y1 and Y2. The LRDG was now split into ten half patrols, with each having fifteen to eighteen men in five vehicles. Each patrol incorporated specialists, a navigator, radio operator, medical orderly and a vehicle mechanic (fitter), each of whom manned a truck equipped for their role, plus a command or pilot vehicle.
>
>   There was now a demand for general recces, going recces, route recces, road watches, offensive patrols, search parties, demolition parties and parties to carry Arab and English agents, wireless set, rations, ammunition and other weapons of war into the general area of the Jebel Akhdar. When all these jobs became too much for us, Y1 and Y2 came under my command. This was too much for Group HQ and they very soon came along to spoil our fun. However, I now had the NZ Patrols under my command, and to avoid losing them I was able to persuade 2NZEF to let me have the men to form a Squadron HQ. Thus, A Squadron became A (NZ) Squadron and any Group orders had to come through our HQ. The New Zealanders were under NZ command. But for all of this R1 Patrol remained under me until Captain Jake Easonsmith, ex-Royal Tank Regiment, replaced me as patrol commander. Without a doubt, the best patrol work was done by this patrol and all the men loved and respected their new upright and fearless leader.

By the end of October 1941, the designations were changed to G1, G2, R1, R2, S1, S2, T1, T2 and Y1 and Y2. The New Zealand patrols comprised A Squadron, while the Guards, Yeomanry and Rhodesians became B Squadron. An expanded

Group HQ oversaw the patrols and was supported by a Signals Troop, Light Repair Squadron and an Air Section of two Waco liaison aircraft. In addition, there was a Heavy Section that transported supplies to forward hidden dumps and between bases.

With its formation in July 1940, there was no LRDG insignia. Any badges that were worn usually reflected their parent unit. The first badge was a commemorative or 'sweetheart' badge to mark the existence of the Long Range Patrol. It was unofficial and made for those who served with W, R and T Patrols, plus LRP HQ. When the Guards Patrol joined in November 1940, the unit became known as the LRDG. The badge was designed in September 1940 by Gunner Bluey Grimsey with the help of Doctor F.B. Edmundson, the medical officer. At first the badge was rejected by Colonel Bagnold for security reasons. However, he later gave approval because it was unofficial and was only to serve as a keepsake for family and sweethearts, but not to be worn on the uniform.

Claude Grimsey wrote on 16 June 1949 his recollections regarding the creation of the LRP/LRDG badge:

> I was the original designer of the LRDG badge, and its history is worth recording. Very early in the life of the LRDG, then called the Long Range Patrol, there was a popular desire for a distinctive badge. So, in September 1940, I designed a badge with the help of Dr. Edmundson, our Medical Officer of the group. He asked me to design a badge using a scorpion as a symbolic emblem of the desert in which we were to work. At that time, I had never seen a scorpion. However, I copied a very poor illustration of one from a dictionary. However, the whole project was dropped as Colonel Bagnold did not want any of us to have any identification of any kind which might fall into enemy hands.
>
> Later I went and saw the colonel and asked if the men could have a brooch made to send to their wives and sweethearts, but not to wear on their uniform. He agreed and Mr Hasseram in the Faude el Awal in Cairo made close to a hundred of these based on a scorpion within a wheel. Colonel Bagnold bought one of these himself.

The LRP badge was silver and stamped on the reverse with two or three Arab hallmarks and manufactured by a Cairo jeweller. It was brooch-mounted and exhibited a fat scorpion within a circle that represented a wheel. Grimsey was a competent artist. So when Dr. Edmundson asked him to make a design using a scorpion as a symbolic emblem of the desert, he had actually never seen a real one up until that time. Consequently he copied an inaccurate drawing of an example he saw in a dictionary. Hence the 'fat' scorpion was also referred to as the 'scarab' badge because it looked like a beetle. Originally the scorpion was gilded with a gold wash. However, on most examples seen today, the gold wash has worn off over time. Close to 100 badges were struck for the LRP men to purchase before they destroyed the die themselves.

In a letter to Jack Davis in 1978, the Secretary of the LRDG (NZ) Association Dick Croucher wrote of his memory of how the badge came about:

> Bluey Grimsey was the prime designer of the badge. When at Abbassia Barracks in June 1940, the then LRP members were asked to exercise their minds and to think of an appropriate badge. There were several suggestions and some chaps even had one made up by the wog jewellers. One was a truck in a circle with a scroll with the letters 1st LRP below, and another was a scorpion in the same format. Unfortunately, however, the scorpion had its legs growing out the wrong way and it looked more like a pineapple! None of these in any case were official badges. Later at the Citadel, Bluey came up with the modified version and as we were then LRDG, incorporated those letters within the circle. He also suggested a scroll below with the motto 'by guile and not by strength'. However, this was not accepted by the hierarchy. It is understood that Bluey did catch a scorpion which he used for his basic final design.

However, by early 1942 the LRDG was finally issued with a cap badge and shoulder titles. Gunner Grimsey also designed the official brass LRDG cap badge, some of which were also made in bronze or blackened brass. He recalled how it came about:

> While with R Patrol at Tazerbo in June 1941, I had laid out my bed under a date palm and went to work on my theodolite. Long after the others were in bed I crept into my blankets and fell quickly asleep. I was rudely awakened by an extremely sharp stabbing pain in my right shoulder blade, in my elbow and again on the back of my hand. In the morning I found a dead scorpion in my blankets. My arm was numb like one's gum after a dentist's needle. I took the scorpion to show our medical orderly Mick Allen. Everyone roared with laughter and said, 'Bluey has been stung by a scorpion and the scorpion died!'
>
> This became quite a joke, and the scorpion was taken back to Kufra in whisky spirit. Time passed and then again at Kufra I received a note from HQ in Cairo with a scorpion enclosed, which I think was mine, asking me to design a badge. This I did and this is how the official badge came to be designed by me.

The scorpion was an emblem used by a number of military forces before the LRDG adopted it as it is a potent symbol of power in a small unit. Its menacing appearance and its ability to strike suddenly and with great effect seemed appropriate to the LRDG.

R Patrol veteran Alf Saunders was with Grimsey when he suffered his scorpion sting. He recalled the incident in an interview with the author:

> During one of our sojourns at Siwa Oasis, Bluey was stung by a green scorpion, a very painful and dangerous thing to happen by any scorpion, let

alone a green one. These things injected a very poisonous venom into the unfortunate recipient; some would be incapacitated for a week or more while the poison worked its way through one's system, a very painful experience. Anyway, this night Bluey was stung by one of these creatures, but by morning the scorpion had died, and Bluey seemed none the worse for his experience. But we gave him hell for killing a poor little scorpion and wondered aloud, within his hearing, as to what sort of blood coursed along his veins; we all decided that all sorts of acids composed his blood to enable him to kill a little scorpion, but he took all our ribbing in good heart.

The scorpion on the new badge was now more accurately represented, with the LRDG letters enclosed within the circle. At first consideration was given to including a crown on top, but the idea was discarded in favour of the clean circle. Most of these were produced in Egypt, where they were either cast or die-struck and then hand-cut. There was usually no maker's mark and the quality, finish and design varied. Some examples displayed slightly different patterns on the back of the scorpion. Moreover, the circle varied in form, either being oval or flat with a single or double raised edge. The Cairo jewellers also offered other LRDG-related items, such as ashtrays, cigarette cases, rings, lapel and tie pins, plus silver and gold LRDG 'sweetheart' badges. One badge was even made to order of gold and studded with diamonds.

Don Steele wrote his LRDG recollections for the NZ War History Branch archive in 1949. He reflected on what LRDG trucks had to endure that contributed to their wear and tear and the good work of the fitters:

> We found that for work out of our Siwa base, the four or five car patrols were most suitable. They were less conspicuous from the air and much easier for the commander to control than the previous eleven car patrols. The shortness of the run necessary meant that far less fuel and rations had to be carried and any greater number would have been uneconomical in men and machines. Another reason for the change was the tremendous demand for our services.
>
> A good word should be said about our trucks, they earned it. They were ordinary commercial-type Chevrolets with a few modifications for our special needs. They had the most gruelling time of it in the desert. There were no roads, and they spent their lives hauling us over the roughest country for thousands of miles. In this area the shortest trip usually averaged about 500 miles and included every type of desert country, steep hills, rough rocks, dry watercourses, sand and dust. In the winter there was often mud and deep streams or flooded wadis. All this and more and they never let us down. It is hard for people used to treating their cars humanely to realize just what those trucks had to put up with.
>
> After the most ordinary patrol, both the men and trucks had to have a spell. While the men could have doubtless stood a great deal more, it was a most wearing business on the nerves. As soon as the trucks returned,

they were stripped of all their guns and equipment and run along to the fitters. There they received all the loving attention that could be lavished on them. Our fitters were probably the best to be found in the Middle East, and they gave their best. It was a matter of pride with them to have the vehicles back on the road with the least possible delay. They would often work right through the night to have a patrol ready for its next task. We owed them a lot!

One veteran recorded his thoughts on the fitters in the field in a document where the writer is unidentified:

> The skill and resourcefulness of the fitters was legendary especially when also operating in the field. Most of the desert in North Africa consists of sand dunes rising to a height of 600 feet, but there are some parts known as ergs which were made up of large pieces of broken rock that were partly buried in the sand, and they made for very difficult going. It was a case of crawler gear and let the truck crawl.
>
> Our trucks were 30cwt Canadian-built Chevrolets stripped of everything such as cabs to lighten the overall weight. They were loaded with rations, water, petrol, oil, mines, grenades and all the other things that might be needed in a patrol lasting up to three months.
>
> On one trip across an erg one truck dropped hard with its diff landing on another big rock. Inspection showed that the diff housing was cracked, and the cover plate was crushed. The hot diff oil was running out and it was obvious that something had to be done. We did not carry a spare diff or any diff oil.
>
> Everyone was requested to chew Wrigleys. When this was done the gum was packed into the cracks in the housing and then we all sat about thinking about diff oil. We could not abandon the truck and it would be impossible to tow it 1,000 miles across the desert. Then someone had a bright idea. Our rations were in petrol cases, and each was numbered for the day to be used. On this particular patrol the cases included some bananas and one bright lad suggested that the bananas be packed into the diff, skins as well, and try it out. No other suggestions were made so the diff was packed with the bananas.
>
> The cover plate was hammered out to near its original shape and bolted and a trial run was made of about 5 miles. After that the diff housing was relatively cool and there was no noise. You may laugh at this, but we started out for Cairo, just a small jaunt of about 1,000 miles. Every 50 miles the truck stopped, and the crew checked the diff for overheating and noise, but all went well, and we reached our base with everything still going.

Buster Gibb, R Patrol NCO, also recalled the work of the trucks:

> Those Chev trucks stood up to the extremes wonderfully well and survived being literally rolled down sand dunes, bounced over obstacles and

crash-landed time after time. The longest jump on the flat over a sand ripple was with a Chev that flew 14 metres from take-off to landing. A bent tie rod was the only damage. A greater distance was achieved with a Ford F30 four-wheel drive. It leapt 16 metres, though all the bolts of both front wheel housings were sheared. The Ford's four-wheel drive saved no end of digging but didn't compare with the Chevs.

Eric Harcourt of R Patrol also recorded his thoughts of the challenges of driving over sand dunes:

> One day we had to turn right out of a wadi and climb up huge sand dunes. We always travelled in a numbered sequence. My truck, No. 9, was second last in line. The dunes were about 600ft high and it was more than a right-angle turn to head up them. The boss in his 15cwt V8 flew up but the 30cwt trucks got bogged down. Me too. I went into reverse and with the steep incline was able to reverse out down the dunes to the wadi. I went up the wadi and then turned round and stirred the old girl up. Not having to make the acute right-hand turn I sheered over to the right of the dune and kept on going until I finally shoved her in creeper gear and ran over the top.
>
> I drove on a way to leave room for the others and went back to the boss, Captain Steele, and Spotswood his driver. Steele congratulated me and remarked on the other nine trucks all bogged down in a heap. 'If a Ghibli (Italian plane) comes over he will wipe out the lot of them!' He wanted to know how I thought of it. I told him I had read *Lily on Sands*, a book written by Colonel Bagnold, the father of the LRDG. He was most emphatic, 'Never run in the wheel tracks of another truck.' To which Steele replied, 'Well, that's something the others will have to learn.'

One of the two LRDG Waco aircraft being greeted as it comes into land; this one is AX697. They were used for liaison duties and, where possible, to transport the sick and wounded. It also carried urgent vehicle spares, mail, supplies and personnel.

(**Above**) General B.C. Freyberg VC, C-in-C 2NZEF. Cairo, 1941.

(**Opposite, above**) R Patrol members pose next to a burned-out Caproni Ca.309 Ghibli light bomber at Kufra airfield. In front left: unidentified, Trooper G.H. Nelson, Trooper M.E. Hammond and Trooper J.W. Eyles, navigator.

(**Opposite, below**) Gunner C.O. (Bluey) Grimsey relaxing in camp playing his flute. He was a talented writer, artist and navigator. He also designed the LRDG scorpion badge.

Paybook cover of Trooper M.E. (Bill) Hammond, R Patrol. Laid out are his LRDG and LRP badges, a shoulder title and silver identity chain. The chain was made by a jeweller in Cairo and measured 35mm × 20mm.

An LRDG Arab headdress and *agal* with LRDG badge and shoulder titles.

An example of LRDG badges and titles. The smaller pins are LRDG (NZ) Association tie or lapel pins. These belonged to Lieutenant A.R. Cramond as pictured.

Lance Corporal C.H.B. (Dick) Croucher, patrol navigator, 1940. He was commissioned and went on to serve with distinction in the LRDG until the end of the war. Note the wooden Shell fuel boxes on the truck; each contained two 4-gallon benzine tins.

A fitter's fantasy! A 1941 cartoon cover on the Cairo-published *The V Weekly Magazine*.

(**Above**) R Patrol members at eleven weeks in the desert. They had come across two barrels of water left by the Italians, so the troops took their first opportunity to wash their clothes. Left, Trooper C. Waetford and navigator Lance Corporal J.W. Eyles. Note the heavy .303 Vickers machine gun mounted on the truck.

(**Opposite, above**) An R Patrol Ford F30 truck, *Rotoehu* F8, at Siwa, 1941. These vehicles replaced the well-served and worn-out Chevrolet WA trucks. The driver is Trooper A.F. Dodunski; standing right is Sergeant C.G. (Curly) Ball.

(**Opposite, below**) Collapsed front wheel of a Ford F30 that jumped a small dune at high speed.

Dressed for the cold, two foremost HQ officers, Jalo 1942. Captain W.K. (Bill) Kennedy Shaw, skilled navigator and Intelligence officer. Captain D. (Shorty) Barrett, Quartermaster LRDG, who had the huge task of keeping the patrols supplied. Their HQ Chevrolet 1311X3 15cwt is parked behind.

Libyan Patrol by Major Charles Gilson, published in 1943 by Blackie & Son Limited, London. This was the first fiction book based on the LRDG.

Chapter Five

Libyan Taxi Service

To take part in the British offensive in Cyrenaica in November 1941, the LRDG was placed under the command of the newly-formed Eighth Army and in October the whole Group was moved from Kufra to Siwa. In August 1941 Major D.G. (Don) Steele had been appointed the commanding officer of A (NZ) Squadron LRDG. He was later awarded the OBE in recognition of his services while in command at Siwa and later Jalo. His citation dated 8 September 1942 read as follows:

> Major Steele was one of the original members of the Long Range Desert Group when the unit was formed in July 1940, and later assumed independent command of a detached squadron of the unit. He was responsible for planning operations of the patrols under his command and for dealing with the supply and maintenance problems involved. The operations included most successful attacks on enemy aerodromes and communications far beyond the front line and reconnaissances deep into Tripolitania. The results obtained were largely due to the zeal and efficiency with which Major Steele commanded his squadron.

Steele had planned operations which included successful attacks on enemy communications and airfields, reconnaissance as far as Tripolitania and the transport of demolition parties, secret agents and search parties (referred to as the 'Libyan Taxi Service') to various points behind the lines. Steele recorded his impressions of Siwa:

> About the middle of 1941 I took R Patrol up north from Kufra to Siwa. We had just returned from a spell of Cairo leave, and, as always after a few days in the Delta area, felt glad to be back in the desert again away from the humidity that made life in the Delta so tiresome. In the dry heat of the central desert, one was never wet with sweat. It dried the moment it reached the surface, and the only sign was a gradual accumulation of salt on the arms and so forth. When it was remembered that we washed only when we were at or near a well it will be seen that this was a great boon. I mean by that of course washing in water. We had another kind: 'dry' washing. On our first run in the desert, we were introduced to this process by Bagnold. One day when we were halted in the Sand Sea he announced to the world at large, 'W-well I'm going to have a b-bath!' and forthwith wandered off into the sand. Those of us in hearing all looked a bit sheepish and there was a certain

amount of head-tapping. He wandered about for a while examining the sand and then for no particular reason that we could see stripped off and started to rub himself all over with the stuff. He returned a few minutes later looking very smug. We tried it (when nobody was looking, and on very small areas) and it worked! The explanation was simple; the sand simply removed a layer of skin. The dirt went with it. The skin was left with a slightly buffed appearance, but sweet and clean.

We left Kufra and, keeping the Kalansho Sand Sea on our left, passed through the Great or Egyptian Sand Sea, coming out on the coastal belt at Garet Khod. Thence east through Giarabub at the western end of the Qattara Depression and so on till we arrived at Siwa.

On arrival we found that the work we could have to do in the future, while basically the same as before, was considerably different in detail. Gone were the carefree days when we were more or less safe from the enemy before and after a raid, safe in our beloved and cursed sand. Up in this narrow strip of dusty, dirty, fly-infested country one had to be very careful. That is, if one wanted to go to some particular spot without the opposition knowing. As a compensation, the patrols were much shorter in time and distance. This meant less time between swims in Cleopatra's pool; a good thing, for the desert near the coast was made up largely of clay overlaid with a thin sprinkling of gravel and consequently was very dirty to travel over.

Life in the oasis of Siwa was fairly pleasant on the whole. We could buy a few fresh vegetables from the locals and at one stage oranges were in fair supply, also the odd egg. Siwa is noted for its dates, but the main attraction was the numerous springs. These varied in size from a few feet across to about 10 yards. The larger ones like Cleopatra and the Figure Eight pools were enclosed with stone walls and deep and made first-class swimming pools. The water was cool, clear and only very slightly saline. Here the troops spent most of their leisure time and inter-patrol water polo competitions were very popular. Near one of the pools, we made tennis courts by rolling the salt mud with trucks and surrounding the area with camouflage netting.

For living quarters we had some native mud huts or houses, though some of the men preferred to sleep in the open where it was cooler. These mud houses of Siwa were rather interesting. They were built from the material available on site; a mixture of mud, salt and water. The salt is there from the evaporation of the more or less brackish spring water. When dry, the mixture sets like concrete and remains so unless there is heavy rain. Since there are only a few brief showers, as a rule, in the winter, this means the buildings are more or less permanent. In the old town, which has been partially demolished by the Egyptian Army for reasons of health and public safety, some of the ruins stood seven or eight storeys high. The roof beams were grown on the spot, being date palm trunks split in two, and made happy hunting grounds for scorpions.

Don Steele also wrote his recollections of the 'Libyan Taxi Service':

> The 'Taxi Service', so-called, was run mainly between Siwa and the Jebel Akhdar. Many gallant souls in Egypt, who spoke fluent Arabic, had joined the General Service branch of the ME Force in Cairo, and had suggested the idea of installing themselves with some of the Arab tribes to find out what they could about the enemy and also to enlist the help of friendly natives. They were very brave men. They lived as Arabs and were in constant danger of being betrayed and shot by a realistic enemy. Such information as they obtained was sent back by radio. They had sets buried in all sorts of places. Our job was simply to take them where they wanted to go and later bring them back. In between times we would take them food for distribution among the natives, batteries for their radios and ammunition and explosives. They had nice habits, those men, and liked nothing better than to play tricks on the opposition. One never knew what was going to turn up on those trips. Aircraft of both sides were often about, and both were hostile. Enemy ground patrols were regularly in the Jebel area and had to be avoided at all costs so as not to give the game away. Sometimes the Arabs would bring an escaped PoW to the rendezvous and the patrol would have the pleasant job of delivering him safely to his own mates again.
>
> Returning from one such run, a patrol got a bad fright. They were steaming along headed for home when someone cried 'Aircraft!' Several fighters were coming along at zero feet almost on their track. There is nothing worse than a fighter at zero feet if you are in a truck and he sees you. However, the planes disappeared over a ridge and appeared to land. Curious, the patrol poked its head over the ridge too and they saw a plane on the ground. They went to investigate, where they found an RAF crew of a Wellington bomber that had been winged over Benghazi and made a forced landing. They were walking home and seemed glad of the offer of a lift by the patrol. Amazingly, there was a New Zealander among them, Lindsay Grey, who I had known as a boy! Our other 'taxi' tasks were, almost without exception, quite interesting. In fact, any old job that was required.

From their new base at Siwa, the patrols were to watch the desert tracks to the south of Jebel Akhdar and to report on the movements of enemy reinforcements and withdrawals. R1 Patrol, now under the command of Captain J.R. (Jake) Easonsmith, undertook several reconnaissance/topographical missions and would drop off and pick up secret agents.

One day as R1 Patrol was travelling on a reconnaissance mission near Gambut, nearer than usual to the rear of the Axis positions at Sollum, they were trying to locate a supply dump of petrol, food and ammunition when they halted for the night and prepared the evening meal. Easonsmith, while waiting for his supper, went for a stroll over a nearby ridge when he found himself looking down on an Italian mobile workshop spread out in a fold in the ground. The light was still good, so he decided to have supper first before dealing with the enemy. When dinner was over, the men took three trucks and attacked the unsuspecting Italians. Surprised, most fled for their lives, but two surrendered. The prisoners begged a moment's notice to collect their kit, and in the meantime the patrol wrecked ten diesel trucks and the workshop lorries.

On their way back to Siwa the cook, at mealtimes as per usual practice, would dig a small hole for his fire. Seeing this, the prisoners became panic-stricken, flung themselves on their knees and begged for mercy. They took some convincing that their graves were not being dug!

On their next mission on 14 October 1941, Easonsmith left Siwa with a patrol of five trucks carrying fifteen all ranks and two Arabs. They crossed the wire at Weshka and, moving by the Wadi Mra, arrived on the 16th at the first rendezvous at Abd el Krim. This was where they were to pick up Captain J. Haselden, a British agent who had been working in the Jebel for three weeks with friendly Arabs. However, he hadn't arrived yet, but the next day they did find three British soldiers who had escaped from a Benghazi prison camp the week before. They had been hiding in the ruins at Garet Tecasis, 12 miles south of Abd bu Krim.

Having waited for the appointed time and searched the area, on 19 October the patrol went on to the second rendezvous at Ain bu Sfia. Two trucks were left at Garet Tecasis, which were to be employed to take Captain Haselden back to Siwa if he later arrived. Furthermore, the two Arabs were sent on to look for him at Marsua about 20 miles to the north where he was eventually found. Haselden, along with three escapees, was taken to Siwa in the vehicles that had been left behind to provide the 'Taxi Service'.

In the meantime, Easonsmith undertook a short reconnaissance on foot and discovered the presence of four enemy trucks and two light tanks close at hand. Taking three days' rations, he continued his observations alone on foot and came across an enemy landing ground which was noted. On 23 October, he climbed to the top of an escarpment where he spotted an enemy camp in the distance at Ain bu Sfia. There he tallied about thirty to forty vehicles and four light tanks. They were parked round the base of a small circular hill with the ruins of a fort on the top which was being used as a lookout post. On another rise there appeared to be low bivouac tents which may have had covered stores. Also there was a constant stream of traffic passing through the camp in the direction of Mechili and Easonsmith decided to make a small 'cutting out' expedition on the truck convoy.

He wanted to seize a prisoner for interrogation, so he decided to lay an ambush with his three trucks on some dead ground close to the track. After a short reconnaissance on foot, he sent two trucks to some rising ground commanding the track, and about 3 or 4 miles from the camp he took the third vehicle to a point on the track about 2 miles away. His intention was to attract the enemy's notice by simulating a breakdown, and therefore turned back along the track dropping some 'specially doctored' boxes of Italian machine-gun ammunition as he went. It was hoped the trucks would slow down to pick up the boxes and later the rounds would prove to be dangerous to the user. Unfortunately, he had not noticed that there was dead ground in the direction from which a convoy of about twenty enemy vehicles was coming and near the spot chosen for the 'breakdown'. They were not seen until they were about 200 yards away and then the deception had to be hurriedly staged.

Of the crew of four, two leaned over the engine, while his gunner Corporal R.O. Spotswood manned his machine gun as he lay concealed under a tarpaulin in the back of the truck. Easonsmith stepped out and held up his hand towards the oncoming traffic. He wrote in his Operational Report what happened next:

> I held up my hand and the leading vehicle that stopped was a large SPA truck. I walked up to it and opened the cab door. Although suspicious, the Italians were still in doubt as to our respectability; I had my Tommy gun behind my back attempting to hide it while coming across. But the time to produce it had come and this I did so very clumsily, standing too close to the driver and he with some guts fell down from the cab on to me and with this sudden move got the gun. We had a short, hand-to-hand tussle, but he got away and ran off. I had a lucky shot with a grenade I threw at him, and he did not get a chance to use the Tommy gun. The passenger, an officer, had in the meantime inaccurately used up all his revolver ammunition and ran, but he was either wounded or killed from fire from our trucks.

All this commotion caused armed soldiers to leap from their vehicles and cautiously advance up beside the column. Fortunately they had no automatic weapons and only carried rifles. Corporal Spotswood had only just managed to fire a few rounds from the back of his truck when his heavy Vickers machine gun jammed. Fortunately, by this time the other two trucks had joined in the fray doing good work with their Lewis guns and small-arms fire. Shouting, 'I must get a prisoner! I must get a prisoner!' Easonsmith ran down the column and threw three grenades among the Italians who sought cover under their transport. The steady and effective LRDG firepower in the surprise attack accounted for damaging at least twelve trucks in the column.

Two Italians were pulled out from under their vehicles, and the leading truck was put out of action with a hand grenade that exploded under the sump, spilling oil everywhere. One of the prisoners was badly wounded and died about two hours later. The other, who was a cook, revealed that the Trieste Motorised Division was on its way to Mechili. Having killed six or seven of the enemy and wounding a dozen, the patrol escaped amazingly unscathed. They got away without any pursuit and by nightfall had covered about 140 miles. The only vehicle damage was a bullet hole in the radiator of Easonsmith's truck. Due to the shortage of water for the leaking radiator and the extra men they were carrying, they curtailed the rest of the mission and set out to return to Siwa. However, they had gained good topographical information on the going, plus intelligence-gathering of the enemy dispositions in the areas in which they operated. Furthermore, they found a crash-landed SM.82 Italian bomber on the ground from which they gained some important papers. Easonsmith wrote the following Intel conclusion in his report:

Enemy Movement

Ground: The two Arabs (reliable) with the party reported a great deal of MT on the road through Maraua. Impossible to keep the track to Mechili under constant observation. The traffic was heavy from 0730 hrs till 1100 hrs on the three days the party was in the area; there was practically a constant stream of MT. During the remainder of the day small parties of a dozen vehicles or so, but no great number. During this period only one tank was seen moving along the road. A check carried out for a quarter of an hour showed:

Open top carriers, men facing inwards, an AA gun in the centre . . . 4
Trucks 5–10 tonners, canvas-covered 16
Motorcycles 6
M/C combinations 1
Omnibus. 1
Small cars 1
No tanks

Note: It was in this area that the party found a crashed SM.82; the plane had apparently been there for over a year. It would appear that with a little attention the plane might be made fit for the air as little damage had been done to the machine in landing. Both propellors were bent and a certain amount of sheeting on the base of the fuselage had been wiped off. Few bullet holes were visible. A considerable number of papers etc. were removed from the plane.

David Lloyd Owen, in his book *Providence Their Guide* published in 1980, wrote in great praise of Easonsmith as a patrol leader as follows:

Jake seemed to have a sort of sixth sense which made him by far the most successful patrol leader the LRDG ever had. Throughout June and July 1941, he was moving freely in and out and around the various enemy posts and patrols and convoys dotted around the Gebel Akhdar and to the south of it. He had an almost uncanny knack of knowing where he would meet danger, and his supreme confidence in his own force's superiority over that of the enemy was of course very quickly transmitted to the men he led, who would follow him anywhere without question or demur.

Not all 'Taxi Service' jobs had encounters with the enemy; many were uneventful in just dropping off and picking up agents. However, often good topographical and general intelligence of enemy dispositions was gathered and sometimes unexpected discoveries were found, as outlined in this routine mission conducted earlier by Easonsmith in September 1941.

Their task was simple: to take two Arab agents to a point from which they could walk into an area bounded on the west by Sidi Timimi and on the east by

Ain el Gazala. The patrol was to wait four days for the agents to complete their mission and take them home again.

They left Siwa on 30 September with two trucks and after several days crossed some rough country to reach their rendezvous point. One truck was left there in reserve while the other proceeded a little further to drop off the agents. Their mission was successful, and the agents returned to the well-concealed LRDG camp in the evening of the fourth day and the small patrol set off to Siwa, arriving on 7 October.

What was eventful on this mission was a discovery they had made along the way. As outlined in Easonsmith's LRDG Reconnaissance Report:

> We found an abandoned Wellington bomber. It appeared to have landed with injury to the crew, who had wrecked the plane most thoroughly. Five men had walked off, but the tracks were too stale to follow, and by discarded equipment we assumed the names of four of the crew to be Sergeants Dodd, McCormick, Leach and Collier. One of the forward guns bore the number 1668 in white paint and punched on it was B3 TIA7668. The only other identification mark was the 'return pipes from engine' panel assembly No. A 70716 A.

Interesting too was that in his report he thought it also worth noting the finding of camels: '5 miles to the north-west of here five young camels were found. The Arabs examined them and passed them as strays.'

Easonsmith also concluded his report with his other observations:

Enemy Movement

> Ground: No MT or troops seen. Very few fresh tracks and none east of the twenty-third meridian. Trig Enver Bei has had considerable use, signs of old camps, benzine drums etc, but only an occasional fresh track.

> Air: Considerable patrolling of the area to the north of where we harboured, largely by Ghiblis. They appeared to work up and down Trig Enver Bei staying within hearing for periods up to two hours. Less frequently they took a tour down to the south-west, probably covering the Gadd El Ahmer-Tengeder track.

In his book *Long Range Desert Group* published in 1945, Kennedy Shaw wrote of how the Arabs viewed Easonsmith:

> Of Jake Easonsmith too tales began to reach us in Kufra. I first heard them from two Arabs: they could not manage his name and thought I was rather stupid not to know it, for surely everyone had heard about his exploits; the Arabs up north, they said, called him *Batl es Sahra*, the Hero of the Desert.

Right: Lance Corporal L.H. Browne, 1940. He was trained as a navigator and won the Distinguished Conduct Medal for his exploits at Murzuk in January 1941, where he was also wounded. Later in May that year he was commissioned. From left: Signalman A. Pressick and Trooper E.W.R. Kitney.

Two iconic LRDG commanders confer. Left: Lieutenant L.H. (Tony) Browne. Right: Captain J.R. (Jake) Easonsmith, who replaced Captain D.G. Steele as commander of R1 Patrol.

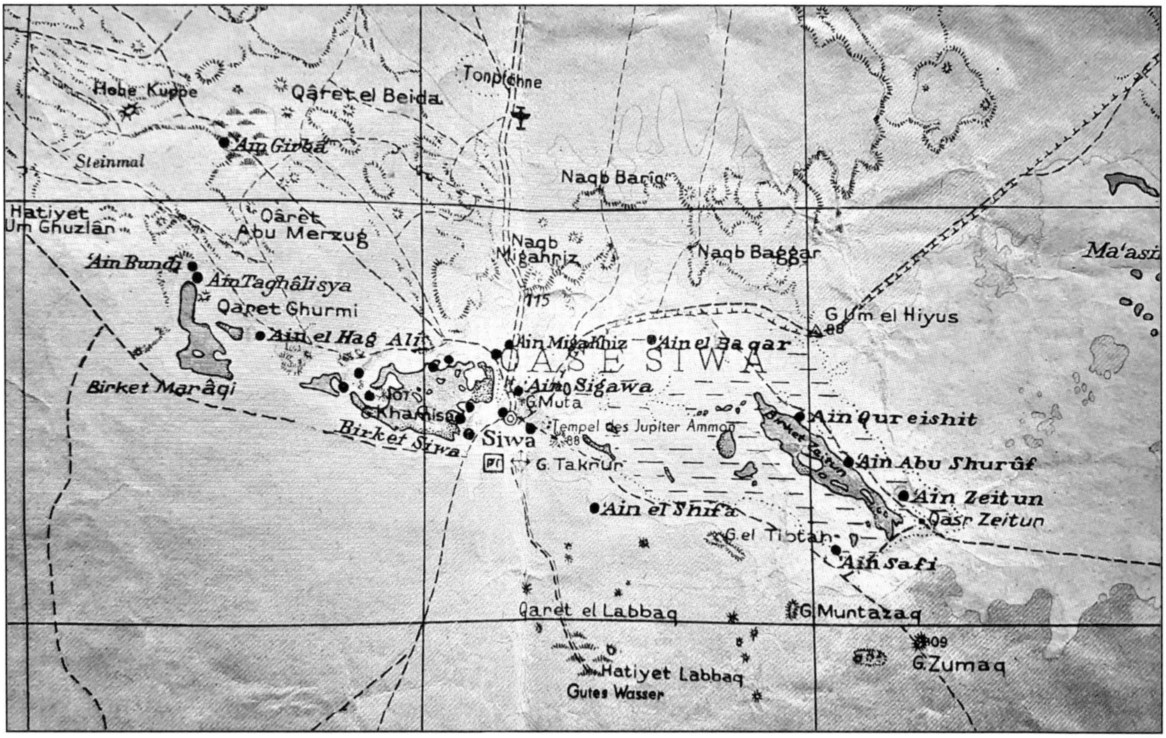

A German *Afrika Korps* 1941 map showing the Siwa oasis where the LRDG had a base.

A wartime French map showing the locations of Siwa, Kufra and Tazerbo.

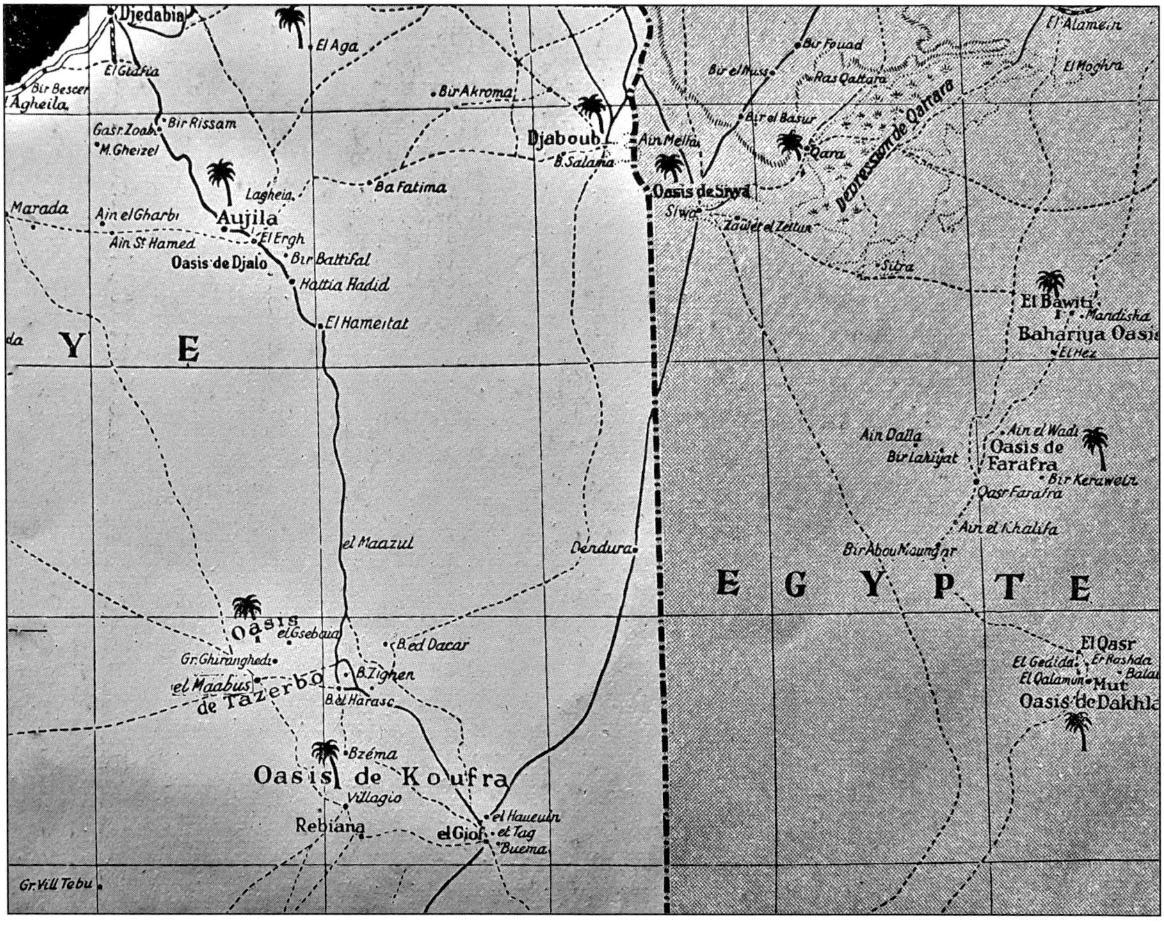

A view of the ancient mud brick buildings at Siwa oasis. One LRDG veteran described it as 'a little New York in the desert'.

LRDG troopers cooling off in the Figure Eight Pool, Siwa.

R Patrol members examining a petrified tree they referred to as Penis Rock. From left: Corporal R.O. Spotswood, Private F.R. Brown and Trooper J.A. Franks.

R Patrol members rest beside Cleopatra's pool, Siwa. From left: Tpr. L.A. Willcox, Sgt. A.D. Gibb, L/Cpl. B.J. Ball (standing), Pte. M. Allen, Pte. E. Harcourt, standing unidentified, Tpr. A.M. Saunders, Gnr. C.O. Grimsey, Tpr. A.F. Dodunski, unidentified, Tpr. L.F. Mather.

(**Opposite, above**) Native women and children of Siwa oasis.

(**Opposite, below**) Left: Captain J.R. Easonsmith and Colonel G.L. Prendergast stand next to the signals truck HQ8 at Siwa. Prendergast replaced Colonel Ralph Bagnold as Commanding Officer LRDG. He was also a prewar desert explorer and a skilled pilot flying the Waco liaison aircraft.

(**Above**) Captain J.E. Haselden, a British agent who worked behind the lines often dressed as an Arab. He was usually dropped off and picked up by the LRDG 'Libyan Taxi Service'. Haselden was later killed in action while working with the Middle East Commandos during a raid on Tobruk on 14 September 1942.

Captain J.R. Easonsmith cleaning his .45 Thompson sub-machine gun, while Trooper F.J.W. McKeown loads a twenty-round magazine for the gun.

A profile of a .45 Thompson M1928 A1 sub-machine gun. The stick magazine contained twenty rounds and the rarely used drum magazine held fifty rounds.

Trooper J.A. Franks cleans his Thompson sub-machine gun.

M36 'Mills bomb' (hand grenade) drawing taken from a wartime military manual. These were carried in the trucks and often used by Captain Easonsmith in close combat situations with good effect.

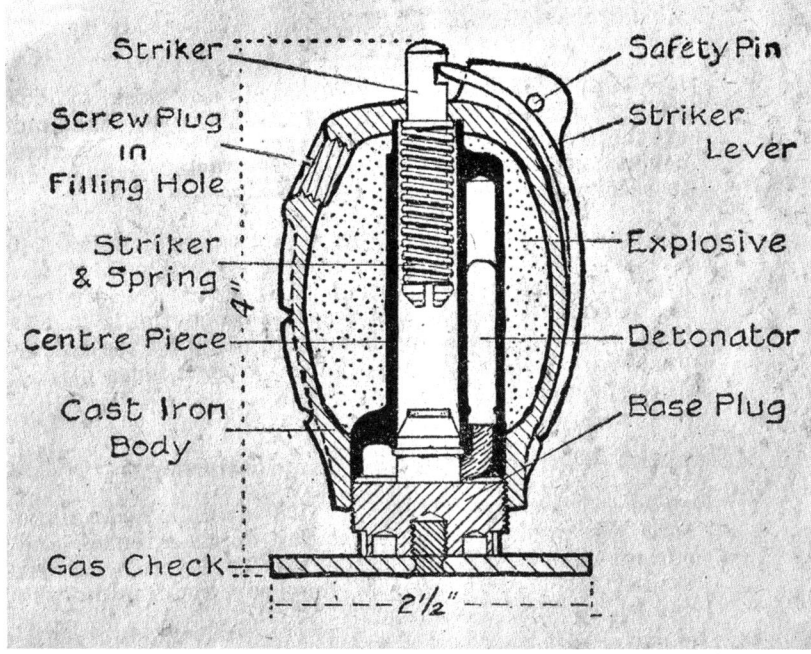

A group of Italian prisoners.

Italian prisoners who look pleased to be in captivity.

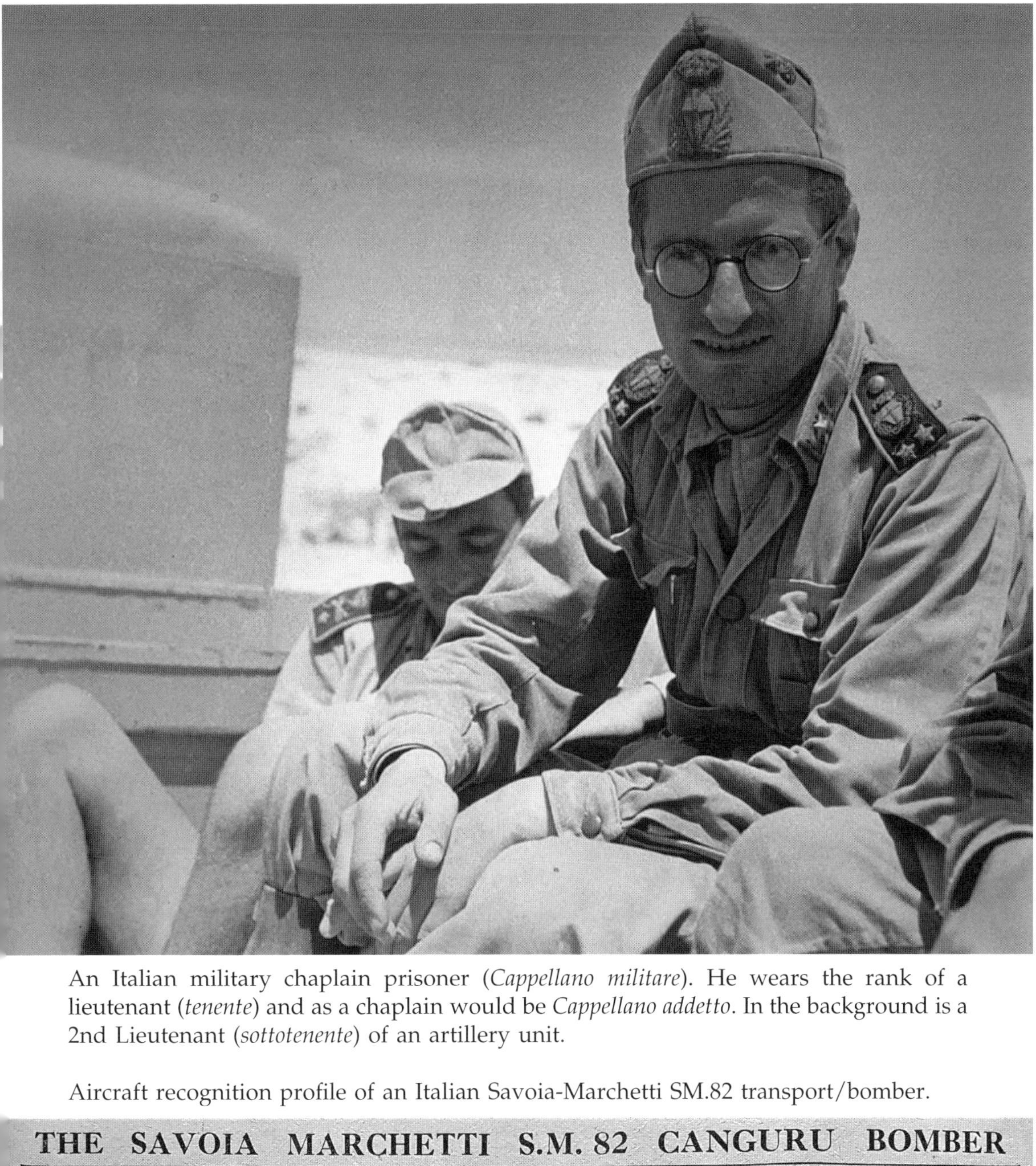

An Italian military chaplain prisoner (*Cappellano militare*). He wears the rank of a lieutenant (*tenente*) and as a chaplain would be *Cappellano addetto*. In the background is a 2nd Lieutenant (*sottotenente*) of an artillery unit.

Aircraft recognition profile of an Italian Savoia-Marchetti SM.82 transport/bomber.

R Patrol Ford F30s parked up in the desert. Foreground left is *Rotoehu* and right the truck *Rotoairo*, which mounts a .37mm Bofors gun.

A crashed burned-out RAF Vickers Wellington Mk II bomber being inspected by members of R Patrol. This variant was fitted with Rolls-Royce Merlin engines. The LRDG often picked up downed aircrews.

Chapter Six

With the SAS

Major Don Steele had also closely worked with Major David Stirling in planning combined operations. He respected their work and wrote of the Special Air Service (SAS):

> The Special Air Service, 'Parashots' to us, were a tough lot of thugs. Their delight was to be dropped on some enemy landing ground or other objective, do what damage they could and then take their way home best they could. This was not very satisfactory for several reasons. First, as it was essential to the success of their operations that they be dropped at night, it was almost impossible for the RAF to drop them in the right place, owing to the difficulties of navigation in an aircraft in darkness. Second, it was impossible to predict conditions on the target. And lastly, there was the problem of getting home. No unit can afford to lose half of its highly trained men in each operation. We first met David Stirling and his merry men after they had made a raid on the landing ground at Ain el Gazala.
>
> It was one of those shows where everything goes wrong. Only some of the planes had found the target and of the men who landed on or near the aerodrome some were lost or drowned when they landed in a wadi which was running bank high with water from a sudden rainstorm some distance inland. We had been told to RV with the SAS men at a point to the south of the field. This we did and brought what remained of the party back to Siwa. Stirling was so impressed with the 'line of shot' about being able to go to any point with absolute certainty that he suggested that we should carry his men into their future tasks. On his return to Cairo, he was able to arrange this and later the patrols were to go on many jaunts with these desperados. They too were very nice men and very brave, but they had strange ideas of fun.
>
> Their main offensive weapon was an explosive mixture of their own making. It was a mixture of an explosive called RDX thermite and old crankcase oil. It is worked up into a soft dough, wrapped round a guncotton primer and detonator and placed in a ration bag. A piece of instantaneous fuse connected the detonator in the bag with a detonator to the time pencil outside. The soft filling of the bag could be placed in almost any position anywhere and, conforming to the shape of the object to be demolished, would stay put. Then a squeeze at the end of the time pencil and all was set for a big bang. Later, when to our relief they got their own jeep transport, they added twin-mounted Vickers K guns to their armaments.

The general method employed while they worked was simply this. We would take them to within a matter of one or two miles of their objective and drop them, the patrol would then go back to the RV and hide itself. The Parashots would go in, do their job, and walk out to the RV. The patrol then put as much distance as it could between itself and the target. On one such raid, on Agedabia landing ground, the score was from memory thirty-six aircraft destroyed. Casualties, one man killed by one of their own planes on their way home.

It was not long before Captain Easonsmith was called out again, this time to pick up Captain A.D. Stirling and his SAS paratroopers. Their mission (Operation SQUATTER) had been to destroy enemy aircraft on the landing grounds near Gazala and Timimi. However, they encountered bad weather, the RAF dropped the parachutists wide of the target and some were lost or drowned in a wadi running bank-high with water after torrential rain. R1 Patrol was to collect Stirling and survivors at the prearranged rendezvous and return them to base.

The patrol left Siwa at 0530 hrs on 17 November with six trucks and two 15cwt Bedfords supplied by Stirling with Lieutenant W. (Bill) Fraser and a crew of four. They were carrying rations and water for the SAS party. In addition, one 3-ton Bedford was supplied by the LRDG as it was considered that the transport supplied by Stirling might not prove adequate. They crossed the wire at Weshka and reached a point some 15 miles to the west for the night. However, the 3-ton truck blew a gasket after 80 miles and had to be left behind.

They reached rendezvous No. 2 in the Wadi-el-Mra at 0800 hrs on 19 November, where they left the two SAS trucks and pushed on to rendezvous No. 1. On their way they met Y2 Patrol which was operating in the Bir Tengeder area. In the evening they reached rendezvous No. 1 which was reported as being 3 miles south-east of Gadd-el-Ahmar crossroads on the Trigh Capuzzo. At 0520 hrs two hurricane lamps were placed on a very high point some three-quarters of a mile from the R1 camp. At 0900 hrs one was seen to be lifted and swung from side to side, the prearranged signal. Contact had been made with the first SAS party of Lieutenant J.S. (Jock) Lewis and nine men.

At 0100 hrs on the 20th following a similar signal, Stirling and a sergeant arrived. That dawn the patrol moved camp for better cover, but left a small party who built a smoke fire on the high point previously used. This brought in Lieutenant R.B. (Paddy) Mayne and eight men. No other SAS men appeared, nor had any been seen by Y2 Patrol which was again met, and in the late afternoon after waiting at rendezvous No. 1 eight hours longer than he had intended, Easonsmith withdrew to rendezvous No. 2 at Wadi-el-Mra.

During 21 November, in spite of having trucks well spread out over an 8-mile front to look for them, no more men came in that day either. At midday on the 22nd, a radio signal was received with orders for Stirling's men to be handed over at Bir Tengeder to R2 Patrol who would take them to Siwa. On the way, R1 Patrol was machine-gunned by a Savoia SM.79 bomber, but vigorous return fire from the trucks caused it to withdraw. No casualties were caused, but apparently the Savoia went off for help as a Heinkel III appeared about forty minutes later. However, it failed to locate the patrol and bombed what were likely derelict trucks about 3 miles away.

The patrol camped about 3 miles from Bir Tengeder on the 22nd, but failed to get in touch with R2. Any further movement the next day was restricted owing to the presence of hostile aircraft. On two occasions, bombs were dropped and there was some machine-gunning, but the patrol was not seen and the targets were probably bushes or derelict trucks. On 24 November orders were received to bring the SAS party in. The return journey was made through rendezvous No. 2 where Lieutenant Fraser was still encamped, but no more men of the SAS came in. The journey was without incident apart from one truck overturning, fortunately with no serious injury to the men or vehicle. Stirling's party was dropped at Brigade HQ at Giarabub at 1230 hrs on the 25th and the patrol reached Siwa at 0700 hrs on the 26th.

The intended raids on the aerodromes were not carried out as the parachutists were dropped over a very wide area and never got together as a fighting force. Only twenty-one men of the fifty-five who took part were picked up.

Gunner Bluey Grimsey was the R1 Patrol navigator on the first SAS pick-up trip and he wrote an account of the lead-up to and rescue events in which he refers to the SAS as 'paratroopers':

15 November 1941: All preparations now seem to be nearing completion for the long-awaited offensive of the coast. Thousands of lorries, tanks and armoured vehicles of all kinds have been churning along these desert roads and one by one our little patrols have come into this our new base at Siwa. R, S, T, G and Y patrols including headquarters are, for the first time since the inauguration of the group, all together in one camp under Lt. Col. Prendergast. Major Steele, our old R Patrol CO, is now HQ-based. Instead, we have Captain Jake Easonsmith, who has most ably filled his place in the patrol. For weeks now – in between recce patrols in which we have been most successful, capturing both Italian and German prisoners – we have been fitting out our trucks for the big push.

Our own patrol, R, has suffered many serious setbacks. The navigators, on which so much of the work of patrolling depends, are getting in the minority. Corporal Ron Tinker has been detained in Cairo where he was meant to be on leave. However, he was smothered in desert sores and unfit for desert work for some time to come and Lance Corporal Joe Eyles was taken to hospital with a swollen leg. Our chief navigator, Lieutenant Croucher, contracted sandfly fever. So I received three days' instruction and within a week was told to navigate our next big stunt for 17 November.

17 November 1941: We left Siwa at 0700 hrs and set out for the Libyan border with six 30cwt trucks under Captain Easonsmith to pick up a party of paratroopers on their way back from a demolition stunt. We were also accompanied by two 15cwt Bedford trucks which were to be left at Gueret el Halib, 100 miles west of the wire, to pick up a party of paratroopers on their way back from a demolition stunt. These men take extreme risks to destroy aircraft and ammunition dumps.

This particular group under Captain Stirling was to attack at three different points hundreds of miles behind enemy lines and to make their raids in the dead of night on five aerodromes: at Timimi, Gazala and Martuba. Luck was against them for a start. They were dropped in the dead of night but encountered a 25mph wind and heavy rain. Conditions that were not expected when they set out from Eighth Army at Bagush. Some of the paratroopers were dragged and badly knocked about when they landed, and their explosives got wet through. One party found it impossible to cross a wadi which had become a raging torrent below an escarpment which bordered the objective. Another party was dropped about 40 miles from the right spot. I do not know what became of the other parties; perhaps they did their jobs and walked back to the coast.

19 November: Leaving our Bedfords at Gueret el Halib, we proceeded north and slightly east to El Teilim where we camped for the night. Two dimmed lanterns were set in the hills by our camp. In the event of them getting away, the paratroopers were to make for this rendezvous, some 40 to 50 miles from their operation area. We were to give a signal by swinging these lanterns from side to side. Our patrol kept an all-night picquet. The password was the tune *Roll out the Barrel*, sung or whistled. At 2150 hrs a sergeant called out that the lights were swinging, and a few moments later there came floating across the still night the password tune. Otherwise, there was not a sound, for we were deep in enemy territory and sitting alongside one of their main roads, from Mechili to Bir Hacheim.

We picked up seventeen men that night. They were cold and hungry after their trying ordeal and long trek. We made them as comfortable as we could with a tot of rum and all the bedding at our disposal. The next morning, we picked up a few more and after spending the greatest part of 20 November in the vicinity we left for Gueret el Halib with twenty-one additional men to our normal complement and we stayed a night and a day there.

We received news by wireless code to contact that other half of R Patrol, under Lt. Tony Browne located on the desert road junction of Bir Tengeder. On the way to this place, we were sighted and attacked by an Italian Savoia SM.79 heavy bomber which machine-gunned us, we vigorously fired back then it flew off. We had no casualties. About 40 minutes later a Heinkel III flew over, but we managed to hide our trucks in a rocky area, and it didn't spot us. For two days we tried unsuccessfully to contact the patrol. At night we heard distinctly heavy bombing 50 to 60 miles to the north and could see the flames hanging like stars on the distant horizon. Planes searching for us continued to fly overhead.

Eventually we decided to return to Giarabub with the paratroopers. We were surprised to be stopped on the way back by Tony Browne's patrol who had seen us machine-gunned two days earlier but failed to attract our attention. The twenty-one paratroopers we rescued had no bedding, very little clothing and practically no food. Each meal was an entertainment and we had to smile at the sight of Captain Stirling eating porridge off a piece of board and using another piece of wood from a benzine box as a spoon.

What became of the other men who were dropped that night I do not know, but it is to be hoped some of them made their way to the coast or were able to make the second rendezvous at Fraser's camp at Gueret el Halib. There is little doubt that some of them must have fallen into enemy hands. Those we contacted were tough and were looking forward to their next job when, they said, they hoped we could meet again.

25 November: At last, we arrived back at Giarabub in the afternoon. It was a great relief, for it had been a responsibility careering about in enemy territory without lorries loaded with men who were ill equipped to assist us in an emergency. As it happened, the truck in which I was travelling turned over at high speed, but by some miracle no one was seriously hurt. Later I learned that one party of paratroopers did succeed in getting onto an enemy landing ground and destroying many planes there.

The co-operation between the paratroopers and the LRDG proved so successful that a further raid was made when S Patrol under Captain Gus Holliman took commandos to a spot where they destroyed planes on the ground and escaped without casualties. Captain Holliman was awarded the MC. It seems that our method of dropping these men safely at the right place is better than dropping them by parachute, where invariably equipment is lost and injuries cannot be avoided.

Don Steele commented further on working with the SAS:

This was the first time we had really worked with the SAS on their raids. After that we continued working with them out of Siwa where it was a matter of taking them to and from their tasks and help where possible. In the main it meant taking them to within easy walking distance of their objective and then, later, picking them up again and returning them home. On one such raid on Sirte landing ground, the only way in was along the main road. The only parking place for the trucks (of S1 Patrol) was in an enemy transport park about half a mile from the LG. The SAS party was spotted immediately, and fired everything they had in all directions. So bright was the display that the tired enemy drivers in the park got up to see the show. They did not notice the return of Stirling's party. Imagine their surprise then when the patrol moved off with all guns firing, about a dozen air Brownings and Vickers K guns, mostly twin-mounted.

It must be stressed that in all our raids it was the element of surprise that gave us success. Without it, the patrol nearly always failed. The patrols could and did pop up anywhere and anytime. When the security was good the few failures were due almost entirely to bad luck.

In April 1942, Second Lieutenant Croucher commanding R2 Patrol was given the task of bringing back Second Lieutenant Roy Dodd and his SAS men, who were unable to be picked up by S2 Patrol a fortnight earlier. They were still at Hagfet Gelgaf to which they had been directed in the message sent them by Captain Holliman of S1 Patrol. It would also be a classic 'Taxi Service' task carrying various additional parties.

R2 was also to take a Commando party of three officers and twelve ORs under Major Glennie to the neighbourhood of Ghedir bu Ascher 6 miles north of Baltet ez Zalagh. They also carried an Arab-speaking officer of the General Staff, plus two ORs of the Libyan Arab Force.

The patrol left Siwa on 5 April and arrived at Baltet ez Zalagh on the 7th. There they met the Arab agent Hamed bu Serawaliya who informed them that Dodd and his party would be at Hagfet Gelgaf, 20 miles to the north, in the evening of 8 April. As this place was nearer Major Glennie's objective than Ghedir bu Ascher, it was decided to drop his party there.

Hagfet Gelgaf was reached after dusk on 8 April. In addition to Dodd and his six SAS men being there, the patrol found Captain Chapman of the General Staff, who was an officer of the Libyan Arab Force, a corporal of the Royal Signals attached to the General Staff, and six men of the RAF who had been brought in by the Arabs. As these unexpected additions to his party greatly increased his load capacity, space and ration supply, Croucher decided to return to Siwa at once and come back again for Major Glennie and his Commando detachment.

The patrol reached Siwa on 10 April and left again on the 11th. On the 13th they picked up the Commando party plus three ORs of the Libyan Arab Force and arrived at Siwa on the evening of the 15th. A good many hostile aircraft were seen or heard during the journey and Arabs gave information of a German patrol which had been seen in the Wadi bu Ascher area and looking for British patrols.

LRDG veteran Ian McCulloch related a story while he was working with the SAS. The patrol was having a quiet rum one evening and Lieutenant Paddy Mayne came up to them and said, 'Hi lads, any chance of a drop?' Obviously his drinking habits were well known to the patrol as McCulloch replied, 'Sorry Paddy, we're all out.' At this, before storming off, Mayne became very irate and replied, 'When you talk to an officer you call him SIR!'

Ian McCulloch said he always had a great amount of respect for the SAS and was in awe of their hardiness and stamina when it came to long-distance walking treks across the desert.

In June 1942 a further mission with the SAS was undertaken by R1 Patrol under Captain A.I. (Alistair) Guild. The patrol consisted of one officer and twelve ORs who left Siwa on 8 June and carried with them a French officer Lieutenant Augustin Jordain and fourteen French ORs of L Detachment SAS. In addition, there was Captain H.C. (Herbert) Buck with his team of fourteen Palestinian Jews of German origin who wore German uniforms, used Axis vehicles and were employed on special missions. They were known as the SIG (Special Interrogation Group). The plan was that the French SAS would pretend to be PoWs escorted by 'German' guards driving in German trucks to gain access to enemy airfields. Buck was in command not only of his own men but also of the SAS detachment. R1 Patrol would carry these men as far as Hagfet Gelgaf, where the passengers would be dropped off to operate independently. The patrol was then to move south, lie up and await their return.

Captain Buck's objectives were the landing-grounds at Martuba and Derna. His party was dropped 10 miles north of Baltet ez Zalagh on 11 June and it was arranged that the patrol would await their return until the evening of the 18th. On 14 June, under instructions from Group HQ, the patrol picked up four men of the RAF and two Libyans at a rendezvous given to them by G1 Patrol which was road-watching in the neighbourhood.

The SAS/SIG attack on the aerodrome was only partly successful for it was betrayed by one of the Palestinians. The whole of the French party was captured, but not until they had destroyed about twenty planes. Lieutenant Jordain, who spoke perfect German, also contrived to bluff the sentries in charge of him and escaped. The remainder of Buck's party was duly picked up on 15 June by R1 Patrol and brought back to Siwa. In Captain Guild's Operation Report, he stated that on 14 June his party viewed from about 5 miles away the destruction by aircraft of the lorries of 'A' Squadron of the Middle East Commando who were operating in the same area attacking Axis transport. The LRDG patrol was well concealed and not observed by reconnaissance aircraft circling the general area at the time.

A contemplative study of Captain David Stirling, founder of the Special Air Service (SAS).

The SAS cap badge, as drawn by Gunner Bluey Grimsey. Their motto: 'Who Dares Wins.'

A studio photo of Captain Jake Easonsmith wearing a traditional Arabic headdress (not a LRDG *keffiyeh*). He led R1 Patrol in the recovery of the SAS survivors after the failure of their first mission under Captain Stirling.

The survivors of L Detachment SAS posing for a photograph after being rescued by Captain Jake Easonsmith's R1 Patrol following a disastrous air drop due to bad weather. Captain Stirling (tall man centre) led the raid, which was to target enemy airfields.

The LRDG/SAS password for locating the dispersed SAS men after their first action was the words of the popular song at the time *Roll out the Barrel*, as illustrated in this Stella beer advertisement from the Cairo-published *Parade* magazine.

Aircraft recognition profile of a Luftwaffe Heinkel III bomber. The LRDG encountered these aircraft on a number of occasions with ground-to-air action.

R1 Patrol men enjoy a meal. Left: Trooper L.A. Willcox, Private F.R. Brown, Trooper R.J. Landon-Lane and Gunner C.O. Grimsey sitting towards the right. He was the navigator for the SAS rescue mission and wrote a diary account of the event.

Lieutenant R.B. 'Paddy' Mayne, second-in-command SAS, L Detachment. Note the 'winged dagger' badge on his cap. By the end of the war he was one of the most highly-decorated soldiers in the British army with the DSO and three Bars.

The LRDG carried SAS men to and from their missions until they eventually acquired their own mainly jeep transport. R2 men in front; left: Trooper J.C. Lucas, who is wearing a German cap displaying an NZ Onward badge; Trooper M.E. Hammond beside a Vickers K machine gun.

LRDG officers in discussion. From left: Captains Alistair Guild, Jake Easonsmith, Tim Hayward, Bill Kennedy Shaw, Tony Hunter and David Lloyd Owen with his back to the photographer.

No entry is to be made which gives any indication as to unit.

Signature of soldier: M. E. Hammond

Book opens on 8 July, 1941.

For the net daily rate of pay see pages 4 and 5 and Note on page 5.
If the soldier was in debt on the above date, the amount to be recovered from the next pay due to him should be stated.

Debt: £ 4 : 15 : 6
(four pounds 15/6)

7. Prideaux Lt Col
(Signature of Officer)

CASH PAYMENTS.

Date	Place. (If on Active Service enter "Field.")	Amount £ s. d.			Signature of Officer.
14/7/41	Field	7	3	1	R.B. Wormnea
21/7/41	"	2	1	1	
25/7/41	1/7/INF	2	7	–	
4/8/41	"	3	1	6	C.A. Holliman Capt
11/8/41	"		10	3	Awbery Lt
18/8/41	"		10	3	Awbery Lt
27/8/41	"		10	3	D.S. Steele Capt.
8.9.41	"		10	3	Easonsmith Capt.
28.9.41	"		1	6	Easonsmith Capt
29.10.41	"	2	1	1	W.P. Costello 2/Lt
1.11.41	"	1	10	8	Easonsmith Capt
15.5.01	"		4	2	
19.5.01	"		2	11	
Total cash payments to date		21	10	6	

When a soldier is granted leave from his unit, an entry stating period of furlough is to be made in second column – i.e., "Place" column.
All sentences of imprisonment, fines, and other stoppages must be entered across the columns above, in addition to record on page 5.

R Patrol Trooper Bill Hammond's paybook, 1941. Identifiable officers' signatures are Captains C.A. Holliman, D.G. Steele, J.R. Easonsmith and Lieutenant W.P. Costello.

EMERGENCY RATION

PURPOSE OF CONTENTS
TO BE CONSUMED ONLY WHEN
NO OTHER RATIONS OF ANY KIND
ARE PROCURABLE

TO OPEN
STRIP OFF BAND INSERT COIN IN
CORNER GROOVE AND TURN
NOTICE. NOT TO BE OPENED EXCEPT
BY ORDER OF AN OFFICER.

BOVRIL, LTD.   W/E. 8/42

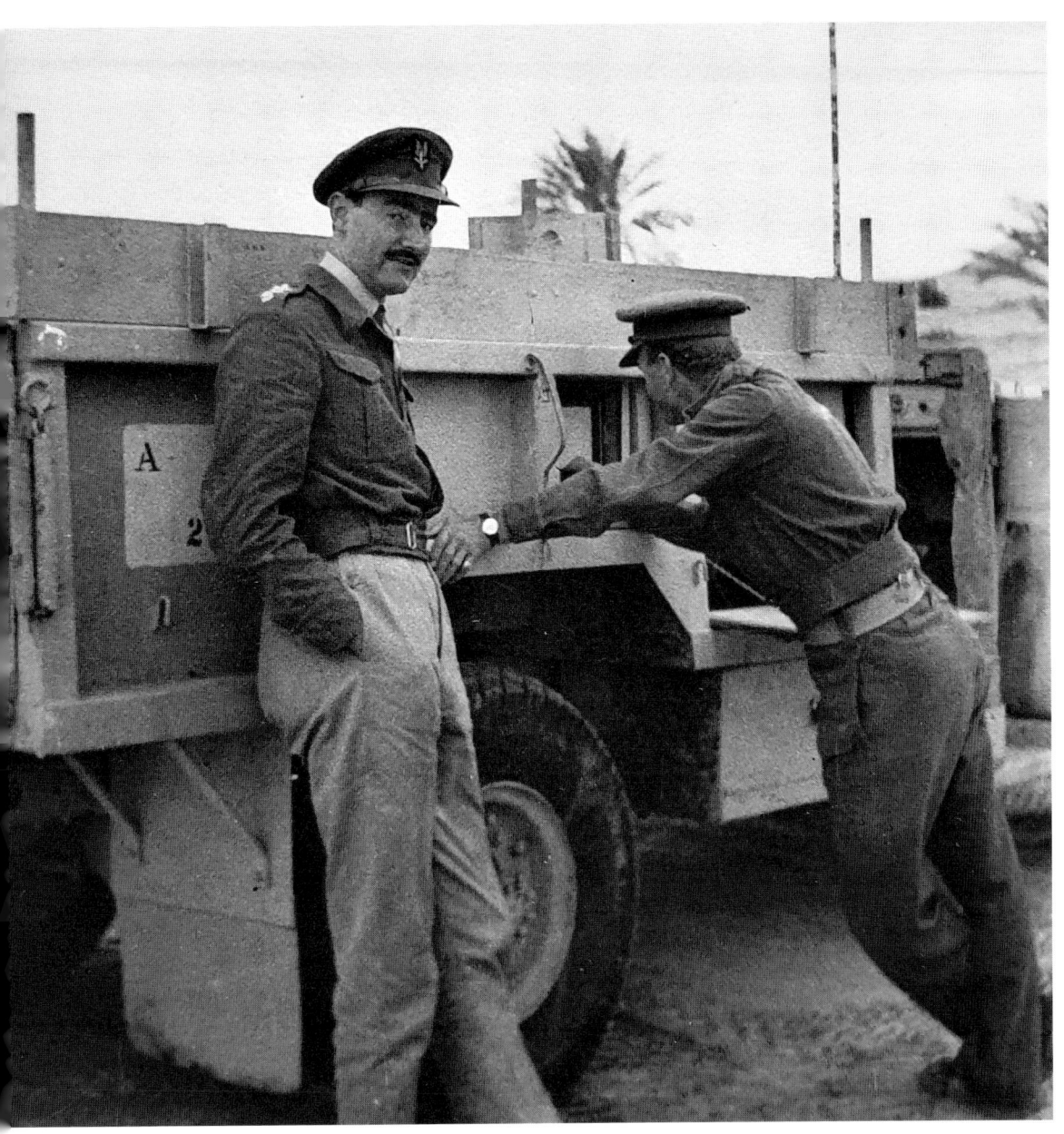

(**Opposite, above**) A wartime 1942-dated emergency ration pack. It states: 'Not to be opened except on the order of an officer.' These were included among other rations plus water and cigarettes in their 'bail out' kits. The bags were placed in a handy position on the trucks just in case the vehicle had to be abandoned in a hurry.

(**Opposite, below**) Left: a Caproni Ca.309 Ghibli light bomber/reconnaissance aircraft and a Fiat CR.42 fighter. Both these aircraft were commonly encountered by the LRDG and among others also targeted by the SAS on their airfield raids.

(**Above**) Left: Major David Stirling SAS with Major Don Steele operating the Philips Type 635 radio housed in the side of the LRDG A Squadron HQ Chevrolet radio truck. These officers organized many successful operations together.

Chapter Seven

Supporting the Eighth Army

On 24 November 1941, when the battle in the Tobruk-Bardia area had reached a critical stage, the role of the LRDG was suddenly changed. The Eighth Army issued orders for the patrols to 'act with utmost vigour offensively against any targets or communications within your reach'. The LRDG referred to these attacks as 'Beat Ups'. For this purpose, Y1 and Y2 Patrols were allocated roads in the Mechili-Derna-Gazala area, S2 and R2 Patrols the Benghazi-Barce-Maraua Road, and G1 and G2 the main road near Agedabia. The combined Rhodesian and New Zealand Patrols (S2 and R2) ambushed nine vehicles and killed and wounded a number of the enemy. Y2 captured a small fort and about twenty Italians, and Y1 damaged fifteen vehicles in a transport park. Mechanical breakdowns prevented G1 and G2 joining forces, so G1 made two independent attacks on road traffic and shot up a few vehicles. Road mines were also laid, mostly in potholes which abounded and so were not easily detected on the sealed road, especially at night.

On their mission S2 Patrol was led by Second Lieutenant J.R. Olivey with eleven ORs in three trucks: S9, S10 and S11. Second Lieutenant L.H. Browne commanded R2 with ten ORs in four trucks: R7, R8, R9 and R11. They left Siwa on 15 November for the north via the Sollum Road. The next day at 0900 hrs they encountered a South African light armoured car making a recce along 'the wire'. An hour later they sighted an RAF armoured car 15 miles west of Fort Grein acting as an OP looking for enemy aircraft. At 1300 hrs the patrol was chased by three unidentified armoured cars for almost 20 miles. They were believed to be British in spite of their failure to respond to signals; however, by 1400 hrs the chase was abandoned. The LRDG always did their best to avoid encounters with enemy armoured vehicles.

They drove on to the road in the evening of 29 November, cut the telephone wires and removed a length of wire to make it more difficult to be rejoined. They then turned eastwards towards Maraua and laid the first ambush at a point where the road dropped through a 20ft cutting. At 2030 hrs a truck approached from the east and as it drew level was engaged by machine-gun fire. Olivey noticed that it was marked with a red cross, but before he could stop his men from firing, enemy troops armed with rifles and sub-machine guns were seen clambering over the tailboard. It was almost a full moon, so the enemy could be clearly seen. After about a minute of sustained shooting on both sides, several of the enemy were killed or wounded and the remainder scattered. The patrols moved towards a vehicle approaching from the opposite direction and engaged it with machine-gun fire. The lorry stopped and fuel, plus a red liquid presumed to be wine, gushed from its load over the road.

Continuing along the road, the New Zealanders and Rhodesians attacked four lorries and trailers. They put each vehicle out of action, probably killed the crew and riddled the load with machine-gun bullets. One trailer tipped sideways and much of its contents were thrown down a bank. In the chaos, a motorcyclist travelling eastbound had a lucky escape, managing to avoid being hit by LRDG machine-gun fire. Taking up positions at a 30ft cutting where they overlooked the road in both directions, they attacked two more lorries and trailers and an oil tanker that leaked its contents over the road. They wrecked the vehicles and killed all the enemy except one badly wounded man. The patrols then cut more telephone wires and retired to the south. They were hoping to attack their next target which was to derail a train, but they were ordered back to Siwa to refuel and get fresh orders. Olivey was very upset that he had been unable to achieve a lifelong ambition of blowing up a train, imitating the deeds of Lawrence of Arabia!

They completed the operation without casualty, the only damage being to a vehicle (R8) with a bullet hole in its radiator, which was quickly plugged. However, after a day's travel the radiator was failing, so it was decided to abandon R8 in a wadi. They removed the springs, steering box, sundry parts for trucks in need of them and the contents were distributed. The success of the convoy attack resulted in Second Lieutenant Olivey being awarded the Military Cross. New Zealander Lance Corporal C. Waetford and Rhodesian Private K.T. Low received the Military Medal. The citations for these awards read as follows:

Military Cross
170243 Second Lieutenant John Richard Olivey
London Gazette, 23.01.42

Second Lieutenant J.R. Olivey's patrol was ordered to attack enemy transport on the Barce-Derna Road, some 150 miles behind enemy lines. During the night of 29 November 1941, having made a personal reconnaissance on foot, he led his patrol in bright moonlight along the road and attacked point-blank range all vehicles which were encountered. His patrol inflicted considerable damage on an eastbound convoy of six heavy lorries with trailers, killing the crews and wrecking the lorries. He then organised an ambush which resulted in the destruction of a further four vehicles with their crews. The success of the operation was largely due to Olivey's careful planning and cool leadership.

Military Medal
RH2990793 Private Kenneth Taylor Low
London Gazette, 23.01.42

On the night of 29 November 1941, a patrol carried out a successful attack on enemy transport on the Barce-Derna Road, some 150 miles behind the enemy lines, during which ten heavy lorries with trailers were destroyed and their crews killed or wounded. The attack was made by driving along the road against the traffic and firing at point-blank range at any vehicles encountered. Low was the driver of the leading patrol vehicle and was therefore frequently under enemy fire. He showed complete indifference to this, and acted with perfect coolness throughout the operation, which culminated in a long night drive, led by Low, over difficult country.

Military Medal
3420 Lance Corporal Clarke Te Ihi Waetford
London Gazette, 23.01.42

Lance Corporal Waetford was a member of a patrol which attacked and destroyed ten enemy vehicles on the Barce-Derna Road on the night of 29 November 1941, some 150 miles behind enemy lines. He played his part in the action with courage and determination and set a splendid example to the remainder of the patrol. Throughout his eighteen months' service with the Long Range Desert Group, Lance Corporal Waetford's excellent work and constant devotion to duty have been outstanding.

Trooper Bill Willcox recalled the unexpected outcome of a raid on a German supply column:

> The Germans' mid-1941 entry into the desert war made life a lot harder for our desert warriors. Suddenly, the enemy did not put up desultory fire, nor did they run or put their hands up. The Germans were a different breed; they stood their ground. They were good soldiers, very professional.
>
> I remember a German supply column we caught one day. We used to take anything of interest then set the rest on fire. There were these crates and crates of what we thought were tubes of toothpaste. But I took one anyway and it wasn't toothpaste at all, it was cheese! They had good rations.

Rommel disengaged his forces from the battle in Cyrenaica in mid-December and began to withdraw towards Agedabia. In an attempt to prevent the enemy's escape from Benghazi, the Eighth Army despatched columns, including the 22nd Guards Brigade, across the desert to the south of Jebel Akhdar to the Benghazi-Agedabia Road. During the move T1 Patrol navigated and R1 and R2 Patrols provided flanking scouts for the Guards Brigade. T1 Patrol waited two weeks at the rendezvous near Bir Hacheim for the Guards to disengage from the battle west of Tobruk. During the wait the patrol survived repeated bombing and strafing attacks by German dive-bombers and fighters.

The advance began on 20 December: R1 and R2 patrolled the country to the north, while T1 guided the main column of the Guards Brigade westwards towards Antelat. Corporal Tinker, with two trucks, was responsible for the navigation of the Scots Guards through Msus towards Sceleidima, 30 miles to the north of Antelat. The operation ended in failure. An enemy covering force including thirty tanks held up the outflanking columns in the Sceleidima-Antelat area on 22 December and this enabled the Axis troops to complete their withdrawal from Benghazi.

Rommel's forces retired from Cyrenaica to strong defensive positions among the salt marshes between Agedabia and El Agheila. From a base at Jalo, an oasis about 140 miles to the south-east of Agedabia, the LRDG continued to harass the enemy's communications further to the west.

As part of supporting the Eighth Army, Lieutenant Tony Browne and his R2 Patrol undertook to mislead the enemy by planting false information. The operation involved the planting near Jalo of a faked map prepared under instructions from Intelligence Eighth Army HQ. The object was to give the enemy the idea that a large British force was about to move to Jalo from the east. The map, which was a copy of the Italian 1:400,000 map of the Jalo area, was a rehash of the plot actually made during a recce around Jalo in September and contained appropriate references to 'good going' for AFVs, possible landing grounds etc., with rough calculations in the margin of distances from Giarabub. The planting went well, R2 Patrol had reached the east of Jalo and after remaining there for a short time and making the usual mess of a cooked meal, an Arab was seen approaching on a camel. The patrol left in a hurry, leaving behind some odds and ends and a petrol box under which Browne had 'forgotten' his map board, scale and protractor. Very shortly afterwards an enemy aircraft flew low over them and returned quickly to Jalo.

The sequel came on 27 November. On that day, two days after the capture of Jalo by Brigadier Reid's forces, Captain Bill Kennedy Shaw, the LRDG Intelligence Officer, visited Jalo at Reid's request to discuss the detachment of an LRDG patrol to his force. He saw on the wall of the Italian commander's office a large-scale map with all the details of the planted one faithfully copied.

(**Opposite, above**) Members of the Southern Rhodesian S Patrol at rest. Seated in the middle, the patrol commander Lieutenant J.R. Olivey reads his book. Note the seats constructed from Shell benzine boxes.

(**Opposite, below**) R Patrol meal break from the back of truck R5. Left, Captain J.R. Easonsmith, and extreme right, Lieutenant L.H. (Tony) Browne.

An RAF Rolls-Royce armoured car observation point. These vehicles were used mainly for aerial reconnaissance and surveillance work to forewarn airfields of incoming enemy aircraft. It mounts a .55 Boys anti-tank rifle and a Vickers K machine gun.

Burned-out Axis vehicles. In support of the Eighth Army, the LRDG undertook hit-and-run attacks on enemy road convoys.

A destroyed Italian Lancia 3Ro truck modified to carry an Ansaldo 90/53 AA/A/T gun.

Trooper Clarke Waetford's portrait studio study taken in Cairo. He wore traditional Arab dress for the photo. He had a distinguished service record with the LRDG and helped in providing the NZ trucks with Māori names. Waetford won the Military Medal for gallant action in a combined attack with S Patrol against an Italian convoy. He went on to serve as a patrol sergeant.

Luftwaffe airmen of a Stuka squadron share a smoke with their Italian *Regia Aeronautica* comrades from a Fiat BR.20M bomber unit. Artwork published in *Der Alder* magazine, February 1941.

An abandoned Ju 87 Stuka dive-bomber. This version has long-range fuel drop tanks. The Stuka was widely used in North Africa against Allied positions and vehicle columns.

An NZ Medical Corps truck badly damaged after a Stuka attack. The men are trying to recover useable supplies.

T and R Patrols provided navigation and scouts for the advance of the 22nd Guards Brigade. In doing so the patrols were subject to air attacks and ground encounters. Corporal R. Tinker (in jeep) with T2 patrol poses in the desert. They navigated for the Scots Guards. Note the dual-mounted .303 Browning machine guns on the truck and the Vickers K machine gun on the jeep.

General Erwin Rommel, commander of the *Afrika Korps*, with Luftwaffe personnel. Wearing a life jacket, he is about to or has completed a flight on a Heinkel III bomber.

A trooper stands next to a destroyed German 88mm anti-aircraft/anti-tank gun.

A heavily-laden Chevrolet truck undergoing a wheel change.

Close-up of the Waco aircraft showing the Kiwi in shield symbol and LRDG letters. In the foreground stands Captain R.P. Lawson, the LRDG medical officer.

R Patrol men at Siwa. Many are wearing the military-issue leather jerkin.

A Kittyhawk P-40 fighter-bomber of the Desert Air Force. The LRDG were always at risk from both enemy and friendly aircraft, especially when they operated behind the lines being mistaken for *Afrika Korps* vehicles. Right: R Patrol Trooper D.O. Beale sits next to an RAF fitter.

A crash-landed RAF Kittyhawk fighter. The LRDG sometimes recovered the .303 Brownings from these aircraft and mounted them on their trucks.

A desert halt on an open plain.

Preparing a meal from the back of the fitter's truck. Note the large vice. A selection of canned food is laid out, including in the foreground a tin of condensed milk which was very popular with the men. The trooper is wearing New Zealand shoulder titles.

Chapter Eight

With the Free French at Zouar

In December 1941, Lieutenant C.H. (Dick) Croucher (a French-speaker) led his R2 Patrol on a reconnaissance mission to the Free French oasis base at Zouar, located in the mountainous Tibesti region of northern Chad. In 1986, Croucher wrote an account for the LRDG Association annual newsletter describing his trip. It was titled *Trip to Zouar with R2 in December 1941* and reads as follows:

> The idea was to follow the tracks of a French expedition a year earlier which commenced at Kayugi and skirted the main massif to Bardai. All very vague. Anyway, we entered the wadi at Kayugi. There had been some muddled tracks presumably left by d'Ornano earlier, but these soon disappeared in the rocky terrain of a wadi. As the wadi itself looked most promising and led in the direction required, we followed it despite the fact that the going was atrocious and involved low-gear work all the way. By late afternoon we had travelled about 50km and seemed to have come to a dead end. The wadi had a pretty well-defined camel trail showing up in the odd soft patches but, when we arrived at the head of the wadi, the camel tracks went up the side of the slope over a saddle into a lovely sandy plain. The trouble was that the track was only camel-width!
>
> We were really in a predicament. Checking up on our fuel supply, we had used far more than expected through all the low-gear work and the situation was not good. We had another look at the track over the saddle and decided we could widen it sufficiently to take a truck, with a bit of luck, in three days, all pitching in. Meantime Clarke Waetford (Tpr. C. Waetford) and his brother Tommy (Pte. E.B. (Tom) Waetford) had other ideas. It was getting dark by then but, working their way along the crest of the hills, they found a branching off the wadi a couple of kilometres back which we had passed without noticing. Next morning, we went to see and found we could get out that way with only minor moving of a couple of boulders. Terrific sighs of relief all round!
>
> Out we went on to that glorious sandy plain dotted with small conical hillocks rather like a moonscape. We headed across the plain in the direction of Bardai (we hoped!). Halfway across we came on a wandering old Tibbu man and his wife. I don't know who was the most surprised. We gave him some cigarettes and were pleased to learn from him that we were on the right track. Shortly after, we climbed a fairly steep dune and came upon the French *Poste* of Bardai. From there to Zouar it was quite a well-defined track

for vehicles and initially quite a climb. The road skirted around the rim of an extinct volcano Mt. Toussidé. The crater was about five miles across and half a mile deep. Having come off the mountain, we were met by the French with great enthusiasm and were escorted into the wadi where they had their HQ.

When we were there, there would have been at least a dozen French officers beside Colonel (then) Leclerc. Also, there were George Mercer Nairne and Bill Barlow, liaison officers. R2 Patrol was allocated a spot amongst the acacia bushes where they set up camp. We were issued with beans (dried), flour, tinned meat, 'Singe' (monkey) which resembled a ball of twine soaked in vinegar, and palm toddy which they called 'Mehrissee'. The first thing to go wrong was that the beans, which were put in the stew, were as hard as rocks and bitter. The grog, which had the kick of a mule, was vile to the taste. The only way to cope with it was to shut one's eyes and hold one's nose. Of course, such small matters never deterred a Kiwi. After some discussion with the French Commissariat, we found that the beans were not haricot, but coffee beans which we were supposed to roast on a tin plate over the fire and then crush with a bottle. The grog was supposed to be used as rising when making bread with the flour. Needless to say, our chaps made dampers and disposed of the liquor in a more direct fashion.

When it appeared that we would not be moving up to the coast immediately, Leclerc asked me to give his officers instruction in Astro navigation, so I ran daily classes. None of the officers taking part could speak any English so the whole thing had to be conducted in French and I was completely lost when it came to translating technical terms in spherical trigonometry.

The rations included the occasional fresh meat (supposedly) brought up by camel from Fort Lamy. The Kiwis in R2 were over-resourceful and did the odd supplementing by barter with the local Tibbus for goat kids. Unfortunately, the locals became rather too greedy for their own good, which led to the need to adopt other methods. It was a daily occurrence for a little boy to drive a herd of goats and kids down the wadi to feed. On a particular day, two of our chaps hid themselves in the thicket and, on the arrival of the herd, quick as a flash, a nice young specimen was extracted and whisked away into the depths of the bush whilst the goatherd was being distracted by others on the other side. Before he was out of sight the beast was slaughtered, skinned, gutted and into the biscuit tin oven in a hole under the fire. All traces of blood, skin, etc. were cleaned up and buried without trace. A most expert performance. I'm sure some of our forebears were sheep rustlers. Some of us, though, regretted the incident later when a man, presumably the lad's father, dragged him down by the ear searching for the missing beast. No evidence was left, but no doubt that lad got his beans.

When we received orders to return to base, we were all lined up for Leclerc to inspect us and bid us farewell. He was most gracious, made a nice little speech and then a couple of Askaris came forward with a box of lettuces and tomatoes which he presented to us for our journey. It was a magnificent gesture because the little vegetable garden of the *Poste* was only designed to feed four or five persons and was under considerable strain with all the additional inhabitants of the mess. Throughout the whole ceremony Leclerc kept a very straight face, but I noticed that a couple of our chaps seemed to be a little uncomfortable. It was not until much later that I found that two of the men had been apprehended by the guards whilst robbing the said garden in the early hours of the morning. I had some correspondence with Leclerc in subsequent months and apologised, but he took it all as a joke.

I seemed to get on quite well with the French. Some of them I managed to keep in touch with: de Guillebon – later killed in action – Dio, a giant of a man, and Fabre, O/C of the garrison at Faya. On our way through there on our return journey we stayed the night and had quite a convivial party. In the course of a poker game, I won a magnificent white, red-lined, *Spahi* cloak from him. It was obviously his pride and joy because next morning when we were lined up to depart, he pleaded with me to let him have it back and I did not have the heart to refuse.

We looked in briefly at Tekro which was unoccupied, then on and camped down for the night at Bishara. Our inveterate fossickers [rummagers] Clarke and Tommy Waetford went for a wander around the dunes and came upon a 15cwt Chev civilian pick-up painted dark blue with narrow road tyres. There seemed to be nothing wrong with it except for a flat battery. In no time it was made mobile, and Clarke and Tommy transferred their bits and pieces to it. They painted on the sides 'Waetford Bros. Country Storekeepers' and as such it was officially incorporated into R2. I am not sure if it did much to assist the *Entente Cordiale*. The French at Kufra were in a cleft stick. It was obviously one of their vehicles left behind or lost on one of their sorties '*vers Kufra*'. On the other hand, they were not prepared to make an issue of it as it meant admitting that they had abandoned or lost a perfectly fit vehicle. We kept it anyway.

It was on the run from Kufra to Siwa that we ran into rain in the Sand Sea. I had struck a course to come out on the track between Jalo and Giarabub. We had only just entered the strip of dune country between the gravel plain and the track when we had light rain. I cannot recall for how long, but in the morning there was a definite low, green fuzz over the dunes and a crust had formed that made it possible to do the craziest of things without getting stuck. Even the Waetford Chev could climb the steepest of slopes with ease. I do not know what happened to the vehicle after that; I wouldn't have put it beyond some of them to have flogged it to the natives!

Gunner Bluey Grimsey, the R2 navigator on the same trip, recorded in his diary in detail his view of the trip and the visit to the Free French fort at Zouar:

17 December: We set out with Captain Easonsmith to watch the roads south of Benghazi and to keep an eye on the deep flanking movements of the enemy around Mechili. On one occasion we encountered an enemy armoured unit near Tedim and had no alternative but to make a hurried withdrawal. As the sun set, we sped westwards with streams of tracer and explosive bullets all around us. No truck was hit and as darkness fell the enemy force broke off the chase. Next morning, we were miles away on our journey via Bir Tengeder to the roads leading from Benghazi and Jedabya.

We returned to Bir Hacheim to join the other half of R Patrol. We set out to move up with the advance which at the time had reached Gazala. Things went so well that the enemy had little time and little inclination to make any sort of deep flanking movement or encircling movement. We were recalled to our base at Siwa. We spent Christmas Eve in the desert, just south-east of Bir Hacheim, but arrived back on 25 December to celebrate Christmas as a whole patrol.

29 December: Three days later Captain Easonsmith gave me an option of taking my overdue leave or of navigating R2 Patrol on a 1,200-mile trip to Zouar in the Tibesti mountains, French Equatorial Africa. Needless to say, I jumped at the offer.

Our journey to Kayugi was almost uneventful until we decided to cut out a large detour and try to follow a wadi, poorly mapped, which seemed to provide a short cut through to a French reconnaissance route to Bardai, a post we had to make on our way to Zouar. All went well until we had passed the landing ground at Tellagoum, where the wadi, which was shown on our map as having been traversed by camels, become narrow and rock strewn. Rock rose on either side perpendicularly, possibly the result of some terrific upheaval thousands of years ago. Here and there were a few shrubby trees and once we passed a small herd of young camels. Presently we came upon a woman and two children sitting in the shade of a tree. Lieutenant Croucher held a dumb show conversation with her, and she tried to make it plain that we could not proceed much further. The woman placed a large stone in the gravel, ran her finger through the gravel and came up against the stone. Some hours later we learned the significance of the demonstration. We found ourselves at the end of the wadi with the camel tracks winding up a steep grade over a saddle, far too steep for a truck to traverse. That night we were a sad and weary patrol.

I set to work with my theodolite to get a fixed position while two others set out on foot across the hills to find some way out. Indeed, we were in a sticky spot as we were carrying only a small margin of petrol, even if it was possible to turn back. We had come down some narrow passes over which it was very doubtful we could reclimb. Late in the night, however, the two scouts returned with news that a branch wadi led off from the one in which we were trapped. In the darkness it appeared this would lead up onto a plain. In addition, my star position indicated we were almost within sight of our objective, Emi Tokolima, a mountain marked on the map, where we could cut the old French route.

After a general discussion, the usual procedure adopted on such occasions, we decided to go ahead in the morning. Little did we know what was in store for us. By working as a road gang, we shifted huge boulders and made our way along this fork. We took our four-wheel-drive (Ford F30s) trucks over seemingly impassable obstacles. Sometimes we had to use a heavy napping hammer to split the rocks before we removed them from our path. All the morning every man worked like hell to get forward and by lunchtime we had covered about 8 miles. Every man was silent, yet worked as I have never seen men work. The crews ran in front of the vehicles, rolling aside boulders, smashing rocks, directing the drivers, and riding in vehicles over the better patches. The going grew steadily worse. A huge cliff reared up in front of us. Hands were bleeding and feet blistered when again we came up against what we thought was a solid wall of rock.

We split up and left our trucks to explore the maze of wadis to find one leading out onto the plain beyond. Only 5 miles away, this plain was visible from some of the higher ground. Our Skipper came back with the news that a tributary of the main wadi, forking off some 2 miles back, wound its tortuous way to lower hills which, he thought, the trucks could climb. After a hurried lunch, we turned back to explore this pass; it was the first time we had turned back. Slowly, hour after hour, we crept forward until we came out into the low hills. We climbed these and found ourselves on what must have been a great mountain lake. To the south-west was what I took to be Emi Tokolima. I set to work to fix our position and to take a bearing on the hills and compare this with our map.

From this position we decided we were now only some 6 miles from the old French route. In the morning we intended to work our way as best we could. I will not forget the effect of seeing a small cairn at about ten o'clock that morning. It indicated that somebody had been exploring the district and had left the cairn as a guide. A few minutes later we crossed double-wheeled tracks and, scarcely daring to give expression to our feelings, we swung onto these tracks and headed in the direction of Bardai, the Free French outpost in the heart of the Tibesti mountains.

I could write a whole book describing the rugged grandeur of the country through which we passed. We followed the narrow winding gorges between the mountains, narrowing in places to mere camel tracks, scarcely wide enough for trucks to pass through, but opening out elsewhere to wide expanses of sand. There at times a few trees and native grasses were seen to relieve the barrenness of naked rock on either side. As we neared Bardai the country opened out.

Bardai itself might have been a picture from one of P.C. Wren's books of the French Foreign Legion. The fort flew the tricolour of the Free French flag. The gun positions were set in crags overlooking the valley in which lived the native population. Their mud and reed huts looked like giant beehives.

The French gave us a royal welcome and, even more appreciated, warm water for a bath, our first wash for nearly two weeks. We had dinner at the fort. Few of us could speak French and our hosts spoke indifferent English, but we got by with dumb show and wine which put an end to any embarrassment there may have been at the beginning of the meal.

Next morning, the French Cameroons turned out with fixed bayonets to form a guard of honour. A grand sight it was their bright red fez-like headgear, glittering bayonets and immobile faces. We drove from beneath the palms on the road to Zouar, our last stage of the long journey. From Bardai we seemed to be climbing most of the time until nearly midday. At the highest point the trucks began to pull badly and even on slight downgrade we had to change down to third gear to prevent stopping altogether. The oil pressure appeared to be very low. This state of affairs continued for about 50 miles. We felt sleepy. We ran into what can be best described as the 'lava' country. The road, obviously made by native labour, passed through rugged, bare hills and mountains and, like a thin yellow ribbon, snaked around peaks and up narrow passes. It was necessary to back and edge round some of the corners. The soft, porous-like pumice ground was of the most delicate pastel shades of mauve and pink. As the country became more even, it looked not unlike the crust of a giant cake of which the rapid baking had caused the surface to crack. About 50 miles from Bardai we saw distinctly the peak of Emi Toussidé (3,265 metres) and soon afterwards, right alongside the road, the largest crater or hole I have ever seen. It was Trou au Natron. We stopped to gaze into this volcanic wonder. A thousand metres deep, it measured 20kms in width. Deep inside we could see three cones surrounded by a white deposit not unlike sulphur deposits I have seen in the New Zealand thermal regions. From there onwards the country was mostly of volcanic formation. Descending all the time, we reached the plain of Tao and early in the afternoon of 8 January 1942 we met part of the French force just outside Zouar. This completed our journey of 1,247 miles from Siwa in eleven days.

We arrived in a country of flora and fauna. To see green trees and birds and to find natural shade after the pitiless glare of the desert was to us something far from commonplace. Zouar is not an oasis and the water, what little there is, had to be drawn from deep wells. It has an earthy taste. There are no palms, but many gum Arabic trees and large green bushes which somehow seem to provide sustenance for the goats and donkeys. Great sandstone hills enclose this wide wadi, stretch east and west and its surface is composed entirely of fine powdery sand from which the trees and bushes sprout.

The natives, Tibbu, live mostly in the hills and the labour of the fort is done mostly by the natives the French have brought with them from around Lake Chad. Huge men with skin like polished ebony and of better physique than small and sinewy Tibbu. The Tibbu used to make raids upon the Saras of the Lake Chad region and enslave them to sell to the Turks. These Tibbu nomad tribes have been a venturesome enterprising people in their earlier history. They cover thousands of miles to make raids and drove their goats and livestock hundreds of miles to sell at other oases such as Kufra, in exchange for dates and grain which are not procurable in their own region.

16 January 1941: We find the French almost overwhelming with their hospitality. They have lost none of their reputation for preparing meals despite the difficulties presented by active service in the desert. The other night I dined under a gum Arabic tree and squatted on a goat skin spread on the sand while the meal was being prepared on a little wood fire built around stones. It was protected from the wind by an old mudguard from a derelict truck. First the soup was prepared; it was brought to the table, benzine boxes, by an obsequious Sara, as dignified as any English butler. Next came a drink of red wine, a cigarette and some *parlez-vous* punctuated by gesticulation and tracings in the sand. Then followed a course of beans and large juicy lumps of pork. Our plates were again removed and washed by the native servant. They were returned laden with little chunks of roasted meat, very tasty. The fourth course was rice, chopped meats and potato with olive oil. Our cups were kept filled with wine until the fifth course of tinned fruit was served. The sixth was sweet black coffee and biscuits. After this, the table was cleared and we settled down to some steady drinking and talking, which by this time proved entertaining for both parties. The whole meal took about two hours, and I could not help comparing it with the manner in which we gobble down our stew of all number of things thrown in together. These French eat no breakfast but dine about midday and at about eight o'clock in the evening. Wine and coffee are their chief drinks, while a spirit called tapia, which seemed to be rather like our whisky, was in much evidence.

30 January 1941: Been here a fortnight now, the flies are getting pretty bloody awful, and I would hate this to develop into another Tazerbo. Fortunately, the days are only moderately warm and the nights cool. Meanwhile, in the camp Clarke Waetford, with his hot sand oven, has been cooking delicious dishes of roast goat and beef, while his brother Tom has worked for days on a Browning machine gun retrieved from a plane. He has made a splendid job of the bolt and sights which we all thought far too complicated a job for any but an expert. He even made use of my theodolite to get the levels right. These two Māori boys put the rest of us to shame for energy and ingenuity. There seems no end to their confidence in carrying out what appear to be almost impossible tasks. Their combined efforts and faith in the wadi from Kayugi played a major part in getting us through that difficult piece of country.

6 February: We have become almost reconciled to the waiting. There is nothing to do but eat, sleep and eat again such poor rations as the French allow us, much inferior to our own. Each time our issue of wine arrives the opportunity is taken for nocturnal parties held around our trucks under the trees throughout the camp area. This is an excusable diversity from the grim monotony, although I weary of the same old coarse songs and stale jokes. Thank heavens we are not all built the same way, for there is something satisfying in the realisation that our boys can make merry and enjoy these little 'dos' with things going from bad to worse up on the coast where again Jerry has pushed east of Derna and Timimi. I have just about brought my maps up to date and Lt. Croucher is now putting the finishing touches to the complete picture.

10 February: Last night there was an electrical storm with much lightning and thunder and a few large drops of rain. I have now completed my maps of Zouar and Lt. Croucher has done one for the French. The flies are becoming a terrible pest and the nights are becoming warmer.

On 16 June 1949, Bluey Grimsey wrote as part of a letter to the New Zealand War History Branch a brief note about navigation and his trip to Zouar:

> I evolved and perfected a method of Astro Navigation for the LRDG, whereby a navigator could get longitude and latitude without the complicated books of figures known as ANT Table and Air Almanac. This method was finally approved and adopted by W.B. Kennedy Shaw and known as 'The Grimsey Method'. It gave a fix on the maps to within one mile of accuracy in the hands of a navigator and could be made from two stars only, without plotting.
>
> My temporary rank of corporal was given to me for leading (navigating) a patrol through Egypt, Libya and the French Equatorial Africa to the Chad Province to meet up with Colonel Leclerc of the Free French Forces. This trip was pioneered through uncharted mountains to Zouar via Bardai. My estimated fix at the end of this journey of some 1,200 miles was a quarter-mile from actual visual navigation on which we came into Zouar.
>
> A full description of the Grimsey Method was provided per document *LRDG/Nav/4* titled *Rapid Determination of Latitude and Longitude, Grimsey Method & Graphic Method*.

(Opposite, above) R2 Patrol members. From left: Tpr. H.L. Mallet, Pte. R.R. Williams, Pte. J.E. Gill, Pte. L.T. Campbell, Tpr. M.E. Hammond and the patrol commander Lieut. C.H.B. Croucher.

(Opposite, below) R Patrol at the French fort at Zouar. From left: unidentified, Pte. G.H. Nelson, Pte. J.E. Gill, Gnr. C.O. Grimsey (navigator), Tpr. M.E. Hammond wearing French military dress, Sgt. C.G. Ball, Sgm. S.J.E. Mahomet (radio operator). On the truck: Tpr. A.F. Dodunski; second right Pte. E.B. Waetford, unidentified.

A Tibbu warrior who they met on the road to Zouar.

A French wartime map of the Zouar region in northern Chad.

A Ford F30 travelling through difficult terrain to Zouar.

Spectacular landscape unfolded after the patrol had to previously negotiate difficult hill country on the way to Zouar. Croucher described the vista as entering a 'moonscape'.

Ford F30 *Rotowhero* stuck in a salt pan. Front left: Trooper R.J. Landon-Lane and Corporal R.A. Tinker.

Ford F30s being towed through rugged country.

Chained French prisoners used as workers in Zouar.

A French soldier of the *Régiment de Tirailleurs Sénégalais du TChad* standing in front of captured Italian flags.

Bluey Grimsey was the R2 Patrol navigator on the journey to Zouar. He also recorded an account of the patrol's time there.

A French 25-franc note souvenired by Trooper Bill Hammond at Zouar.

Ford F30 *Rotomahana* deeply sunk in sand.

R Patrol passing an upturned Free French Air Force Lysander liaison aircraft.

French troops drying meat at the Zouar oasis.

Left: Trooper C. Waetford sitting on a benzine tin enjoying a tea break with his comrades. Middle: Trooper A.F. Dodunski. A Ford F30 truck is seen in the background.

LRDG/NAV/4.

RAPID DETERMINATION OF LATITUDE AND LONGITUDE

GRIMSEY METHOD & GRAPHIC METHOD

GRIMSEY METHOD.

       This method, suggested by Gnr. GRIMSEY, "A" Squadron, enables one to obtain a reasonably accurate position by one observation on one star. G.M.T. must be known and the Air Almanac and Abridged Nautical Almanac are required, but not the A.N. Tables, and no plotting is involved.

       The method consists in observing the time and altitude of a star's meridian passage. Either North or South stars may be used, but in Libya south stars will be found more convenient.

formulae:-   Latitude and Longitude are obtained from the

       Latitude = Zenith Distance + or - Declination.
       Longitude = 360° - (G.H.A. Aries + S.H.A Star)

Procedure.

1. Decide the time at which the observations are to be made. This is determined by the L.M.T. (i.e., interval after Local Mean Noon) of the meridian passage of a suitable star. The L.M.T. of the star's meridian passage can be found with sufficient accuracy by subtracting R at 12 hour G.M.T. from the star's R.A.

Example:- Required the L.M.T. of the meridian passage of a Piscis Australis on October 30th. 1942.

	H.	M.
R.A. Star	22	54
R 12 hours	02	33
L.M.T.	20	21

2. Place the Theodolite in the meridian. This is done by calculating the azimuth of Polaris (i.e. the amount Polaris is east or west of the Celestial Pole) at a convenient time, say 15 minutes before the meridian passage of the selected star, setting this azimuth on the horizontal plate of the Theodolite, intersecting Polaris at the proper moment, and then moving the Theodolite back to zero on the horizontal plate when it's axis will be in the meridian.

Example:- Required the azimuth of Polaris at 2000 hours L.M.T. on 30/10/42 in D.R. Lat. 24° 10' Long. 23° 15'.

	H.	M.
L.M.T.	20	00
Long E	1	33
G.M.T.	18	27
Long E +	1	33
R +	02	34
L.S.T.	22	34

       Then from P.158 N.A. (1942) the azimuth of Polaris at 22 h. 34 m. L.S.T. is 0.85° (= 51 Minutes) East.
       Set the horizontal plate to read 00° 51'., intersect Polaris at 18 h. 27 m. G.M.T., turn the upper plate back to 000 00' 00" and the axis of the theodolite should be in the merid

Copy of original document LRDG/Nav/4: Rapid Determination of Latitude and Longitude, Grimsey Method & Graphic Method, page 1.

- 2 -

3. Assuming a South Star is to be used, turn the upper plate through 180° and clamp it. Elevate the telescope so that the star will pass across the field. Keep the star on the horizontal wire and when it crosses the vertical wire note the time and the altitude.

4. Example of Computation.

Date 30/10/42 D.R. Lat 24° 10' D.R. Long 23° 15'
Star - a Piscis Australis. Watch 2 m. 35.5 s fast.

	H.	M.	S.
Watch time	18	50	05
		2	35.5
G.M.T.	18	47	29.5
G.H.A. Aries 18h. 40m.	318°	27'	
Increment 7m. 29.5s		1	53
G.H.A. Aries	320	20	
S.H.A. Star	16	23	
	336	43	
	360	00	
Longitude	23	17	E

	°	'	"	
Observed Altitude	35	55	00	
Refraction		1	16	
Corrected Altitude	35	53	44	
	90			
Meridian Zenith Distance	54	06	16	N
Declination	29	55	36	S
Latitude	24	10	40	N

(N.B. The correct position of the place of observation was Lat 24° 12' Long 23° 16' 30").

The method is liable to error because:-

(a) The azimuth of Polaris is only given to a tenth of a degree in the N.A. and there may therefore be some inaccuracy in placing the Theodolite in the meridian.

(b) Only one face of the Theodolite is used to obtain the altitude of the star. If there is an instrumental error between the two faces this error must be applied to the observed altitude.

The method is not as accurate as the position line method and should not normally be used instead of it.

LRDG/Nav/4: Rapid Determination of Latitude and Longitude, Grimsey Method & Graphic Method, page 2.

- 3 -

GRAPHIC METHOD.

This method is applicable to both sun and star observations.

Procedure:

Calculate the time of meridian passage as explained above. About 10 minutes before the time of meridian passage, begin to observe the star, recording the altitudes and the corresponding times. Continue to observe for 4 or 5 minutes after transit. Then, on squared paper, draw a graph showing altitudes against times. Draw a smooth curve through the points. Reading from the top of the curve to the altitude scale gives maximum altitude of the star, and reading to the time scale gives watch time of transit.

Computation.

Latitude:-

(a) Star)   With the altitude obtained as above
(b) Sun)   compute the latitude in the usual manner.

Longitude:-

(a) Star)   Compute as shown in Para.4 above.
(b) Sun)   Compute from the formula:-

East Longitude = 24 hours
                 - (G.M.T. plus E)
(N.B. The value of E is given in the
N.A. for every two hours of G.M.T. &
must be interpolated for the exact
time of transit).

Do not forget to correct the altitudes
for refraction and the Watch times for
error.

An example of the graphical plotting can be seen in the I.O.'s Office.

Chapter Nine

Road Watch

In 1942 Rommel's *Afrika Korps* had broken out of El Agheila on the Gulf of Sirte in Libya and the Allies were desperately in need of reliable intelligence for their planned counter-offensive in Cyrenaica. To help gather this information the LRDG established the 'Road Watch'. This entailed the observation of the Tripoli-Benghazi Road (*Via Balbia*), which was 643 kilometres behind enemy lines and was kept under constant twenty-four-hour watch over several months in 1942. It was along this road that the Axis forces brought almost all their armour, supplies and troop reinforcements. A large percentage of the information received by the Eighth Army about enemy movements came via the radios of the LRDG stationed behind the lines.

The classification, markings, loads and other details of all troop and supply transport, armoured vehicles and artillery were recorded as they passed. Even Allied PoWs were seen being trucked to the rear. Yet rescue was not an option, as the Road Watch could not be compromised. If the information was considered vital such as large numbers of armoured vehicles, it was immediately transmitted to LRDG HQ in Siwa. Otherwise, it was sent when the patrol was relieved and clear of enemy territory. This intelligence gained proved invaluable to GHQ in Cairo in assessing the enemy's strength in Cyrenaica. It took three patrols to do this work: while one was watching the road for a week or ten days, another was going out from the base at Siwa to relieve it, and the third was making the 965km journey back. All the LRDG patrols shared this vital yet tedious work. This put a heavy drain on the unit and sometimes made it very difficult for them to carry out other tasks without overtaxing the men and trucks. Ron Landon-Lane of R Patrol recalled that of all the patrol duties, this was the most hated.

Don Steele of R Patrol wrote in his wartime reflections his view of the Road Watch:

> The curse of our life up in the north was the Road Watch. The curse because to the men it meant a week of sheer boredom and to HQ it meant that at all times three patrols were always tied up. The Road Watch had been going for some time when we took over in Siwa. It had been established by Major Mitford near Marble Arch. As Benghazi was always subject to raids by the RAF, vast quantities of material and men too were landed at Tripoli and then sent to the front by road. The idea then was to keep an eye on this traffic; the information gained gave GHQ in Cairo a fair idea of what was on the enemy's mind.

The two watchers equipped with powerful field glasses and books of silhouettes of enemy vehicles would take up a position where they could see the road without themselves being seen. They would lie there all day: one would watch the traffic through the glasses and the other would write down what was seen. The men had to take up their position during the few minutes before the dawn and lie still all day. Movement was impossible without giving the show away. As soon as it was dark, they made their way back to where the patrol was hidden in some shallow wadis to the south, their place being taken by two more men who would lie up as close to the road as was possible in the darkness.

Most of the time it was just a case of sitting there bored stiff and reporting an unending stream of uninteresting traffic. The watchers were seen, once or twice, by Arabs who, fortunately, did not give them away to the enemy. And on one occasion they were surrounded by an enemy convoy which left the road and dispersed in the area. But the men were not seen and although they spent a few uncomfortable hours, they got back to the trucks safely, and so the watch went on.

An example of a comprehensive report on a Road Watch mission was produced by Captain J.R. Easonsmith of R1 Patrol as per Operation Report No. 17 dated 1 April 1942. This provides in detail an insightful account of a typical road observation which all the patrols had to perform at some point. The report was laid out as follows:

Detail: Patrol left Siwa on March 12th with two LRDG officers and twelve other ranks, also Lieutenant Graham of the Army Photographic Unit. The party was carried in four 30cwt Chevrolets. At dawn on March 17th, a rendezvous was kept with T2 Patrol at a point some miles S.S.E. of the Marble Arch and the Sirte-Agheila Road. From there it was possible to move up a further 4 miles to a position in an offshoot of the wadi at Turchi where good cover made it possible to harbour the trucks. From this point, the patrol operated until the evening of March 28th, when T2 returned and took over again. The return journey was without incident, the patrol arriving in Siwa on the night of March 31st.

Method: The camp was situated about 3 miles from the road at its nearest point. One man was kept on watch on a nearby vantage point. From this point, vehicles using the road could be seen without glasses, and with glasses a general idea of their size could be obtained when visibility was good.

Daily leaving the camp at 0330 hours in the morning, a picket of two men walked down to the road, arriving there just before first light, and making their arrangements for a hideout for the day. This was usually selected about 350–400 yards from the road. Cover in the whole area of the road is extremely scanty. The ground bordering the road to the south is a flat plain, some 2 to 3 miles broad. The surface consists of small stones and the only vegetation is small patches of a dry heather-like plant with a maximum height of 2 feet. There are no shrubs. Fortunately, K.D. (khaki drill) fits in well with the prevalent colours and the picket might be unnoticed considerably nearer to the road save for the daily presence of gangs of road workers who operate at no fixed point. These men are apt to wander about during their midday break.

Another source of danger if the picket is too close comes from vehicles or convoys that pull a few hundred yards off the road to have meals or effect repairs. During the hours of darkness, the picket moves up to some 20 or 30 yards from the road, but even so, very few details can be distinguished. They leave at daybreak and return to the camp, making a complete period of duty about 26 hours.

Accuracy of Reports: Too high a standard of accuracy should not be anticipated, as although all ranks are extremely keen, they have had no previous training in this type of work and had no special knowledge of guns or armoured vehicles. Nearly all are well versed in the looks and weights of British M.T. and used our own trucks as comparisons for 30cwts – the Bedford for 3-ton trucks. Some confusion arose over five- or ten-tonners, as I think that many of the heavy Italian trucks lie between the two weights at 6 or 7 tons and whereas one would classify them as 5 tons, another patrol would make them 10 tons.

Watch Notes

March 21st: Reports on this day are accurate up until 1230 hrs GMT. From then on until darkness, the road pickets were unable to look up or move to do their job as a convoy moved in behind them with the nearest vehicle at 150 yards. The approximation for the remainder of the day is based on reports of the camp pickets and the average traffic in the afternoons.

March 22nd: Numerically quite accurate, but detail poor as owing to a large quantity of vehicles being parked between the wadi mouth of the road. The picket had to operate from about 2 miles from the road.

March 23rd and 24th: On both days there were heavy sandstorms and at times the visibility was very poor, but this was slightly offset by the fact that pickets were able to get close to the road.

Daily Notes

March 18th: Largest convoy, nineteen trucks going west. No troop movement.

March 19th: Largest convoy, seven vehicles going east. Only troop movement noted, approximately 100 Germans in six 5-ton trucks going east. 1 light, 1 medium tank, self-propelled, 1 medium on 4-wheel transporter.

March 20th: Largest convoy, twelve vehicles going east. No troop movement. The eight AA guns were mounted on 4 wheels. Tractors had German white cross on side. Two field guns (25-pdr type) towed by 30cwt trucks. Two long-barrelled probably AA guns, about the size of our Bofors, mounted on 3-ton trucks with German white cross on side.

The light tank resembled a three-man German light tank. The two medium tanks were equipped with short heavy guns, about 3 feet, probably howitzers.

Going westwards were two 7- to 10-ton lorries and trailers and loaded in each were three guns of size approximating to our 25-pdrs on two-wheel mountings. (Two on trailer, one on truck.)

March 21st: Six guns going west, 25-pdr size, but with longer barrels, each towed on two wheels by a gun tractor.

1230 hrs: First party of a convoy consisting of thirteen vehicles including two or three staff cars, a motorcycle and an ambulance.

1330 hrs: Second party, twenty vehicles in all, five or six W/T trucks and remainder 3-tonners.

1500 hrs: Third party, remaining twenty-seven vehicles, included eight gun tractors, four of which were pulling guns of our 25-pdr type.

All these vehicles pulled off the road behind our picket. Two or three small green bivouac tents were erected; they stayed until 0745 hrs the next morning when fifty of them moved off. The remaining twelve followed after an interval of two hours. The convoy was moving east, and it was probably only a coincidence that their departure synchronised with the passing of two Ghibli aircraft flying westwards very low, obviously doing road patrol. The party had a field kitchen with them; there were about 200 men dressed in light overalls in some cases. Vehicles appeared to be German. Bugle calls were sounded for some sort of inspection parade in the evening, reveille and breakfast. All movements were done at the double. At night a picket was placed on each of the four corners of the area in which the vehicles were parked. Every 5 to 10 minutes the first man would flash a torch and the other three would follow suit in turn, apparently to show that all was well. Their departure in the morning seemed a very leisurely affair about three hours after sunrise. Some of the guns, which would be the slowest-moving components, were not in the first section to leave. After all had gone, two men remained who seemed to be systematically pacing up and down where the convoy had been. They eventually left sometime in the afternoon. The pickets could see little as the convoy was too close to them to look up, but six gun tractors were seen to pass going east. Earlier in the day nine of the 30cwt trucks going east were W/T trucks.

March 22nd: Few details available as picket unable to get near the road owing to the convoy already described.

March 23rd: Heavy sandstorm. No troop movements. Largest convoy sixteen vehicles going east.

March 24th: Conditions slightly better than yesterday. Observation good. Largest convoy, twenty-six vehicles going east followed by one of twenty-five; they may have been one and the same. Both convoys consisted largely of 5-tonners. At the front of the first were three scout cars, followed by a staff car and at the rear was a touring car. The second was led by a motorcycle and a staff car and the rear brought up in a similar manner.

Only troop movement consisted largely of twelve 30cwts, each with what appeared to be a 20mm Breda gun mounted on it, pointing forward and elevated to an angle of approximately 45 degrees. Each truck had a crew of six Italians in the back. There were also two 3-tonners similarly equipped. The two eight-wheel and one light four-wheel armoured cars had German crews who appeared to be wearing the light-coloured cricket cap.

March 25th: Largest convoy was of twenty-six empty covered 30cwts going east, followed later by one of nineteen and another of fourteen also empty 30cwts. No troop movements. Twelve 5-tonners and trailers going east had been covered by tarpaulins on the trailers, what the picket took to be light tanks. No crews were visible. Three heavy tanks thought to be Mk IVs went east under their own power. One heavy tank passed during the night, also under its own power.

March 27th: Largest convoy, twenty-eight vehicles eastbound. The ten tanks appeared to be medium in size, but as they passed at 0400 hrs no details could be seen. They were on transporters and must have been travelling at night as they had not spent the night within sight of our pickets. The eighteen armoured cars were not identifiable by any photos that we held. They had four wheels, no visible gun mounted, high circular turrets and fairly long chassis. Crews wore dark, tight-fitting berets and dark overalls. No markings were seen on the cars. Two aircraft transporters passed going west with what appeared to be fighters on them.

March 28th: Largest convoy twenty vehicles. No troop movements. Light howitzer on two wheels towed by gun tractor (7.5cm German approximately for size). The tanks seen were in three parties. Identification is not definite. Two thought Mk IVs, two Mk IIIs and one light tank with two staff cars. Second party, six Mk IIIs with three staff cars and third party eight Mk IIIs with five staff cars. All three parties passed between 0745 hrs and 0845 hrs.

General Notes

Not a very high percentage of captured British vehicles were seen, probably 5%. Those recognised were Macks, Whites or 3-ton Bedfords. The condition of this heavy transport appeared to be good, and the littler stuff, not noticeably bad. A great number of vehicles in the 3-ton and 30cwt class had a white transverse bar about one foot wide painted across the radiator end of the bonnet. Some vehicles with cabs had stripes of green, white and red, each about one foot wide painted over the cab roof along the axis of the car. In the 10-ton and trailer class, many civilian lorries were being used for military purposes. They were painted in non-military colours such as red and blue and had large names painted along the side of the body such as Monti, U Signorette and Trucchi. Loads were difficult to judge, as easily 90% of the traffic was covered and in most cases the back laced up. Quite a lot of loads of metal fuel drums were seen, but usually on 3-tonners. The bigger trucks and trailers were usually high-sided and when not covered the load was difficult to distinguish. Several loads of rough timber for fuel were seen going east. Vehicles going west were often empty. A common arrangement was to see a 10-tonner with an empty trailer loaded onto the truck towing a second trailer with a truck on it.

As so many of the largest convoys seen were about 20/25 vehicles, it looks as though larger numbers are split up and sent off at intervals. This was borne out by the arrival in sections of the convoy noted on March 21st. For the first couple of hours each morning, the preponderance of movement is westwards by a large margin. It seems probable that a lot of traffic reaches Agheila or thereabouts for a halting-point for the night. For two hours in the middle of the day, traffic slackens off considerably. The busiest periods are 0900 hrs to 1030 hrs and 1330 hrs to 1530 hrs GMT daily. Very few trucks carried any form of AA defence that could be seen, but a lot had a man sitting in the back, probably as a spotter. Previous patrols have reported an armoured car patrolling the road. This was not seen during our stay. This task seemed to be carried out by Ghibli aircraft which flew on average at about 500 to 1,000 feet.

The condition of the road is maintained by gangs of Italian soldiers wearing uniform. They do not appear to be attempting any major repairs but just stopping any serious deterioration, working in a different place each day. Parts of it are tar-sealed and parts stone and gravel finish. The telephone lines bear three lines.

Opposite to our camp on the northern side of the road, some vehicle pits had been dug, but not being used. Similar pits were on the southern side of the road and at the base of the scarp in the Dor Lanuf area some 7 or 8 miles east of us. Nearly all the traffic at night used lights. No Arabs were seen in the area during our stay, but there were obvious signs that the camel tracks are well used at some periods during the year.

Key to Pickets

March

17/18th	Lt. Graham	Cpl. Tinker	23rd	Lt. Guild	Pte. Allen
18th	Capt. Easonsmith	Tpr. McKeown	24th	Capt. Easonsmith	Lt. Graham
19th	Tpr. Rawson	Tpr. Bowler	25th	Tpr. Rawson	Tpr. Bowler
20th	Cpl. Spotswood	Tpr. Franks	26th	Pte. Gorringe	Pte. Williams
21st	Tpr. Brown	Tpr. Parkes	27th	Cpl. Spotswood	Tpr. Franks
22nd	Pte. Gorringe	Pte. Williams	28th	Lt. Guild	Pte. Allen

As per the watch list, the task was shared by both officers and men. On this occasion even Lieutenant Graham, an army photographer who was with the patrol to observe, was allocated a watch duty. It was considered an uncomfortable and tedious job, but was of great value in gathering vital intelligence on the movement and dispositions of the Axis forces.

In November 1942, Lieutenant R.J. Talbot of R2 Patrol undertook a Road Watch mission where he had some close encounters with the enemy. His task was to carry out a traffic census on the coastal road at the former LRDG Road Watch site near Marble Arch. He had to ensure that all his men were instructed by the Intelligence Officer in recognition of enemy vehicles and equipment, plus high-powered binoculars were to be drawn before leaving.

They would travel in five trucks with one officer and seventeen ORs. Water and rations for thirty days would be loaded in Kufra. Also forty-five jerrycans per truck and these would be refilled at Zighen on both the outward and return journeys. When on watch they had to report immediately any large troop movements and the movement of all armoured vehicles if numbered more than five in any period of twenty-four hours. The ground-to-air signal would be a chequered sand mat. On the ground it would be the use of flag signals. They would be relieving Y1 Patrol and would remain for ten days when they would be replaced by another patrol.

On 22/11/42 Talbot recorded the events of the watch in his Operation Report No. 48:

> Patrol left Kufra on 1/11/42 and arrived at Two Beacons at 1800 hrs on 7/11/42, meeting Lieutenant Spicer of Y1 Patrol. He guided us to Wadi Hatema from where the Road Watch was being maintained. The patrol camouflaged vehicles next morning and the watch was taken over in the evening with Y Patrol moving out at dawn on 9/11/42.
>
> The patrol remained camouflaged until the night of the 15th, while maintaining a traffic census from the flat ground between the escarpment and the road. During the day of 14/11/42, two small working parties of Germans in two 30cwt trucks drove and walked around the flats on both sides of the road and appeared to be marking out the ground and putting in pegs. One party came within 150 yards of the two watchers who were concealed in a small bush. Also, in the late afternoon, a reconnaissance plane circled round the mouth of Wadi Hatema, and then followed the many tracks made by watchers going to and from the watch site, passing only 20ft over the bush. In view of this I decided to take the traffic census from the escarpment on 15/11/42.
>
> In addition to taking a tally of vehicles using the road, much enemy activity was observed in the area on 15/11/42. As the two wadis to the west and the wadi east of Hatema appeared to become occupied and Wadi Hatema seemed certain to be occupied very soon, I decided to withdraw during the night.
>
> This was carried out and the patrol moved south towards Hofra to get cover from air observation, and to signal summary of information and to

get further information instructions. However, when about 15 miles northeast of Hofra an enemy force of at least two armoured cars or patrol trucks and at least five other vehicles were seen approaching, I decided to avoid an action if possible and circled west then south for 12 miles. The enemy vehicles followed for several miles and then stopped. The patrol therefore entered a steep-sided wadi and vehicles were camouflaged from air patrols for the rest of the day. Two hours after stopping in the wadi, a plane was seen north of us and about an hour later was seen in the south, while most of the afternoon it could be heard.

A check of the vehicles disclosed nine broken centre bolts of rear springs and leaves broken in three other springs. Advice was signalled to Group HQ who instructed me to return to Kufra. Until 1400 hrs the next day we spent on vehicle repairs and summarising the traffic census for signalling to Kufra.

Five long messages were enciphered but WT contact with HQ faded out after three had been sent. It was decided to push on south and complete signals later. All messages were cleared next morning. The patrol then proceeded to Kufra on evening of 20/11/42. The 'chorehorse' charging set was handed to T1 Patrol. We met G1 Patrol at Bun Hill, gave them the high-power binoculars and information, and arrived at Kufra on 21/11/42.

Appendix 1: Enemy Activity

Enemy activity observed from escarpment near Wadi Hatema.

On 15/11/42 the traffic census was taken by two watchers on the escarpment on the west side of Wadi Hatema. Apart from road traffic the following enemy activity was observed during the day by them.

Many working parties on the flat between the escarpment and beach (both sides of the road) from Marble Arch LG (Landing Ground) to the small wadi east of Wadi Hatema. Over 1,000 vehicles were dispersed in the same area, principally round the LG.

Vehicles were also entering Wadi El Hagiag, Wadi Turchi and the wadi east of Wadi Hatema. The vehicles between the road and the wadi east of Hatema were in one line at regular intervals of about 300yds.

Six marquees were erected along the road between the LG and Wadi Hatema. Five tents were erected near the road, around the small bush which had been used the previous day for cover by the road watchers. The LG was used both by fighter and transport planes. Fighters patrolled the road both east and west and appeared to be using the LG for refuelling, though they could not actually be seen while on the ground.

A cruiser lay a short distance from the beach all day until 1600 hrs when it was bombed by six planes. The ship was hit and moved out to sea. It still appeared to be burning when darkness fell.

Attached to Talbot's Operation Report No. 48 were thirteen pages of and statistics of road transport, aircraft and coastal vessel observations. A sample of four of these pages is shown in this chapter. This particular watch was very high risk as it was situated close to a large concentration of Axis forces and low-flying aircraft, so the patrol had to keep well concealed while gaining much valuable intelligence on enemy dispositions.

A pair of American-made Bausch & Lomb 6 × 30 binoculars as used on the Road Watch and other duties by Trooper Bill Hammond, R2 Patrol. The binoculars with a tan leather case were not official War Department issue, but acquired by the LRP in 1940 from whatever source they could find to meet the needs of the new patrols. The inside of the cover is marked 'Bill Hammond 1104, LRDG 1940'.

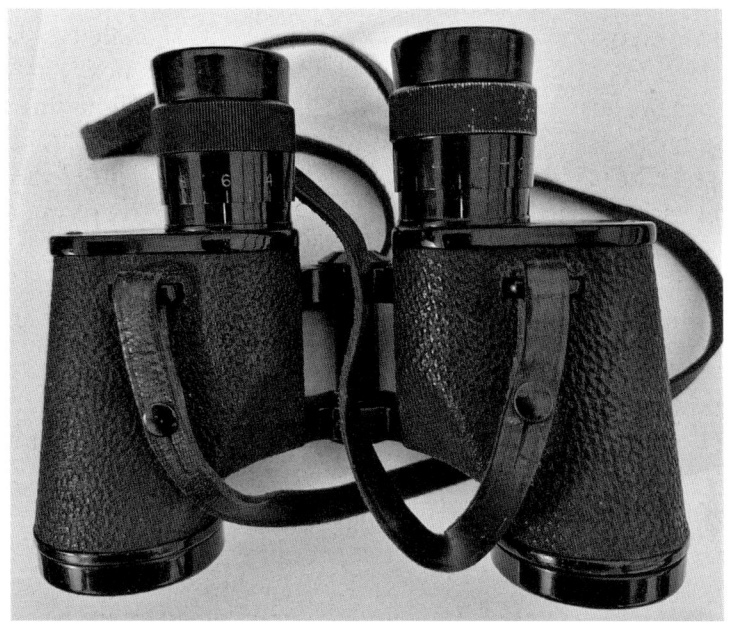

Corporal R.O. Spotswood dressed for the cold stands next to his heavily loaded Ford F30 truck. Note the leather binocular case hanging on the side of the truck below the camouflage net, both essential items for Road Watch.

Captain J.R. Easonsmith enjoying his pipe and studying a map while on a patrol halt.

A Chevrolet patrol truck driving through a wadi on their way to find a concealed place to set up the Road Watch camp.

Jake Easonsmith scrubbing his plate with fine sand as per the usual LRDG practice for cleaning plates and utensils. Note he is wearing comfortable desert shoes.

R Patrol members rest between watches with their camouflaged truck behind them. Left: Private R.R. Williams.

Private R.R. Williams on watch with his binoculars.

British army issue compass as used by Trooper Bill Hammond of R Patrol. These were used when men were operating on foot such as walking to and from their Road Watch position.

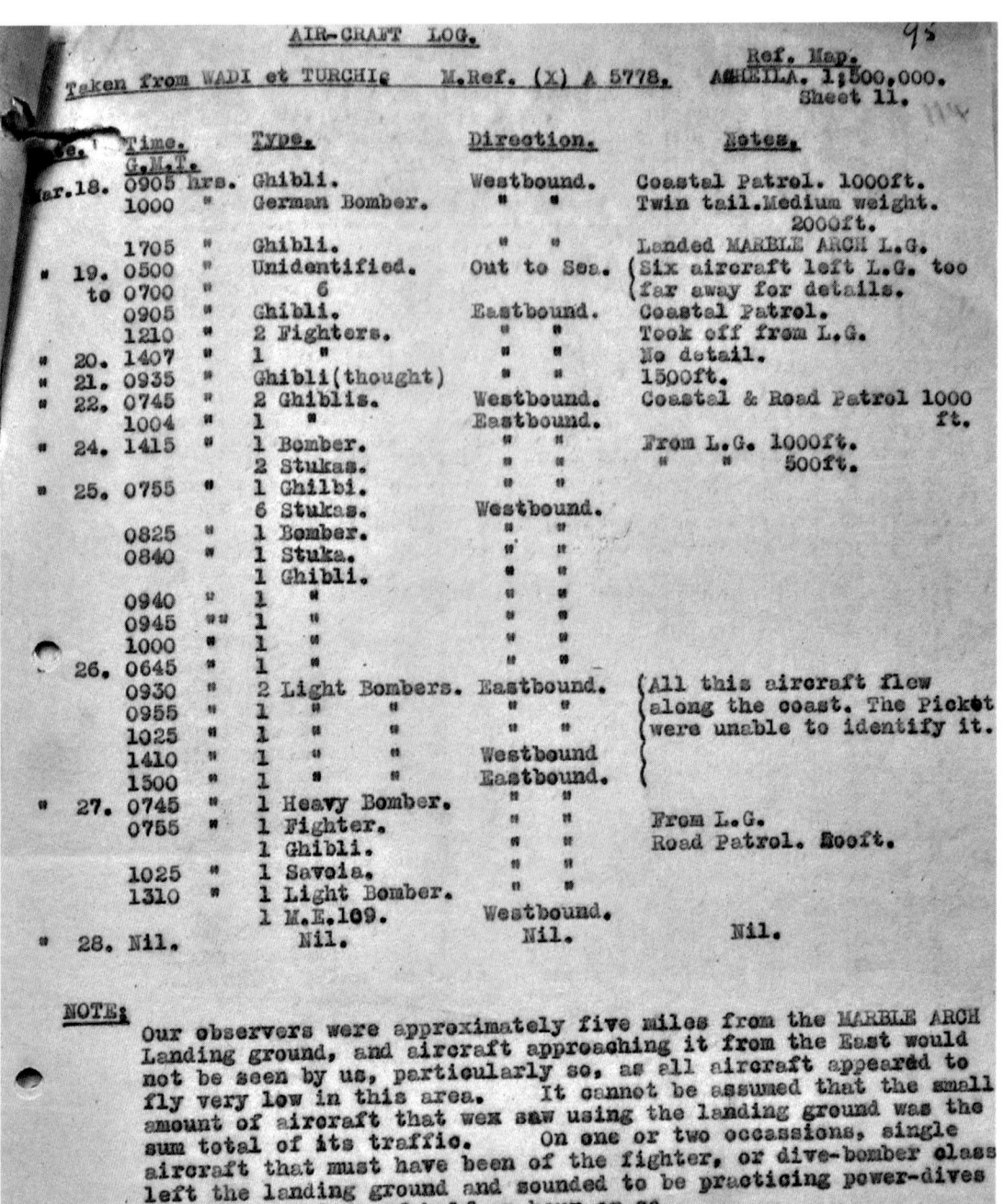

A copy of the original aircraft log that was attached to Captain Easonsmith's *Operation Report 17* Road Watch report. A great variety of aircraft observations were recorded.

A Luftwaffe aircraft recognition reference booklet, *Kriegsflugzeuge* (*Aircraft of War*), dated 1941. This captured example was useful in identifying German, Italian and Allied aircraft in both silhouette and photo profiles.

A captured Panzer Mk IV Aust.G with its 75mm gun. When these were first sighted by the Road Watch in mid-1942 it caused a big concern for GHQ in Cairo. The watchers had to be able to identify the variety of Axis vehicles that travelled along the main highway. They carried a book of silhouettes of enemy vehicles to help identify them, or if they could not find an image they drew the outline in their notebook for later evaluation.

An Italian Carro Armato M13/40 medium tank. It was armed with a 47mm gun and three 8mm machine guns.

An *Afrika Korps Demag* Sd.Kfz.10 half-track towing a Pak 38 anti-tank gun.

A Horch Kfz.12.901 staff car undergoing maintenance. Note the *Afrika Korps* palm tree symbol painted on the left mudguard.

Good old Marble Arch, the scene of many a 'road watch'.

(**Opposite, above**) The Road Watch also observed prisoners being transported, but no intervention could be made by the LRDG. In this case Indian PoWs rest during a halt. Note the Horch staff car in the background.

(**Opposite, below**) In 1942 the Road Watch was established 8 kilometres from Mussolini's *Arae Philaenorum*, which the troops called the Marble Arch. This photo was taken in December 1942 following the Allied advance.

(**Above**) A drawing by Bluey Grimsey of an RAF Westland Lysander aircraft flying over the Marble Arch.

Using his No. 11 radio housed in the side of his truck, the R Patrol operator transmits its watch observations. Trooper J.A. Franks looks on.

9th November 1942.

EASTBOUND.
LOADS.
- EMPTY. — 3/10ton, 18/5ton & 1 Trailer, 2/3ton,
- Troops. — 3/5ton, German, 2/5ton & trailer, unidentified. In addition on other loads, 18 German, 10 Italian, and 20 mixed.
- Large Cases. — 1/10ton & trailer. (Engines ?)
- Boxes. — 1/10ton & trailer, 2/5ton & trailer, 1/3ton.
- Drums. 40gal. — 2/5ton, 1/5ton & trailer, 1/3ton.
- Sacks. — 1/10ton & trailer, 1/5ton.
- Ammunition Boxes. — 1/10ton & trailer.
- Mixed. — 1/3ton. (Tyres etc.)
- Cement. — 1/10ton & trailer.
- Barrels. (Wooden) — 2/5ton.

NUMBERS. 1/5ton & trailer with SATA on side and 381 on door.

FORMATION SIGNS. 5/5ton HIKER with [symbol] on door.

6/5ton Fiats, new and painted yellow, with eagle with outspread wings and short tail painted in black on doors.
1/Tanker with a tank(AFV) painted on side of cover

WESTBOUND.
LOADS.
- Troops. — Italian, 1/10ton & trailer & 1/3ton. In addition the following were carried on other loads:- 12 German, 10 Italian, and 14 mixed.
- Cases. — 1/3ton, 1/5ton & trailer.
- Large Crates. — 3/5ton.
- Aero Fuselages. — 1/10ton & trailer, 1/3ton, 1/5ton and trailer. (5 fuselages.)
- Drums. — 1/10 & trailer, 4/5ton, 1/5ton & trailer.
- Timber. — 1/5ton.
- Baggage. — 1/5ton, 1/3ton.
- Furniture. — 1/5ton.

Formation Signs. 1/5ton with [symbol] 8 painted with black lines.

GENERAL. Over half the vehicles were covered and loads not seen.
Many 5ton trucks with canopies and roll up sides, and with seating accommodation for troops.
About 50% of vehicles without canopies have canvas covered over loads.
No AA spotters and no AA guns mounted.
No camouflage nets. Some vehicles mottle painted.

Lieutenant R.J. Talbot's Road Watch observations for 9 November 1942 as attached to his Operation Report No. 48.

10th November 1942.

EASTBOUND.
LOADS. Troops. 3/3ton, 10/3ton & trailer, 4/30cwt.
(All Italian.)
Timber. 3/30cwt.
Tyres. 4/3ton.
Coal. 1/3ton & trailer.
Boxes. 1/5ton, 1/3ton.
Ammunition Boxes. 1/3ton & trailer.
Bales. 1/3ton.

WESTBOUND.
LOADS. Troops. 1/10ton & trailer, 1/5ton, 5/3ton, 5/3ton & trailer, 1/30cwt. Plus 158 carried on other loads.
Tyres. 2/3ton, 1/3ton & trailer, 6/30cwt.
Baggage. 1/3ton, 3/3ton & trailer, 6/30cwt.
Machinery. 2/5ton.
Crates. (Engines) 1/3ton, 1/3ton & trailer.
Drums. 3/5ton & trailer, 2/3ton, 3/30cwt.
Timber. 1/3ton, 1/3ton & trailer.
Fuselages. 1/10ton & trailer. (2 Fuselages.)
Black Boxes with
  Green Bands. 1/3ton.
Mixed. 1/3ton.
Bedding. 1/3ton, 1/30cwt.
Furniture. 3/3ton.

GUNS. 2 AA mounted on 1/30cwt. & trailer.
1 AA mounted on 1/3ton.

GENERAL. Many vehicles had a white stripe across mudguard and bonnett.
Several 30cwt. & trailer marked with TURIN on side.
6/30cwt. trucks covered with a sign on the side of the body, as follows:-

```
┌─────────┐
│White    │
│    ╱    │
│   ╱     │
│      Red│
└─────────┘
```

Talbot watch report for 10 November 1942.

13th November 1942.

EASTBOUND LOADS. All vehicles appeared to be empty, except 4/5ton, 1/5ton & trailer, and 5/3ton with 40gal. drums.

WESTBOUND LOADS.

Troops. Mostly Italian, 1/10ton & trailer, 29/5ton, 18/5ton & trailer, 60/3ton, 37/3ton & trailer, 1/30cwt. Plus 592 carried on other loads.
Cases & Boxes. 9/5ton, 25/5ton & trailer, 37/3ton, 5/3ton & trailer, 2/30cwt.
Drums, 40gal. 2/5ton, 1/5ton & trailer, 3/3ton, 1/30cwt.
Baggage. 2/5ton, 6/5ton & trailer, 7/3ton.
Aero Fuselages. 1/5ton & trailer, 1/3ton. (5 fuselages.)
Sacks. 3/5ton, 5/5ton & trailer, 4/3ton, 1/3ton & trailer.
Tyres. 1/5ton & trailer, 1/3ton.
Timber. 1/3ton.
Clothing. 2/5ton & trailer.
Tents. 1/3ton & trailer.
Mixed. 1/5ton, 4/3ton.
Furniture. 3/5ton, 7/5ton & trailer, 26/3ton, 3/3ton & trailer, 2/30cwt.
Civilians. 2/5ton & trailer, 6/3ton, 3/3ton & trailer, 1/30cwt.
Natives. 2/5ton, 8/3ton, 2/3ton & trailer, 1/30cwt.

Miscellaneous Vehicles included:-
7 Buses, 40 Caravans, 35 Ambulances, 5 Jeeps, 21/3wheeled small cars, 7 tank hunters or assault guns, and 3/3ton breakdown lorries.

GENERAL.

GUNS. 1/20m/m Breda mounted on 1/3ton lorry, and 12m/m Bredas mounted on each of 3/15cwts. 1/2.8c.m. Hotchkiss AT Gun. Twin mounted Spandaus on each of 2/30cwt. lorries.
ARMOURED CAR. Italian 4/wheeled.
TRACTOR. Small caterpillar tractor transported.
TANKERS. 2 covered with nets and 1 not covered.
FORMATION SIGNS:-
1/3ton & trailer with SATA on side.
1/3ton with TOERS.
2/5ton with Eagle clutching S and K painted on front of truck and C on side.

Talbot watch report for 13 November 1942.

GENERAL OBSERVATIONS.

TRAFFIC. There was a sharp increase in WESTBOUND traffic each day from 9/II/42 until 14/II/42, when vehicles were passing in a steady stream from before dawn until midnight, when it would ease up. During the days of 14th and 15th it was impossible to identify many of the loads, or the nationality of the troops carried as the traffic was so heavy.

THE FOLLOWING PASSED WESTWARDS.

SHIPS.
- 9/II/42. 2 large and 1 small vessel.
- 10/II/42. 3 small coastal vessels.
- 11/II/42. 3 small coastal vessels.
- 12/II/42. 1 Tanker, 4 large, 9 small vessels, and 1 E boat.
- 13/II/42. 2 ships and 1 small sailing ship.
- 14/II/42. 3 freighters, 2 small ships and 1 Cruiser.
- 15/II/42. 5 small and 1 large ship.

The ship, presumed to be a cruiser, on 14th was bombed by six planes at about 1600hrs. Smoke was seen pouring from it the remainder of the afternoon.

PLANES.
- 9/II/42. 18 troop carriers and 17 fighters.
- 10/II/42. 2 Bombers and 46 fighters, and 25 troop carriers.
- 11/II/42. 54 Bombers, 54 fighters, 22 troop carriers.
- 12/II/42. 14 Bombers, 13 fighters, 6 troop carriers.
- 13/II/42. 30 Bombers, 25 fighters, 14 troop carriers.

On 14th and 15th, planes were so numerous, passing each way, chiefly WEST, that no tally was made.
It appeared that many fighters were used as road patrols and were more numerous in late morning and late afternoon.
One recce plane circled round WADI HATEMA on 14th and followed our many tracks down to road watch site.

Talbot watch report on shipping observations.

Chapter Ten

Air Attack

Buster Gibb recorded his recollections about coming under air attack in the early days of the LRDG:

> In the early days we weren't afraid of the Italian troops in ground actions, but it was their aircraft that gave us the most trouble and we had to show respect for. We usually drove them high with our gunfire, as they were easily frightened, which would make their bombing inaccurate. If we were on a flat area, it was easier to avoid the bombs because we had room to disperse and manoeuvre. We had a trick while driving where we would allow the plane to come in and commit to a bomb run on our tail and then suddenly turn at a right angle and go like hell the other way. When he dropped his bombs, you would see the little spinners on them that released the primers. They would glitter when they let them go. Our tactics worked well, and it was hard for the Italian bombers to ever hit us, though on occasion we suffered bomb splinter damage to the truck bodies and tyres.
>
> The greater risk was if the bomber used its air gunners, who could whip their fire from one side to another, but our concentrated return fire tended to make them fly higher which made the gunners still dangerous, but less accurate.
>
> On one occasion, Sandy Sanders (Gunner E. Sanders) while driving during an air alert lost one of his sand mats from the front of his truck. He simply jumped off and walked back to retrieve the mat when a load of bombs dropped. We thought God! Goodbye Sandy, they got Sandy! When the dust cleared away, there he was nonchalantly walking with his sand mat under his arm; somehow, he came through it unharmed.

On 14 September 1942, R2 Patrol led by Lieutenant J.R. Talbot departed from Kufra to undertake a reconnaissance patrol around the Jalo area. The patrol consisted of six vehicles, seventeen other ranks and one officer. They carried sixty jerrycans of fuel per truck and had the option of refuelling from a dump established close to Jalo. In addition, they took supplies of rations and water for a month's operation. For recognition from the air, they used the chequered sand mats. From the ground any flag waved above the head (challenge) and flag held out horizontally to left (to reply). Their task was to patrol the area for 70 miles daily and work in conjunction with operations at Jalo by 'Z Force'. (This was a code-name for the Sudan Defence Force and Y2 Patrol operating against Jalo.)

Talbot wrote an account of the mission per Operation Report No. 44 dated 23 September 1942:

Report

The patrol left Kufra on 14 September 1942 and arrived in the evening of 16 September 42, passing through Z Force B Echelon area in Wadi El Farigh at 1200 hrs. Just prior to reaching Wadi El Farigh, two Savoias (Savoia-Marchetti SM.79 bombers) attacked the patrol for about twenty minutes, but only tried to machine-gun three trucks. The trucks swerved about and whenever not being directly attacked, all stopped, and the crews opened fire. The planes flew off in a northerly direction and the patrol continued on its way.

At 0730 hrs on 17 September, Lieut. Talbot, with three trucks, patrolled from the camp area to hills at Bir Quwetin and return. There was absolutely no cover from air observation on this route. No enemy movements were seen. Tracks, possibly two weeks old, of many vehicles were found. In the evening they moved to an area with excellent cover in a large depression with a high escarpment on the southern side and high sand hills on the northern side. No W/T contact could be made with Z Force.

On 18 September, Sgt. Willcox, with three trucks, patrolled along our tracks made the previous day; no vehicles had crossed the tracks, and no enemy vehicles were seen, but a plane spotted the patrol near Bir Quwetin. An unsuccessful attempt was made during the day to make W/T contact with Z Force on the emergency frequency. However, in the evening, a message was received from Y2 Patrol who was with Z Force to come to Jalo for a closer reconnaissance role.

The patrol broke camp at 0630 hrs on 19 September and proceeded towards Jalo. When approximately 8 miles west of the oasis we observed an enemy air raid was on there. We waited for nearly two hours until no more planes could be seen or heard before proceeding. We arrived within sight of the Jalo oasis, about 4 miles out, and stopped to make sure of Z Force positions before going further.

An enemy plane suddenly appeared, diving towards my truck. The patrol accordingly turned away, as the going ahead was soft, and prepared to take evasive action and open fire. My truck avoided the stick of bombs aimed at it and as the plane turned away, we saw five other planes approaching. From then it was a case of each truck for itself as each plane singled out a target. I set course for the Wadi Farigh, which was the nearest cover of which I knew, and the other trucks followed as well as they could while swerving about.

After we had gone about 5 miles, I saw R12 truck go to the north-west and no planes appeared to follow him. The truck found cover in some hummocks about 5 miles south of Augila and was not spotted again. Cpl. Waetford, the truck commander, went into Jalo later in the afternoon and joined Y2 patrol there.

After having travelled 25 miles towards Wadi Farigh the planes left us. During the whole distance we were attacked with bombs, cannon and machine-gun fire, sometimes by three planes at a time. We returned fire all the way. R7 truck (Sgt. Willcox) was followed towards the south-east until he found cover in a small scarp.

A separate report by Sgt. Willcox was completed:

R10 truck (Tpr. Dodunski, fitter) followed Cpl. Waetford and found cover near Augila fort. Later in the afternoon he headed south and picked up the crew of R9 and met Sgt. Willcox in the desert. R9 truck (L/Cpl. A.D. Sadgrove, navigator) went about 5 miles, but a bomb landed near one side just as it swerved, with the result that it overturned. The crew was later picked up by R10 and the truck was eventually righted, towed away and picked up. I did not see R8 truck turn away during the fight.

When the planes left me, I stopped, but had to carry on before I found cover and lost the sound of the planes in the vicinity. However, we could still hear planes all the afternoon at intervals until 1700 hrs, when we backtracked and searched around the area where the attack took place, until 2300 hrs. We then went 10 miles back along the tracks we had made before the attack as this was to be the RV. Here we found a piece of case timber with a note reporting R8 was OK. This truck had apparently gone further back along the tracks. We went on a further 10 miles and camped for the night.

At 0500 hrs on 20 September we returned to the RV, but no other trucks had reported there. We then followed tracks of R8 for another 16 miles but turned south as we expected a plane to reconnoitre the route. About 6 miles south we stopped and heard a plane going from east to west, apparently along the tracks.

We made three attempts to get into the SDF (Sudan Defence Force) area, but each time an air raid took place there. We then decided to go 10 miles west of Wadi Farigh, camouflage the truck near the tracks we had made going from the SDF area and contact R8 or any other of our trucks which came that way.

We went to Wadi Farigh at 1800 hrs and found the SDF on the point of evacuating the area. I could not send any message as they had sent their W/T truck ahead. I decided to wait in the wadi for any patrol trucks until 2230 hrs and then follow Z Force to Zighen, where Y2 Patrol were expected to arrive the next morning. We had been informed that some of R2 Patrol had joined Y2 at Jalo.

We met Y2 Patrol at Bir Harasc on 21 September at 1700 hrs and found R12 was the only truck which had joined Y2 Patrol. However, we received a message in the evening, which indicated that R7 and R9 trucks were on the way back to Kufra.

On 22 September we returned to Kufra with Y2 Patrol and found the trucks R7, R9 and R10, so that R8 is the only truck not yet returned. As I had arranged with the patrol to make their way back to Wadi Farigh in the event of any untoward incident, I expect this truck will go there. As the crew will find the place deserted, they should carry on to Zighen, though they were not aware that Z Force had left Jalo.

General

Personnel: The spirit of the men of the patrol was excellent throughout the attack. No crew abandoned their vehicle while it was possible to keep up the running fight. I wish specially to mention the very fine work done by Sgt. Willcox in contacting two trucks, attending to the wounded men, recovering the truck which was overturned and getting the three trucks back to Kufra.

I also wish to bring to notice the excellent effort of Signalman R. Atkins who, although painfully injured when thrown from the truck which overturned, finally succeeded in getting his wireless set working and making contact with Kufra by emergency cipher. His devotion to work, his conduct and his cheerful personality are always of a very high order.

Casualties: Evacuated to hospital: 4. Minor wounds: 3. Missing, believed safe: 3.

Signed: J.R. Talbot, Lieut. O.C. R2 Patrol.

Veteran Rowley Talbot recalled the action in a letter to the author dated 16 March 1997:

I took command of R2 Patrol and for the next six months led the patrol on six operations behind enemy lines which varied from 10 miles to 1,000 miles. It was much safer to be 1,000 miles than 10 miles. The boys were artists at camouflage of the trucks when there was little cover. Amazing!

When the Sudan Defence Force went from Kufra to attack Jalo Oasis my patrol's job was to patrol a line about 70 miles further west to watch for German or Italian reinforcements coming to help repel the SDF attack. We were finally ordered to go into the oasis but when we were some miles away, we were attacked by six dive-bombers, three of which concentrated on my truck. The only hope was to keep moving which we did staying out in the open which was all flat sand and gravel. The planes each dropped two sticks of bombs, but as we could see the bombs leave the planes it was comparatively easy to dodge them. We covered 25 miles in an hour when the bombers were out of ammunition and left. Our plan in this situation when we were all scattered was to return 20 miles on our tracks and regroup. However, after crossing and recrossing our tracks and finding no other trucks we went back the 20 miles by about 11.00pm. I did not know that my other trucks had gone into the oasis so as we were not far from the HQ of the SDF, we went into their area and found that our trucks had gone into Jalo Oasis and the whole force was to withdraw from the oasis and return to Kufra.

Sergeant L.A. Willcox MM of R2 Patrol wrote on 23 September 1942 an Appendix to Operation Report No. 44 by Lieutenant J.R. Talbot giving his account of the action:

19 September 1942: Broke camp at 0630 hrs and set out for Jalo. At 10 miles we spotted two planes bombing Jalo. We then stayed for one and a half hours while planes in relays of two continued to pass overhead bombing Jalo and returning. Also during this period two planes dropped bombs due west of us at approximately 1030 hrs. We also heard light AA fire considered to be Vickers K guns. About 1030 hrs we proceeded to continue on our bearing for another 5 miles. Lieutenant Talbot then stopped when he saw palm growth so presumed it to be the outskirts of Jalo. He then gave us the signal to advance. Upon doing so, I perceived Lieutenant Talbot running towards his truck and on looking up I saw one plane flying overhead; all trucks then scattered, as by this time five planes had spotted us and were coming into attack.

There being no cover, we decided to make a running fight. On turning to scatter, I saw explosions on the skyline which I judged to be artillery fire from the oasis. This was later confirmed by other members of the party, definitely not caused by aircraft or bombing. We were then bombed and machine-gunned, and with twisting and turning to avoid attack, we lost contact with the others. During this time our 20mm Breda, manned by Tpr. Campbell, opened up with good effect, after which four planes came in to attack, three machine-gunning and one bombing. We then found some small cover where we stopped, our gun being jammed. While Tpr. C.L. Fisher and Tpr. Campbell made for what little cover could be found, I tried to retrieve maps and escape kit, during which time we were being continually machine-gunned by four planes and during which I sustained a slight wound in my left arm.

This attack having lasted about an hour, the planes then disappeared, after which we decided to return to look for the other trucks. Following back on our tracks 5 miles we came upon R10 commanded by Tpr. A.F. Dodunski, making towards us with the crew of the wireless truck, two of whom were wounded. We then decided to return to our cover to dress these wounded men.

L/Cpl. A.D. Sadgrove was wounded in the arm and leg, Tpr. Ellis wounded in the knee and Sgm. R. Atkins with a slightly injured back. We then washed and dressed the wounds with field dressings. Tpr. Dodunski had previously found cover and during the raid had seen planes diving and machine-gunning in the distance. After the raid, he made in this direction and found the wireless truck had overturned; here he had picked up the wounded and made in the direction of my truck. We had now three crews and two trucks, R7 and R10. We stayed in cover as the wounded needed attention. We kept a picket on until sunset as a lookout for other trucks or smoking vehicles. Nothing was seen. Also during this time planes continued flying overhead in relays of twos, presumed to be looking for us, but we were not spotted.

At sunset we all proceeded towards the wireless truck to salvage maps, theodolite, wireless set, etc. On arriving at the vehicle, we decided to upturn it and try to tow. We were hoping we could fix it to run by daylight. We spent about one and a half hours at the truck, during which time I was continually flashing prearranged signal 'R' with torch, hoping to attract the attention of the other trucks, but without result. Not knowing our present position, we decided to head in the general direction of south-east with the wireless truck in tow. At midnight we hit Landing Ground 1. There having fixed the wireless, we tried unsuccessfully to contact Kufra. We could not contact Z Force or Y2 because the cipher was held by Lieutenant Talbot who is missing, together with two other trucks, R12 and R8 and their crews.

The morning of September 20, a plane was heard but not seen. The wireless truck was fixed and still unable to contact Kufra. I decided to make for Kufra with the wounded. On this run R7 jumped a razor-backed dune, causing head injuries to Pte. J.E. Gill and I suffered a cut in my back.

We finally arrived at Kufra on 21 September, 1700 hrs. In conclusion, I wish to make special mention of all personnel who, both under fire and later during our return journey, and in spite of injuries, behaved with cheerful determination and willingness to get the party through.

Though he played it down in his report, Sergeant Willcox had been hit in the shoulder by cannon shell fragments and had to spend three weeks in hospital to recover. He said, 'It was like being hit with a hammer!'

Of the four SM.79s that attacked the patrol, AA fire from the trucks seriously damaged one aircraft and slightly damaged another. They both returned to base with three airmen wounded. The concentrated fire from the LRDG caused the aircraft to fly higher and therefore more inaccurate with their strafing and bombing.

Another air attack action was when Captain L.H. (Tony) Browne, R1 Patrol was undertaking a Libyan Taxi Service mission between 12 and 30 November 1942. The task was to transport an undercover radio operator along with 998 kilograms of stores for his hideout at Bir Tala, 1,600 kilometres from their starting-point at Kufra. The patrol consisted of six patrol trucks with two officers and fifteen other ranks. In addition, travelling with them was an observer, Captain M. Pilkington of the Life Guards attached to the Arab Legion, acting as Intelligence Officer.

On 5 October 1943, LRDG HQ agreed to an attachment for one month of fourteen members of the Arab Legion. It was to include a high proportion of British officers and some technicians plus an Intelligence Officer. They would be based at Kufra, and the personnel would be spread among the patrols as observers and have instruction in navigation skills.

Captain Browne recorded the mission in his Operation Report No. 49 dated 2 December 1942:

The patrol left Kufra at 1500 hrs on 12/11/42 and arrived at Tazerbo Landing Ground at noon the following day. Here petrol containers were refilled from an existing dump. The journey continued without incident until the morning of 16/11/42. At about 0900 hrs the patrol was crossing the Kufra depression. On rounding the western end of a large rocky hill, I saw six to seven men and two vehicles in a cleft in the hill about 40 feet up. At least two machine guns were ground-mounted. It appeared to me that they hoped we should not see them and that either they had laid mines further on, or intended to open fire when all our trucks were in view. Consequently, as there was a wadi offering good cover about 800 yards to westward, I swung gradually round with the object of disguising the manoeuvre as one not caused by my having seen the enemy post. Fire was opened by the enemy when only two of our vehicles had reached cover. We replied while still on the move with accurate shooting, particularly by our .50 Browning gunner, who caused the enemy to take cover.

I then ordered my Breda truck to take up a strategic position in the wadi and to attempt to dislodge the enemy from their post. About a dozen trays (12 × 20mm rounds per tray) were fired and by observation the range was found, and the shooting appeared to be excellent. It was obvious, however, that a serious attempt to take the position would involve loss of much time and the risk of jeopardising the success of the task. Therefore, I decided to continue northwards and signalled the necessary information to Group HQ. It has since been ascertained that the two enemy vehicles were put out of action by our fire.

On the morning of 17/11/42 we arrived at a prearranged RV, where we were joined by Y2 Patrol and a detachment of the Heavy Section. After refilling with petrol, we continued north-westward, having arranged to meet Captain Hunter (Capt. A.D.N. Hunter) with Y2 in the Wadi Tamet.

Shortly before reaching the wadi, we were seen by a Ghibli recce aircraft. There are steep cliffs on either side of the Wadi Tamet and each of my vehicles selected a cleft with bonnets facing downhill. Half an hour after our arrival a Heinkel flew over and was then joined by two Capronis which flew round in a wide circle but took no action. At about midday several CR.42 Italian fighter aircraft arrived, and machine-gunned our vehicles half-heartedly. All our guns were firing and none of the enemy pilots seemed disposed to make a determined attack. About 1230 hrs all the aircraft disappeared, and I took the opportunity of moving my vehicles to new positions.

Within half an hour a larger number of CR.42s arrived (fourteen were counted). At least two of these disregarded our fire and low-level attacks were made. During these attacks it is regretted that Captain M. Pilkington, Life Guards, and Lance Corporal N. O'Malley, NZEF, patrol navigator, were mortally wounded and died within two hours. Both men were shot while firing machine guns. Private M.F. Fogden NZEF was shot in the legs. The W/T and patrol commander's truck were both damaged beyond repair. At dusk Captain Pilkington and Lance Corporal O'Malley were buried in one grave on the western side of the wadi.

The patrol was divided into two parties, each having two trucks. One party commanded by me was to continue to the destination and complete the task, the other commanded by Sergeant R.J. Landon-Lane to return to Kufra with the wounded man, Private Fogden. Having stripped the two damaged trucks and transferred the W/T sets, the two parties set off in opposite directions about 2200 hrs. Sergeant Landon-Lane's party returned to Kufra without incident, Private Fogden having been collected from Tazerbo by air.

My party drove westward from Wadi Tamet for five hours during the night 17/18 November and halted in thick tall bushes. The natural camouflage was excellent and searching aircraft failed to locate us. We continued westward at 1500 hrs, 18/11/42 and crossed the Hon-Misurata Road. The following day we again laid up until the afternoon. After continuing for 20 miles the going became very bad and movement at night was not considered advisable.

We arrived at our destination at sunset on 20/11/42. It was found, however, that we had approached the RV by a wadi too far north which debouched on to the Bir Tala Landing Ground. As the actual RV was at the top of an escarpment some 500 ft above, it was necessary for us to find a track up the cliff. A native guided us to a narrow camel track and during the night 20/21 November under a high moon, we widened the track and built it up where necessary so that the trucks could ascend. We reached the actual RV where Major A.I. Guild had dropped his men last August at 0500 hrs, 21/11/42. We left for the return journey at 1000 hrs, 21/11/42. We crossed the Misurata-Hon Road and Wadi Tamet without incident. As we had extra petrol from the two abandoned trucks, it was found unnecessary to refill at the Heavy Section dump.

On the evening of 23/11/42 we were observed by two enemy fighter aircraft. It was already dusk, and they made off in the direction of Zella. We continued southwards without further incident, arriving at Tazerbo on 28/11/42. Here we met by arrangement the LRDG aircraft for the purpose of evacuating the Sudanese W/T operator whom we had brought from Bir Tala. He was suffering from desert sores and weakness due to undernourishment. We arrived at Kufra at dawn 30/11/42 after a 1,017-mile journey. There were no mechanical breakdowns on the journey and few punctures and blowouts due to excellent driving and maintenance.

Interestingly, in his report Browne does not mention that he was also slightly wounded which made him uncomfortable and in difficulty with sitting for a few days. Merle Fogden, in an interview with the author in 1998, described the attack in more detail:

> When we came under attack from the CR.42s the six trucks dispersed to make less of a target. We took cover in the wadi banks and fought back with all our weapons. While manning their guns, the navigator, Lance Corporal N. (Nui) O'Malley received a fatal wound to his stomach and Captain M. Pilkington, an observer attached to the patrol, was killed outright. I was hit by an exploding bullet and suffered splinter wounds in both thighs.
>
> Captain Browne had a very lucky escape. He was firing a Vickers K and as ammunition was running short, he handed the gun over to Pilkington so he could get more pans. Meanwhile, the CR.42s had swept round for another attack coming in low, and as Browne was bending over an ammunition box a bullet grazed his buttocks. Pilkington, however, was killed. Such are the odds of war; Browne could have also been fatally hit if he was standing up.
>
> My truck R2 *Rotowhero*, the wireless truck, was damaged, as was Lance Corporal Murray Richardson's Chev *Rotomahana*. There was no time to try to repair these vehicles in case the enemy returned, so they were stripped and abandoned. The dead were hastily buried nearby, and I was given morphine to ease my substantial pain. Sergeant Ron Landon-Lane was assigned to take me with two trucks, the other commanded by Lance Corporal Jack Jones, on a three-day journey to Landing Ground 165. From there I was evacuated by an RAF Blenheim to Kufra, then after a few days I was flown to hospital in Cairo. Tony Browne, though slightly wounded and unable to sit comfortably, continued his mission in the remaining two vehicles. The day after the attack a sandstorm blew up, which enabled the men to all get away on their separate tasks without further incident.

There is a postscript to this story that was not known to Merle Fogden until 1992. Two months after the air attack, Lieutenant Duncan McRea, a transport officer with the 28th Maori Battalion was operating with his troops in the Wadi Tamet area when they came across the abandoned LRDG truck *Rotowhero*. McRea said he had found it in a wadi about 15 miles south of Tripoli on 22 January 1943. They saw it had been strafed and nearby lay two graves, but they were mystified as to how the vehicle came to be there and what had happened to its crew. The men soon got the Chevrolet running and adopted it for the rest of the desert campaign. It was employed to transport wounded and used as a hearse to carry those killed in action to a Tunisian burial ground.

For long after the war Duncan McRea had always wondered about the fate of *Rotowhero*'s crew. Consequently, in 1992 he wrote a letter to the New Zealand Returned Services Association newspaper, the *RSA Review*. They published his story about finding the truck and asked whether anyone knew its history. Merle Fogden saw the article and corresponded through the newspaper explaining the story. He was pleased to hear that his Chev had not been left to rust, but was recovered and went on to provide good service until the end of the desert war.

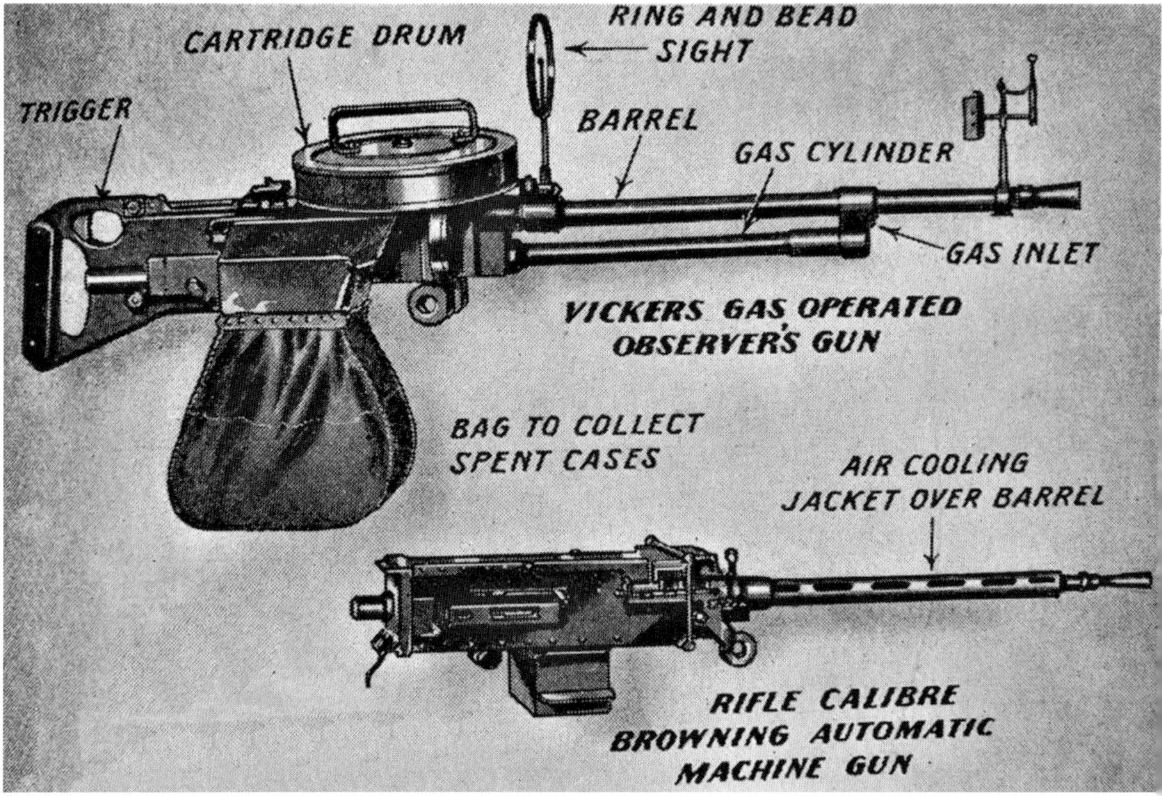

From a wartime reference drawing. Top: a .303 Vickers K, an RAF air gunner's weapon. Below: a .303 aircraft Browning as fitted to RAF fighters. Both these guns were adopted by the LRDG, which considerably improved their truck-mounted firepower.

A pair of Italian Savoia-Marchetti SM.79 bombers. These bombed and used their air gunners to attack LRDG vehicles and positions throughout the desert war.

Sergeant L.A. Willcox's Breda gun truck R7. While escaping an enemy aircraft it flew at speed over a razorbacked dune and landed heavily, injuring Willcox and Private J.E. Gill.

Trooper A.F. Dodunski's fitter's truck R10 at Siwa. Note the spare truck springs attached to the side and the supply of jerrycans.

Members of the Sudan Defence Force. They were part of Z Force, who with Y2 Patrol attempted to take Jalo oasis from the Italians. R2 Patrol under Lieutenant J.R. Talbot worked in conjunction in support of the force.

R and Y Patrols meet in the desert. The R Patrol radio truck is seen in the foreground.

R2 Patrol members looking weary after returning from a desert operation. Left: Sergeant L.A. Willcox MM, Trooper M.E. Hammond MiD and Trooper H.H. Cleaver.

Captain Alistair Guild's R1 Patrol having a tea break from the back of a truck, November 1942. Top left: Sgm. T. Evans, Tpr. A. Connelly, Capt. M. Pilkington (observer Arab Legion), Pte. F.J. Whitaker, Pte. L.J. Middlebrook, L/Cpl. N. O'Malley. Sitting left: Sgt. R.J. Landon-Lane, Pte. R. Rawson, Capt. A.L. Guild, Tpr. P.G. Reid, L/Cpl. M.D. Richardson, Pte. M.F. Fogden. A few days after this photo was taken the patrol was strafed during an air attack. Capt. Pilkington and L/Cpl. O'Malley were killed and Pte. M.F. Fogden wounded.

LRDG truck-mounted Breda Model 35 20mm anti-aircraft gun in action against enemy aircraft. The loader holds the twelve-round clip in readiness.

A captured Caproni Ca.309 Ghibli light bomber under RAF guard. These aircraft were general-purpose light reconnaissance bombers and had many encounters with the LRDG over their three years in the desert.

A trooper poses next to a memorial tomb of an Italian CR.42 fighter pilot.

An Italian Fiat CR.42 Falco fighter abandoned at Sollum after a forced landing in 1942. In the desert operations these aircraft successfully attacked LRDG patrols on several occasions, resulting in fatalities and the loss of vehicles.

R1 Patrol lined up. While on this trip they were attacked by seven Italian CR.42 fighters. An observer, Captain M. Pilkington of the Arab Legion, was killed along with Lance Corporal N. O'Malley, patrol navigator. In addition, Private M.F. Fogden was wounded and two trucks were damaged beyond repair.

Private M.F. Fogden at the wheel of his truck R2 *Rotowhero*, the radio truck. On 18 November 1942, his patrol was attacked by Italian CR.42 fighters, Fogden was wounded in the thigh and his vehicle put out of action. The truck was later recovered by the 28th Māori Battalion who got it running again and used it as base transport.

Lance Corporal M. Richardson rests against his truck *Rotomahana* which was lost due to enemy air attack on 18 November 1942.

Private Fogden had to suffer a three-day journey in the back of the R1 Patrol Breda gun truck to reach a suitable landing ground for a Blenheim bomber to airlift him out. Members of the Sudan Defence Force look on.

R2 radio truck and its operator wearing headphones. In the foreground a trooper cleans up after a meal.

Large timber beams being recovered and loaded on truck R6. No doubt they had a use for them to warrant the heavy load. Captain L.H. Browne looks on.

A crash-landed Messerschmitt BF110 found in the desert during a patrol. These aircraft were widely used by the Luftwaffe in North Africa. The LRDG had shot down at least two of them.

A souvenired *Afrika Korps* 1943 calendar. It belonged to *Unteroffizier* Willi Kain, who was killed in action on 23/03/1943 during the Battle of the Mareth Line, Tunisia.

(**Left**) An *Afrika Korps* prisoner. Note the sand goggles around his neck.

(**Right**) Private T.E. Ritchie wearing an *Afrika Korps* cap with a neck cloth. The LRDG occasionally wore these to deceive observing enemy aircraft while operating behind the lines.

Chapter Eleven

Ground Actions

In early December 1942 HQ Eighth Army asked for a patrol to guide a force in a movement to outflank the El Agheila position which was still held by Axis forces. R1 Patrol under Captain L.H. (Tony) Browne was assigned this mission. His first task was to guide the 2nd NZ Division round the enemy's right flank at the Wadi er Rigel and later to the Wadi el Nizam west of Nofilia. They were also required to establish the 'going' or topographical mapping of the country, plus general reconnaissance in the El Agheila sector.

Browne left the patrol for a short time to attend conferences with Lieutenant General Freyberg and General Montgomery at the HQ of the 51st Division. Now back with his patrol on 11 December 1942, R1 was honoured with an informal desert inspection by both the generals. On 16 December, the patrol guided the 6th NZ Field Company to the landing ground at Bir el Merduma and on the 17th it again guided the 2nd NZ Division round the southern flank of Nofilia.

On 19 December, Browne was told to reconnoitre the 'going' through the Wadi Tamet, the Wadi el Chebir and the Wadi Zem Zem to report on the suitability of the Zem Zem area for tank action. He was to also take navigational Astro fixes in the Chebir and Zem Zem wadis which would help in the interpretation of air photographs. These tasks were entrusted to Sergeant E. Gorringe with nine ORs in two trucks, who acted under the orders of the 2nd NZ Division. Accompanied by two South African officers to take the Astro fixes, the party moved to Nofilia and left there on 22 December.

In the meantime, Captain Browne continued with the rest of his patrol in a jeep accompanied by a South African officer Captain F.E. le Roex. After covering about 80 miles, they arrived at El Machina where they unfortunately ran over a German teller mine. The wounded officers were immediately driven to Nofilia, arriving at 0200 hrs on 23 December. Unfortunately, Captain le Roex died about an hour after the incident. Browne suffered from severe shock and bruises and a broken collarbone. Consequently the rough journey in the back of a Chevrolet truck to proper medical help was very uncomfortable for him. For his valued work Browne was awarded the Military Cross. The following citation appeared in the *London Gazette* on 22 April 1943:

> For most distinguished services during the operation that resulted in the turning of the Agheila position. Captain Browne carried out the initial reconnaissance of country several hundred miles behind the enemy lines, the information he obtained being invaluable in making plans for the approach

marches. During the operation he personally navigated and led the New Zealand Division column from Haseiat to Merduma and then on to Nofilia. While carrying out a further reconnaissance before the next advance he was wounded when blown up on an unmarked minefield near Wadi Tamet. Captain Browne displayed excellent judgement and the greatest enterprise at all times.

Second Lieutenant K.F. (Paddy) McLauchlan took over patrol command from Browne and continued the mission with orders to make an additional reconnaissance further south in the direction of Bu Ngem at the Hon-Misurata Road. He was accompanied by Lieutenant Colonel Pyman from the 7th Armoured Division and Captain W.G. Alexander of the South African forces, plus ten ORs, all transported in one jeep and three Chevrolet trucks. While travelling north to Wadi el Chebir he met an armoured car squadron of the King's Dragoon Guards (KDG) at the landing ground of Bir el Zidan and was told of the positions of the squadron's patrols and that the area between them was clear of the enemy.

What happened next is recorded in the LRDG Operation Report No. 65 by Second Lieutenant McLauchlan, R1 Patrol. The event took place on 27 December 1942 while undertaking reconnaissance around the Gheddahia-Bu Ngem track. An extract of that report is as follows:

> After lunch, our intention was to proceed to Fortino, and the South African captain was going to make a fix and if possible, the patrol was going to recce the area to west of the road. At 1545 hrs we were proceeding in desert formation making our frequent close inspections of the area. Had just started moving again when I was told there was an A/Car (armoured car) coming up to us from the rear through the patrol. I stopped and stood up and saw a four-wheeled A/Car approaching about 50 yards from the rear. The commander had no hat on and was smiling, and I wrongly assumed he was from the KDGs. As he drew alongside, he picked up a rifle and covered the three of us in the truck. Then he ordered us in English to put our hands up! For a moment I thought it was a joke, but then realized the A/Car (Sd.Kfz.222) was hostile.
>
> The ambush was well planned, but the execution as far as R1 truck was concerned was not well done. The A/Car had drawn up about 5 feet away from us and in the same axis. I concluded we had a reasonable chance of getting out and instructed the driver to drive on. This he did admirably and the A/Car manoeuvred to bring his 'fixed line' 20mm gun to bear upon us. The commander with his rifle was loath to pull the trigger on us until we had moved some 5 yards. They turned left to head us off, we turned right and then turned right around to make towards safe territory. As we swung, we saw a similar A/Car alongside the W/T truck and the entire personnel had surrendered.
>
> We were chased for approx. 2 miles. The enemy scored a direct hit with a 20mm A.P. round and also succeeded in putting some baggage on fire.

We crossed a wadi at 30 mph and the enemy called it a day, contenting himself with having a few pot shots as we crossed the skyline. The following personnel were captured unhurt:

Capt. W.G. Alexander, 45 Company South African Engineer Corps

L/Cpl. H. Norton (jeep driver), 45 Company South African Engineer Corps

L/Cpl. C.O. Grimsey, LRDG R1 Patrol navigator

Pte. K.C.J. Ineson, LRDG R1 Patrol

Tpr. R.D. Hayes, LRDG R1 Patrol

Sgm. T. Evans, LRDG R1 Patrol, attached signaller

Losses:

One W/T 30cwt Chevrolet complete with signal instructions and ciphers. Navigational equipment on R2.

One jeep and navigational equipment carried by Captain Alexander, South African Forces.

Half an hour after the attack Lieutenant McLauchlan got back to the KDGs at Bir el Zidan and they radioed their patrols to close in on the area where the ambush had taken place. He then went on to 4th Light Armoured Brigade HQ in order to report to the Eighth Army and then on to 7th Armoured Division HQ to communicate with LRDG HQ. On his return on 30 December, Lieutenant Colonel Pyman told the rest of the story. They saw that the jeep was forced to surrender first, and he told the LRDG driver to retrace his tracks to get help from the KDGs. However, about a mile back they got stuck in a wadi and walked about 6 miles, arriving at the KDGs at dusk.

When the fitter's truck R10 escaped, they saw that the occupants of the radio truck R2 together with the jeep carrying Captain Alexander had surrendered to a third armoured car. The driver of the truck was Trooper R.D. Hayes, and the crew were Private K.C.J. Ineson, Lance Corporal C.O. Grimsey the navigator, and the W/T operator Signalman Thomas Evans (Royal Corps of Signals). On 17 January 1943, the Italian destroyer carrying Grimsey and Evans across the Mediterranean to Italy was sunk. Grimsey survived, but tragically Evans was drowned.

The surviving men and trucks went back to Nofilia, where McLauchlan reported to Eighth Army HQ. There he met Lieutenant Colonel G.L. Prendergast, LRDG commander, and was given orders to go to Zella. The patrol arrived there on 5 January 1943, by which time it had covered 2,540 miles.

As a footnote to this story, both Italian and *Afrika Korps* armoured cars were always a threat to LRDG trucks and skilful manoeuvring was required to evade them. There were several encounters with these vehicles recorded in LRDG history with losses on both sides. The vehicles McLauchlan faced were three four-wheel-drive Sd.Kfz.222 Horch armoured cars mounting a 20mm gun and a 7.92mm machine gun.

In December 1942, Lieutenant R.J. Talbot leading R2 Patrol was tasked with a mission to destroy aircraft on a landing ground at Sebha. The orders were to attack on the night of 11/12 December 1942, not before, after which he was to withdraw to a safe position and await further orders. The patrol would consist of one officer and eighteen ORs who would travel in five Chevrolet trucks. Their fuel supplies would be forty-five jerrycans per truck taken from Kufra and these would be later refilled at both Tazerbo and Olivers dumps. Water and rations were provided for twenty-one days. Their recognition signals ground-to-air were to be the chequered sand mat and ground-to-ground by flag signals.

This mission is an example of how unexpected climate conditions, along with misleading maps, affected the outcome of the mission. Lieutenant Talbot wrote in his Operation Report No. 52 on 26 December 1942 of how the journey unfolded:

> The patrol left Kufra on 3/12/42 and on 7/12/42. All the jerrycans were refilled at Tazerbo and again from a dump at Wadi Bu Sceberem. The patrol remained there until the afternoon of 9/12/42 when a move was made to the low hills. Rain fell during the night and the next day. On that afternoon we moved through a depression to a camp site.
>
> On 11/12/42 at 0730 hrs three vehicles moved to a position 3 miles west of us and took up positions covering the exit from the depression where we were camped. Two more vehicles were located a similar distance south of us. A Ghibli aircraft twice searched the hills in the depression, the second time passing overhead at a few hundred feet. A heavy shower of rain prevented us being observed. I decided that our presence was known, though perhaps not our exact location, and that if we disclosed it, we would be attacked by both ground and air forces. Therefore, just before darkness fell the patrol moved out in a N.E. direction for about 12 miles where W/T contact was made with HQ. But before a reply was received to our message the W/T set broke down, so it was decided to move back 30 miles for cover in the hills.
>
> Rain fell continuously all night. At 0300 hrs on 12/12/42 we started east but what had been perfect going before the rain was now a quagmire, and it took over 6 hours to cover the distance. We moved another 10 miles into the black hills and camouflaged the trucks with blankets. We remained there until 16/12/42 waiting for the serir to dry out.
>
> Another attempt to carry out the attack was made on 17/12/42. The going was good enough though 3rd Ruxtel gear was often necessary over soft patches. From the above position to Sebha the map shows serir with one escarpment, but what we found was mostly soft depressions with many low scarps, rough, uneven stony serir, a rock belt, sand sheets with rocky outcrops and a very rough, rocky gravel plain.
>
> On the last stretch of plain the main propellor shaft of the Breda truck was bent and almost broken. The fitter straightened it, and we carried on though expecting it to break at any minute. Also, a brake drum on the fitter's truck was badly dented and was scraping badly on the brake band. Owing to the unexpected bad going we did not arrive at our destination until midnight.

The intention was to go through a wadi to get on to the Umm el Araneb track and attack the landing ground from along the road. However, the wadi was found to have many dead ends, deep-sided wadis leading from it, and the main wadi leading east could not be found. The trucks stuck in soft sand repeatedly and could not climb out of the wadis once in them. Therefore, owing to the state of the country and the state of the vehicles, it was decided to withdraw and abandon the attempt that night.

After travelling east for about 10 miles the brake on the fitter's truck became red hot and a piece had to be cut out of the band housing. Shortly afterwards the Breda truck propellor shaft broke in two. As the going was rough in some places and soft in others it was necessary to use two trucks to tow the Breda truck. The patrol travelled all night on 18/12/42. In the morning we saw motorable tracks running north from Imessa that had been used by dozens of vehicles during the previous three days, i.e. since the rain.

Instructions were received on 19/12/42 from HQ to return to Zella via Wadi Bu Sceberem. We reached Zella on the evening of 22/12/42.

Vehicles: One broken propellor shaft, two badly dented brake drum housings, and two blown out tyres.

Another important task was topographical reconnaissance missions. This was to report the nature of the landscape known in the LRDG as 'the going' for the creation of a 'going map'. This would describe main obstacles, accessibility, cover, wadi crossings, scarps and possible lines of march, along with water supplies such as wells and springs. Furthermore, it would report on areas with prominent landmarks for navigation which were suitable for landing grounds with little work needed and did not require graders. By January 1943, all the LRDG patrols were engaged under the command of the Eighth Army to obtain information for the making of 'going maps'. It was considered a priority job and the LRDG was taken off all other work to complete it.

Major D.G. Steele recorded his thoughts on these operations:

> A favourite job the Army had for us, though not very popular with us, was 'Going Recce'. We would be asked to find out if a force of all arms could travel from point A to point B. We would then have to plod over the route indicated, imagining we were tanks or armoured cars or army lorries with a lot of bloody fools sitting behind the wheel, making notes all the way on the nature of the surface and gradients etc. Still, these recces were nearly mostly in safe country and so in a way were a rest from worrying about the enemy.

It was not long before Lieutenant Talbot and his R2 Patrol were sent out again on another task. Talbot was accompanied by Lieutenant A.H. Kinsman of the Grenadier Guards. This time it was a topographical information-gathering mission and one from which the officers were not to return. It was also to prove to be a very difficult mission for the fitters due to the high number of breakdowns encountered on the journey. Four areas mainly along the coast road region were targeted for evaluation. The Operation Instruction No. 56 dated 25/12/42 stated what the requirements were:

> The information is required from the point of view of the advance of a force of all arms on a wide front. It should include the following:-
> (a) Going
> (b) Wadi crossings
> (c) Cover
> (d) Water supplies – wells – depth of water – drinkable or not – accessibility for MT in rock or sand. Springs – flow – accessibility
> (e) Landing grounds. Possible sites where LGs can be made without the use of graders. A prominent landmark is desirable. Size, 1,500yds square.

Recce instructions were given and the location of known enemy posts identified. A permanent escape base with food and water had been established to which stragglers could go. Water and rations were supplied for thirty days, and forty-five jerrycans would be loaded per truck from their base at Zella. A refill of cans was established at Bir El Communia. The patrol would consist of two officers, thirteen ORs and five 30cwt trucks. The final report had to be available to Eighth Army HQ on 20/01/43.

On 21 January 1943, on returning from the operation Sergeant C. Waetford recorded the details of the mission in Operation Report No. 56. Normally the officer would complete the report, but both patrol officers had been captured. It was thought that the fort and town of Esc Sciuref was occupied by the Free French, but unbeknown to R1 at the time when they arrived, the French had withdrawn to be replaced by an Italian garrison. What follows is an edited version of Sergeant Waetford's report:

> Patrol left Zella at 1600 hrs on 27 December to do a topographical recce. At noon 28th it was necessary to send back to Zella for a new gearbox for R12. On 29th at noon the patrol moved to a position where a camp was made. On the 31st we reached the dump at Bir El Communia. Here jerrycans were filled and the patrol moved on again to cross Hon Road. A Heinkel 111 flying north from Hon spotted us at 1400 hrs, we hid and remained in position until dusk. Crossing was made in daylight on 1st, but repairs to R10's sump caused a delay of approx. 7 hours. We received instructions that the recce for the intended area was changed, and the patrol was to proceed to the western end of Wadi Zem Zem to act as a reserve for G Patrol.
>
> By the night of the 4th, we reached Wadi Ghirza where further instructions were awaited. Here the less serious defections were repaired (springs, centre bolts, steering boxes, etc.). On the morning of the 9th at 0930 hrs instructions were received to proceed to Bir Cau to contact Lieut. B. Bruce. On the afternoon of the 10th, we reached the other party that was contacted earlier. Here it was found that Lieut. Bruce had left to contact Colonel Stirling's HQ and had left four men with one unserviceable truck. This truck

took 6 hours to repair. Instructions on the night of the 11th were to follow Lieut. Bruce's tracks back but owing to the nature of the country this was impossible. We arrived on the morning of the 13th where it was found that Colonel Stirling had moved his headquarters. Here instructions were received on the 14th to proceed to Esc Sciuref and proceed along the line of Wadi Crebir down which we had come.

A party of five men were seen standing on the sand hills on the southern side of the fort and at a point about 3 miles from the fort. When a mile from the party of men, the OC (Lt. Talbot) decided to display the recognition signal which was not acknowledged and then to contact the party on foot. At this time the unidentified party broke up and ran in different directions disappearing from view. The OC walked about 250 yards towards the place where the men were last seen, turned round and came back to his truck. Here he told the patrol that he thought the men sighted were natives and instructed Lieut. Kinsman to go with him on a foot reconnaissance of the fort which from this point seemed entirely deserted. As the two officers disappeared over the ridge a mile away in the direction of the fort, a close watch on all points of the compass was kept.

When a reasonable time for contact had elapsed two bursts of machine-gun fire from the direction of the fort attracted attention and at this juncture a truck was noticed in the hills north-west of the fort making for the fort. When this truck was about a mile from the fort five men appeared from within but disappeared simultaneously with a burst of machine-gun fire from this truck. After a five-minute interval two vehicles were noticed moving towards the fort on a different route from the first and several bursts of machine-gun fire were heard. Owing to the nature of surrounding terrain it was impossible to observe the target or direction of fire. Afterwards these bursts were thought to be recognition signals between vehicles etc. Two men were observed to proceed from the fort towards parked vehicles, all three of which proceeded rapidly towards the hills on the route of the first truck.

At 1515 hrs, when I was a mile away from the patrol, a 5-ton truck was observed to be parked outside the fort where it remained stationary for quarter of an hour. Several men were observed moving between the truck and the fort before the truck moved off to pick up two more men about a mile away from the fort on the edge of the vegetation of the wadi itself. This vehicle was seen to move towards us, worming its way through the hummocks on the wadi bed. A mile from the ridge over which the two officers were last seen to disappear, the truck stopped. After an interval of several minutes, I noticed two figures on top of this ridge, who as soon as they saw us adopted a crouching position and doubled back out of sight. As it was dusk, I decided that the fort must be occupied by the enemy and the two officers to have been captured. Accordingly, I at once moved the patrol away to the east for a distance of 5 miles to the nearest hills.

There we wirelessed HQ of the disappearance of the two officers and again experienced the difficulty of getting in touch with HQ. At first light on the 16th contact with resident natives was made and our suspicion that the French were not in Sciuref fort was confirmed. A good hiding-place 8 miles from the fort was found and a close watch was kept on all movements in and around the fort. At 0745 hrs two vehicles were observed to come down from the hills north-west of the fort and parked on the landing ground for one hour. At the end of this time the larger vehicle moved nearer the fort and considerable activity between the two was observed. At 1515 hrs several vehicles appeared from the hills and took up position on the west side of the fort at the foot of the hills.

One-quarter hour later Y1 Patrol under Lieut. E.F. Spicer contacted us at this point. Owing to the inability of contacting HQ by wireless, Lieut. Spicer decided to proceed from this locality across country to Hon. After travelling 30 miles mechanical troubles held us up and instructions were given to us to proceed to a point and wait for S1. At this position Lieut. R.A. Tinker was contacted on the 19th on which date we were instructed to proceed at once to Hon where we arrived the next day. Our current strength is 13 ORs and two officers missing.

Vehicle repairs: 17 × springs, 12 × U-bolts, 5 × steering boxes, 10 × shackles and pins, 1 × radiator, 2 × engines to be changed, 2 × engines to have valve grinds, 2 × defective gear boxes, 2 × track rods, 2 × hangers and bearings, 6 × tyres and tubes, 10 × kingpins and 1 × speedometer.

By April 1943 the Axis forces were near to capitulation as their defeat in Tunisia was only a month away. By this time the LRDG had 'run out of desert' with most of the topographical work done. Their tasks were mostly limited to 'taxi service' and liaison duties with the regular forces in cleaning up the desert. This included activities such as transporting engineers for mine-clearing and guiding and assisting with vehicle recovery missions of LRDG, Allied and Axis vehicles. One example was on 20 January 1943, when Corporal R.O. Gorringe of R1 Patrol was sent out to salvage the abandoned Guards Patrol truck G3.

Yet despite the enemy being long defeated in Libya, the desert still had its dangers. One example of these final trips was undertaken by Lieutenant J.M. Sutherland of R2 Patrol, setting out from Hon on 23 March 1943. His task was to proceed to Agedabia and pick up an unspecified number of Royal Army Service Corps (RASC) officers, then to proceed via Jalo to Kufra and return via Jalo and Giarabub to Sollum. There would be one officer, fifteen ORs and attached was one Royal Engineers officer and an RASC officer. They would be travelling in four trucks and two jeeps.

Lieutenant Sutherland wrote of the mission in his Operation Report No. 62 dated 10 April 1943:

> The patrol left Hon on the 23rd of March and proceeded to the main road and then 24th to Marble Arch, arriving at Agedabia on the 25th. On reporting

to the Political Officer, Agedabia, we were informed the RASC officers would not be ready to move until the 28th. Patrol then proceeded to Zetina water point and made camp. On reporting to the Political Officer on the 27th a further task was given to the patrol to search for any recoverable vehicles between Agedabia and Jalo in conjunction with a Recovery Section. This information was passed to LRDG HQ, and the patrol was ordered to spend three days on recovery.

To shorten the trip Sergeant Waetford and one truck were detached to the Recovery Section and the remainder proceeded with passengers to Kufra on March 28th. That night they camped at Hasiet and reached Augila on 29th. Arrived Kufra 1st April. All beacons were put up between Agedabia and Kufra. Spent one day at Kufra and left for the return journey on the 3rd of April.

The first day out of Kufra the patrol encountered a severe sandstorm, and it was necessary to camp for the day. Reached Jalo on 5th April, here passengers were dropped, and the sergeant and his truck picked up. Left on 6th April for Giarabub via the Sand Sea. Giarabub was reached early on 7th April. Going into Giarabub the patrol had to pass through a mine field. I was leading in my jeep. I took the track which I considered was cleared and got through.

The navigator's truck (R9) followed me through, but the rear wheel struck a mine. With the help of Sergeant Waetford, I cleared two more mines in the vicinity of the truck. The truck was then unloaded, and ropes were attached in order to tow it well clear of the mine field. On moving it back the near rear wheel went over another mine. A search for a vehicle to obtain the necessary spare parts from was made but could not be found. All moveable parts such as spare tyres, wireless, batteries and navigation equipment were removed, and the truck was covered for later recovery. The patrol camped north of Giarabub. The following morning, we moved off due north for 20 miles then north-east until meeting the wire, then up the wire to Sollum then onto Alexandria, arriving on the 10th of April.

On the journey the patrol had four blow-outs and the wireless failed to function as from 28th March. There were no casualties.

Sergeant's Report on Recovery

Sergeant Waetford and one truck left Agedabia on the 28 March with the Recovery Section. For three days they scouted for vehicles, the Recovery Section dragging them to the road. The section then proceeded to Jalo via Jikerra and awaited my return from Kufra.

During the siege of Giarabub in early 1941, the LRDG laid many mines on roads and tracks leading to the fort. It is possible that Sutherland's patrol may have run over some of its own mines laid two years earlier. It cannot be proved, but at the time it was reported as a possibility.

R1 Patrol desert meeting, 11 December 1942. They pose with (centre, L to R) Generals Freyberg and Montgomery. On the right is Captain L.H. (Tony) Browne, patrol commander and Second Lieutenant K.F. McLauchlan.

A Chevrolet 1533x2 racing down a small dune.

An LRDG Willys jeep in its bare state alongside an unidentified trooper. This is unusual in that they had been experimenting with an armoured plate in front of the driver. There is no photographic evidence of it being used in action. Note the front white-walled tyre.

A Marmon-Herrington armoured car named *Weymouth* of the King's Dragoon Guards. The LRDG occasionally encountered both Allied and Axis armoured cars on their operations. In front is Trooper E. Ellis of T2 Patrol. While on a Road Watch, he was cut off from his patrol by the enemy and had to endure a five-day desert trek. He was later picked up by the KDG and received the Military Medal for his action.

An *Afrika Korps* Sd.Kfz.222 armoured car. Armed with a 20mm gun and a 7.92mm machine gun, these vehicles had several encounters with LRDG patrols.

A signaller operating his No. 11 radio housed in the side of his truck. The vehicle mounts both a Lewis and Vickers K machine guns.

A sketch by Bluey Grimsey done while he was a prisoner in Stalag VIIIB in Germany; described as having Xmas dinner of 'roast pork and spuds' near Nofilia, 1942.

Xmas dinner 1942. near Nofilia. Roast pork & spud

A drawing of Bluey Grimsey who was captured on 27 December 1942. He is being escorted by an *Afrika Korps* soldier and the local inhabitants appear sad. This was done in December 1943 by a fellow prisoner 'Steve' in Stalag VIIIB.

An R Patrol Chevrolet drives out of a wadi.

Having a meal from the back of a truck. Left: Captain Peter McIntyre, the official NZ war artist, Lieutenant J.R. Talbot and Lieutenant Chevalier. McIntyre went on a trip with R Patrol and produced various watercolours and drawings of the men and their activities.

A nice watercolour study of Private R.R. Willams of R Patrol by Captain Peter McIntyre.

Front view of truck R11. Note the large towing chain hooked in front.

R Patrol crossing a flooded wadi.

Truck R9 tows another vehicle out of the bog.

Truck R6 bogged, with sand trays at the ready.

Digging deep with a shovel to clear the wheel and place a sand channel.

Sand mats are being employed here to negotiate the front wheels of R6 over soft sand.

R Patrol examines the burned-out remains of a Heinkel III.

A tail-end view of a downed Heinkel III. Some of these aircraft were fitted with a fixed machine gun in their tail.

A page from the September 1942 *LRDG War Diary* entries.

Place.	Date	Hour.	Summary of Events and Information.	References to Appendices.
KUFRA	25	1130	Low level bombing + mg attack by 6 HEINKELS and 2 JUNKERS 88. Capt Lloyd Owen + Gdsm Harkness wounded. 5 ORs Welsh Regt killed. 3 BOMBAYS & 1 HUDSON destroyed. 2 JUNKERS 88 brought down 1 crew of 4 latter prisoner. No LRDG damage.	
	26	1000	Capt Ashdown arrived with Light Repair Sec.	
	28	1200	Capt LAWSON & officers of 1 SLD arrived	
	29	0700	Major EASONSMITH & Capt OLIVEY left for CAIRO	
		1000	Capt SHAW & Capt MCINTYRE (NZ artist) arrived	
	30	0700	Lieut TALBOT with R2 and personnel of T1 & G1 Capt MCINTYRE & Lieut CHEVALIER left for CAIRO.	
		0730	Lieut SWEETING left for Operation No —	
		1000	Sgt LANE arrived with R1 & 2/Lieut BARKER.	

In 1943 the LRDG assisted with navigation in enabling the Army Recovery Section to uplift abandoned vehicles in the desert. The tank appears to be an Italian M11/39.

A Diamond T recovery truck uplifting a Panzer Mk III.

Chapter Twelve

On Leave

Major Steele reflected on the welcome journey from their desert bases to Cairo for leave:

> Cairo leave from time to time was a welcome change and provided some innocent fun on the run into town. The road from Matruh to Cairo was strewn with checkpoints manned by the British MPs who had a habit of detaining people who had no leave pass and movement orders. As we never issued either, there was at first a certain amount of hold up until we hit on the idea of driving straight through or round the roadblocks. As we always travelled fast there were some exciting chases and when we finally stopped and asked the MPs what they wanted, they would nearly burst a boiler. We would then say, 'We are from the LRDG, you can report on us to whom you please, stand back, good day!' And we drove on. They did not like it, but Bagnold had always said there was too much red tape in the army, and we believed him. It worked at any rate, and we never heard any more about it from the provost. No doubt it was bad from the point of view of general army discipline, but it was good for patrol morale.

The troops always looked forward to going on leave to enjoy a nice meal, a cold drink and for some, visiting the brothels. There were areas that were considered unsafe for troops and so these areas of Cairo were established as out of bounds. At times there was anti-British sentiment or just plain robbery of an unsuspecting soldier, especially if he was drunk. However, despite this some troops ignored the warning signs and took the risk, though even those in the secure areas could get into trouble with unsavoury members of the Cairo populace. Buster Gibb recalled the time he was unexpectedly attacked in the streets of Cairo:

> One time while I was walking along the street, a couple of Arabs hit me on the head with a tyre lever and I quickly flattened them in return. I hit the first one and knocked him out and he hit his head on the kerb and didn't move. The other one started to run away so I rushed after him and grabbed him by the shoulder, swung him round and hit him. When I looked up, I was surrounded by twenty to thirty Arabs, in white gowns, blue gowns, all around me. I walked out of there as fast as I could, I didn't want to run, and headed out to the main street with about four following me. Every time I would stop, they would stop; they were waiting for an opportunity to have a go and kept following me. Then I saw around the corner a carriage with the driver asleep

with his horse whip in a side socket. I rushed over and grabbed the whip, turned around and lashed these blokes who were following me. I chased them down the road, and they disappeared. Next thing the carriage driver was screaming at me wanting his whip back, which I threw back at him.

Fortunately, the next person I ran into was Bill Williams, one of our radio operators. He looked at me and nearly fainted. My head wound was bleeding badly, and my jacket and woollen singlet were soaked in blood right down past the waist. I must have looked a gruesome sight. They tried to get a taxi back to base, but the driver took one look and refused to take us. Then a finely dressed gentleman arrived and asked what happened to me. I thought he was Egyptian; I said your bloody countrymen hit me with a tyre lever. Ooh, he said, and offered to bind my wound with his perfectly white handkerchief. I said it doesn't need binding and I would be grateful if he could get us a reliable taxi. We thought that would be the last we would see of him. But no, he soon turned up with a taxi and we returned to base to get fixed up. I was very grateful to him. As it turned out he was a Scotsman living in Cairo.

On another occasion Buster Gibb had an encounter with an SAS man in a bar in Alexandria:

I was down in Alexandria one day and there was one of Stirling's boys at the bar. I said something about the SAS and there was a hand phone at the end of the bar. He grabbed the cord, wound it around his wrist and was going to belt me with it. I said you think you are tough! If you think so have a go, I said I would kill him. We have been carting you buggers around, you need us. I am bigger than you and have had more experience than you. And I said a bloody telephone hand piece is not going to do you any good. A lot of this was bluff by me, but in the end, he backed off. The problem was I mentioned Stirling in the bar, and he took exception to this, like be like mum, keep your mouth shut. I apologised, I said I had no right to bring up the name anyway and we finished up drinking together.

Alf Saunders was a founding member of W Patrol, and then later joined R Patrol serving alongside Buster Gibb. He told the author of one of his recollections of a trip to and from Cairo:

In the early days when a patrol would depart Cairo, they would first have to wind their way through all the city traffic. We played a game with the barrow boys selling fruit, sometimes a barrow was side-swiped, and the fruit would spill over the road. We would then leap off our trucks and throw as much fruit as possible into the back.

Usually there were apples, oranges, grapes, pomegranates and pineapples. This was all done in about 15 seconds, then we would catch up with the truck in front. Before moving off we always threw a handful of small change at the boys. This had become a ritual, and even if we did not tip over their barrows, they would tip it themselves screaming blue murder. Then we would do our stuff, and chuck what we could in the trucks, throw them some money and move off.

One thing that always puzzled me was the fact that it did not matter if we changed our route, the barrow boys were always waiting in ambush for us. Their Intelligence Section was certainly on the ball, and they never missed our departure from Cairo. After a while we got to know them by name and enjoyed yelling at each other in the street. For the first few days in the desert the patrols gorged themselves on fruit.

When I think of the manner in which the fruit seeds were scattered over the desert wastes, I often speculate on the possibility that in the future if those areas ever received a regular rainfall, what would historians think. They would ponder on how fruit trees came to be there, and talk of lost civilizations, ancient cities, or a dried-up oasis. No one would consider it to be New Zealanders travelling in a foreign land, spreading a few seeds in nature's way.

One day we captured an Italian convoy bound for Ethiopia. On one of the huge diesel trucks we found a few cases of what we called 'Wog silver jewellery rubbish'. Some of us filled a couple of sandbags with this jewellery and threw them in the back of the truck and forgot about it. When we had finished our patrol we came back to Cairo, following the Nile River. We passed through a number of villages, and when we saw a group of women and kids, we would throw them handfuls of the jewellery. This was received with great joy and amazement.

When we got back to Cairo, we had a few pieces left, so had them valued. As it turned out the joke was on us. The patrol had apparently tossed away an average of £200 sterling worth of jewellery per two sandbags. We had a good laugh at ourselves and forgot it. No wonder those women and kids were overjoyed; in the general scramble some of them would have received a very nice nest egg indeed.

Alf Saunders also recalled another incident in Cairo where a patrol member took umbrage at how one local was treating his wife:

I remember one incident when some of our group took drastic action against an Egyptian man riding along on a donkey. The animal was much too small for the person's size, who was as fat as a pig. Struggling along behind him was what they presumed to be his wife, a tired-looking woman carrying a lot of bundles. So our 'Hero' took the matter into his own hands and promptly made the 'Wallad' (man) get off the donkey and placed the woman on it and made the man carry all the bundles himself, then escorted them both to their house. I am sure the troops did not make any impression on the man to change his ways, as the system they were so upset about had been going on for hundreds or even thousands of years!

Buster Gibb always seemed to run into trouble when he visited Cairo bars. Except on this occasion when it was his drinking mate Joe Eyles who caused a ruckus, as Buster recalled:

> On another occasion a bunch of us, myself, Joe Eyles and Rex Beech while on leave in Cairo were drinking at the bar in a club. There was a large group of Pommy (British) sailors drinking around a table and singing a song. Can't recall the song but one of their number was standing on the table and every time a verse of the song was sung this sailor would remove an article of clothing. He had removed all his clothes and was now putting on an item for every verse. He had got as far as one sock. At the same time a couple more of their group were working their way around the bar with their hats soliciting donations from the other bar patrons. They got as far as Joe Eyles and rattled a hat under his nose. Joe looked the guy in the face and said, 'Bugger off or I'll pistol whip you' (we were wearing our service revolvers).
>
> The sailor responded, saying 'You'd be too scared to pull the bloody thing out of its holster!'
>
> With that Joe pulled out his revolver and put a shot through the chandelier. There was pandemonium and a mad panic amongst the group of singing sailors. They all made a stampede for the door. One half of the double doors was fixed closed creating a bottleneck and they were all jammed there fighting to get out. The sailor in one sock was last to the door and disappeared out the door by scrambling over the heads of his mates. The last we saw of him was his bare arse.

(**Right**) The *Services Guide to Cairo* booklet. The cover art is painted by Peter McIntyre, the NZ war artist.

(**Opposite, above**) Wartime map of Cairo showing the LRDG base at the Citadel.

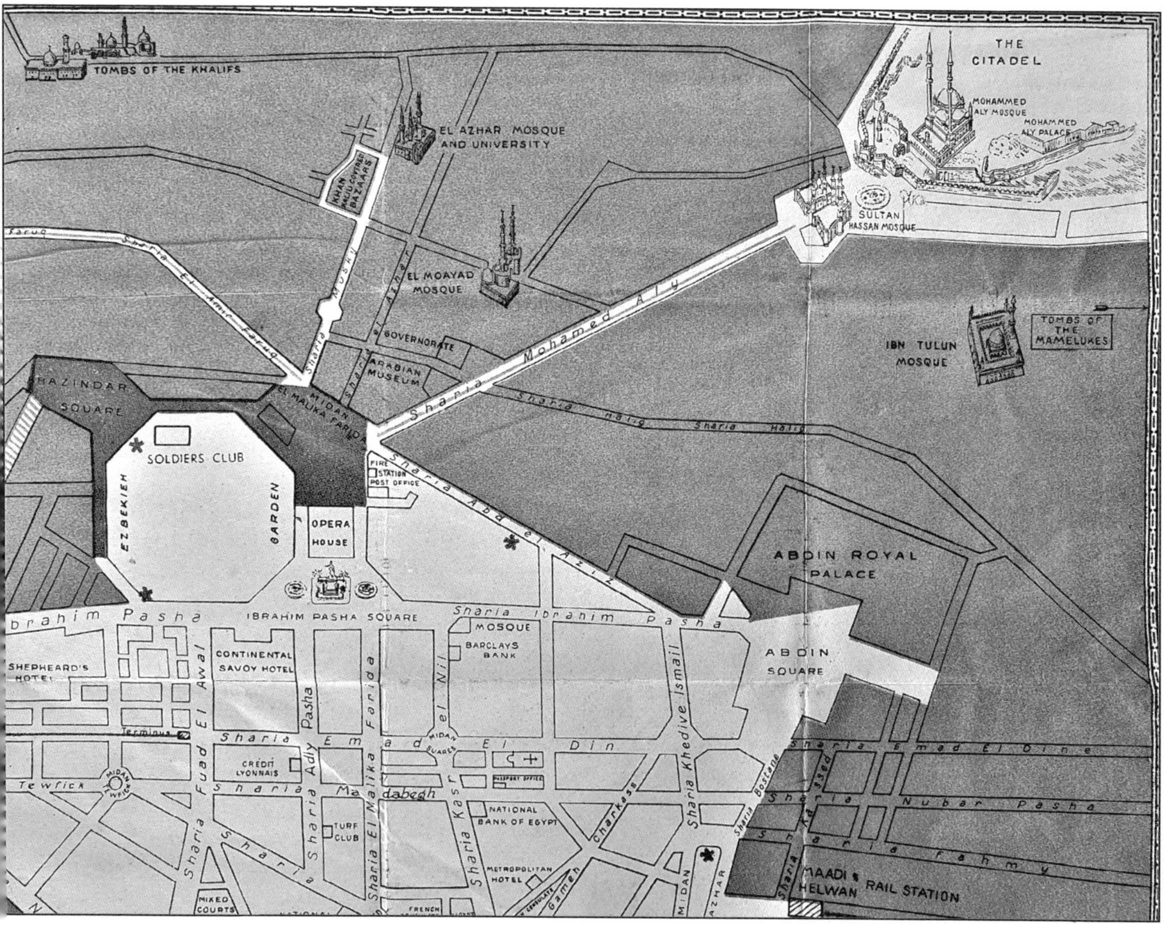

56 - Cairo - The Citadel

'Out of Bounds' sign in Cairo.

Entrance to the licensed soldiers' brothel at No. 27 the Birket, Cairo. A prophylactic centre was also in the building. Military Police stand at the front as New Zealand soldiers enter the building.

(**Above**) A New Zealand soldier enjoys the company of a prostitute. This was in the licensed Sharia Wagh el Birket brothel in Cairo.

(**Opposite, above**) NZ soldiers showing off the variety of beers available in Egypt. Right: LRDG Trooper I.H. McInnes. He won the Military Medal for his effective 2in mortar shooting with T Patrol at Murzuk fort in 1941. The following year on 24 October 1942 he was killed while serving with the Divisional Cavalry at El Alamein. The others are unidentified.

(**Opposite, below**) Photo of R2 Patrol still unshaven, taken in a Cairo bar after returning from a long trip to Zouar. Top left: Pte. E.B. Waetford, Pte. J.E. Gill, Phil Mannering (bar manager), Sgt. C.G. Ball, Sgm. S.J.E. Mahomet, Pte. J. Emslie. Middle: Tpr. A.F. Dodunski, Pte. A.A. Murdoch, Pte. J.C. Lucas, Sgm. R. Atkins. Front: Pte. A.D. Sadgrove, Tpr. M.E. Hammond, Gnr. C.O. Grimsey, Pte. G.H. Nelson, Tpr. C. Waetford.

R Patrol members pose for a photo at the NZ Forces Club, 1942. Top from left: Cpl. R.O. Spotswood, Dvr. J.H. Jones, Tpr. F.J.W. McKeown. Sitting middle: Cpl. R.A. Tinker, Pte. E.F. Gorringe, Pte. F.R. Brown. Front: Tpr. R.J. Landon-Lane, Pte. M. Allen. They are enjoying Castlemaine Bitter Ale, an Australian beer.

R Patrol members Trooper J.C. (Sam) Lucas and Trooper A.M. (Alf) Saunders. They are wearing their LRDG-issued *keffiyehs*.

A Christmas 1941 invitation to celebrate at Shepheard's Hotel in Cairo, a popular place with LRDG officers.

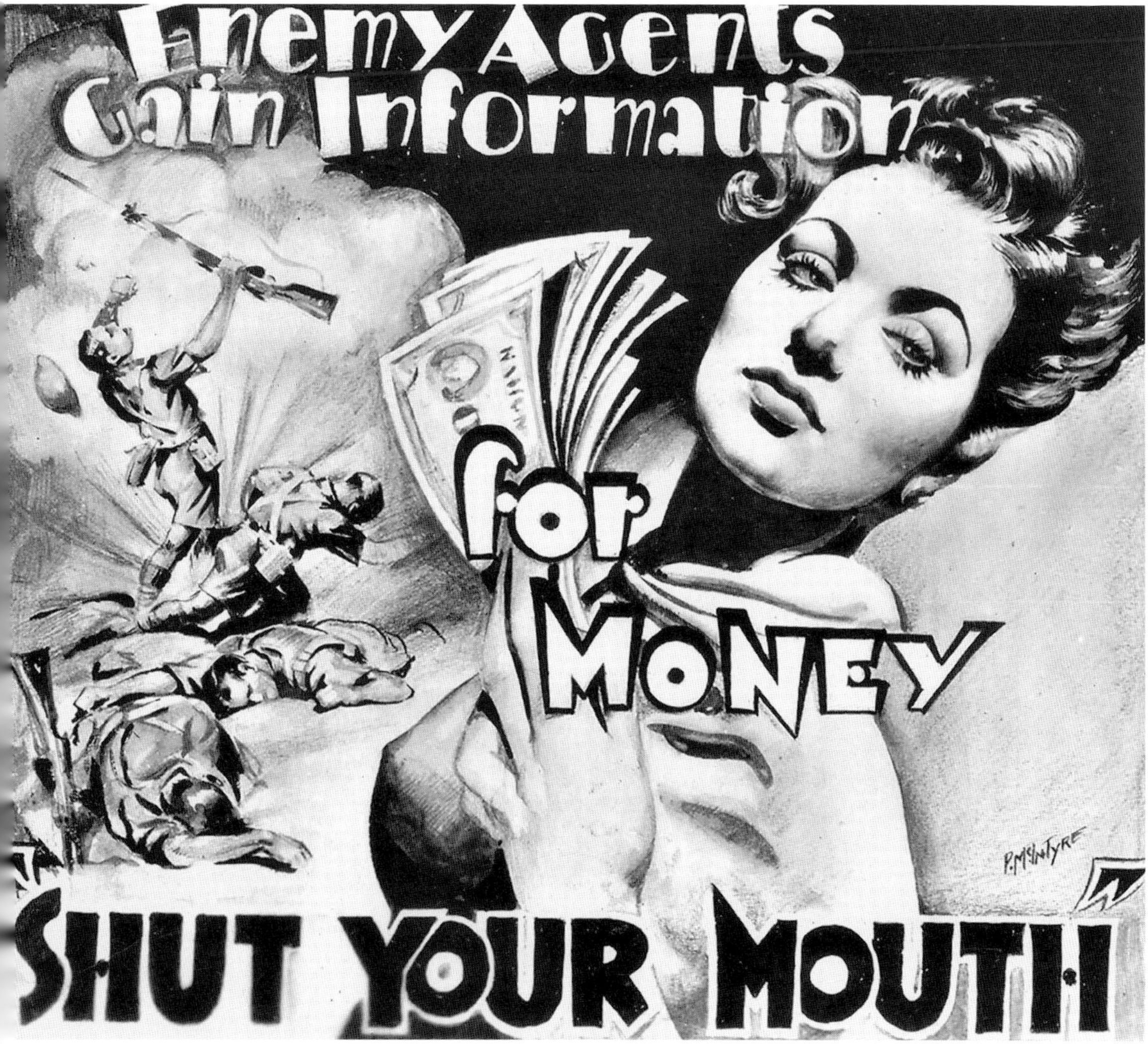

Security was important when out entertaining in clubs and bars where spies could always be listening. This 'Shut Your Mouth' message was illustrated by Peter McIntyre, NZ war artist.

A studio photo of Trooper M.E. (Bill) Hammond displaying his LRDG beret badge and shoulder titles.

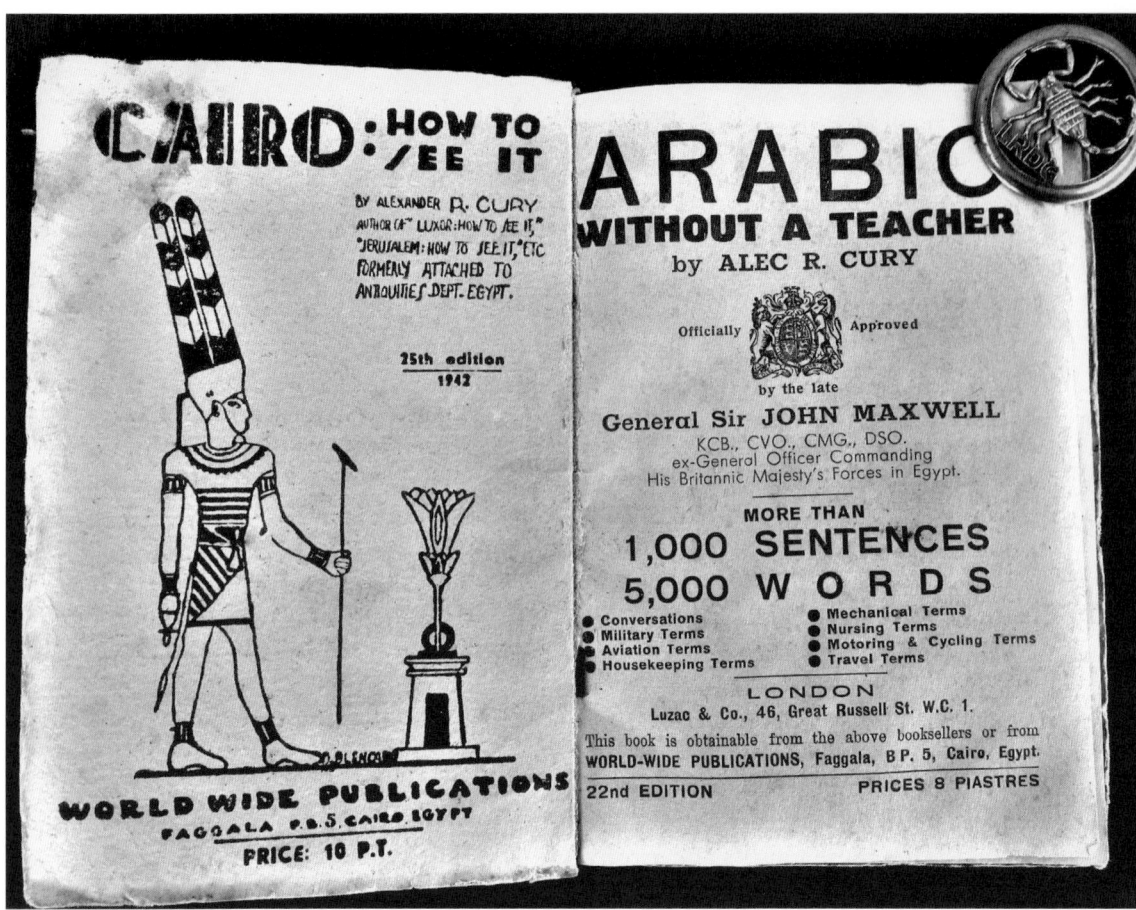

Booklet on how to learn Arabic. A number of LRDG men endeavoured to study the language and culture to enable better interactions with the Arabs.

Chapter Thirteen

R Patrol Gunner / Medical Orderly

Lance Corporal Mick Allen, Royal Army Medical Corps, was attached to R Patrol in a dual role as both their medical orderly and a gunner. He also had to be a capable driver if required. On 4 May 1943, at A (NZ) Squadron LRDG HQ, he presented to Warrant Officer R.L. Kay of the NZ Official Archives a detailed personal overview of his duties and service with R Patrol:

> If I was caught with my pay book and gun, I would be shot. We medical orderlies are protected by the Geneva Convention, but as LRDG patrols were such compact units, with no room for passengers, we travel with them as gunners or drivers with a definite job to do. I have never gone out with an LRDG patrol but as a gunner, and if I had been caught in possession of my gun, I would have got rid of my pay book and would have given a false name and number. Thus, I would have become an ordinary prisoner of war. If, on the other hand, I could have got rid of my gun upon being captured, I would have come under the protection of the Geneva Convention and would have stood a chance of being repatriated.
>
> I was, however, never in danger of being captured. Although we medical orderlies had been in the Medical Corps before joining the LRDG, which we did at our own risk, we are not protected by arm bands or the Red Cross. Colonel Bagnold instructed medical orderlies to leave their pay book at base when going on a trip, but I always took mine with me.
>
> There is only one specialist in an LRDG patrol, the navigator. All the other men are primarily fighting men, even if they are fitters, wireless operators or medical orderlies.
>
> At first the LRDG did not have medical orderlies and on the first two trips none were carried with the patrols. When a truck overturned and Fred Kendall split his knee open, no medical assistance was available. Dan Ormond stitched Kendall's knee with a needle and a piece of string. He did as good a job as a Harley Street specialist would do, but this accident resulted in the introduction of medical orderlies to patrols.
>
> I joined R Patrol at the time W Patrol was absorbed into R and T Patrols. Even then, the members of the patrols knew that they could expect only the minimum of medical attention and they appreciated the difficulties of evacuating seriously wounded or sick cases or of getting expert attention when it was most needed. In those days there was no means of transporting a wounded man except by patrol truck and it would usually take days to get

him back to base or to a hospital. This was not as serious as it would appear, however, for the total casualties suffered by R Patrol, for example, other than those captured, were only one man killed and three wounded.

We had been told how to administer a fatal drug, in case it could be necessary to resort to such measures, if the best thing under the circumstances would be to release a man from days or weeks of suffering or a lingering death, but fortunately that did not have to be done in R Patrol. Nonetheless, we always were prepared.

We received every possible assistance from the officer commanding the patrol. If we ever were in doubt about a patient, we always looked on the pessimistic side, and if we could not diagnose a case but thought it sufficiently serious to evacuate the patient, the skipper always took the orderly's advice, and the man was evacuated.

Malaria and Desert Sores

The most serious complaints among members of the LRDG were malaria and desert sores. There was no incidence of malaria until we arrived at Siwa. There was very little malaria at Kufra and what cases did occur it was probably a recurrence of a dose contracted at Siwa. Sometimes malaria lay dormant in men, especially if they have been taking prophylactic doses of quinine and it might then develop when the men were away on a patrol. As a matter of fact, I was one of the three. Four days after we returned to Siwa we were evacuated to hospital by plane. When we arrived at hospital, we had had malaria for 21 days and our temperatures were still 103 degrees.

The desert sores were a most irritating complaint, but men were not put off duty by it. My observations were that desert sores always occurred on a part of the skin exposed to the sun, when men were unable to drink beer and perspired a good deal. I have seen an eighth of an inch of salt caked on a man's spectacles; such perspiration might have had something to do with it. Men used to drinking beer developed desert sores when they were unable to obtain beer, but soon recovered from their complaint when their beer supply was resumed.

Some men developed the complaint when they were in the desert and recovered when they returned to Cairo. Others were free of the complaint in the desert but came out in desert sores when they returned to the city. That is something for which I cannot account.

During two years' service with the LRDG, the great majority of men enjoyed very good health, but during the summer that R Patrol was stationed at Tazerbo, there was a marked deterioration in the general standard of fitness. The heat at that time, 130 degrees in the shade, was so great that the men had to lie in the shade of their vehicles from 0800 to 1700 hrs daily. Although they were used to walking about barefooted, they could not stand the heat of the sand on their feet. At that stage malaria, dysentery and desert sores began to occur among the veterans of the unit.

Those who had joined the LRDG only recently were not affected in this manner.

Hygiene and Sanitation

One thing that confounded the critics was the fact that members of the LRDG could go so long without a wash, shave or haircut. We have gone for fourteen weeks like that, and yet in all that time not one man became lousy or infected by any kind of vermin. I have not known a man to suffer any trouble through being dirty, except on one occasion when some men picked up camel ticks at an Italian camp. For that reason, we avoided all Italian camps. The Italians have very filthy habits; they had no organised system of latrines, they do not dream of burying anything, and their places of habitation always attract millions of flies.

Tazerbo is the worst place we have known for flies. When the flies ceased to pester us at nightfall, we were at once attacked by mosquitoes. At daybreak, the man on piquet invariably found his back literally covered with flies. There was not room among them to place a pin. Yes, I think I know where the flies go in winter. At mealtimes they used to drive the men practically crazy. In sheer desperation, I have also seen men sit over a fire with their faces in the smoke in order to eat their meals in comparative comfort.

Our manner of finding water at Tazerbo was rather extraordinary. Bluey Grimsey was considered the authority on water-finding. He selected a spot to sink a well and after we had dug 12 or 14 feet, we struck solid rock which we could not penetrate. Another man selected a site, and we dug a well to 18 feet, still without finding water. And then a third man found a place where we struck water after excavating to only 4 feet. There was as much good water there as we could use. In an area of about 200 yards square, we found water at levels varying from 4 to 25 feet.

Only on one occasion was a patrol seriously short of water. While this party was travelling to Hon, where it was expected to get fresh water, a vehicle developed a leak, and most of the water the patrol was carrying was poured into the radiator of this truck. The water at the well at Hon was found to be like sheep dip. The party reached the stage of drinking the water from the heavy Vickers gun, which was better than that from the well, but nevertheless took some of the brackish water on the return journey. The damaged 15cwt truck was placed on a 30cwt vehicle. The brackish water was strained three times through a towel before it was boiled, but even with generous proportions of tea and sugar, it made the men who tried to drink it vomit immediately. These men suffered from great thirst until they returned to their base.

When a man did his usual morning task, he went away from the camp and dug himself a hole. The patrols always buried every single item of refuse, not only to avoid fouling the area and attracting the flies, but also to avoid attracting the attention of the enemy. In order to avoid affecting the subterranean water supply at Tazerbo, refuse was buried in drums, of which there was any number. Latrine boxes were constructed out of petrol cases.

While the LRDG was in the Kufra area, a shortage of medical supplies occurred. Sufficient quantities of all supplies had been provided in the first place, but liquids evaporated in the excessive heat and other supplies and equipment deteriorated rapidly, until at one time we were right out of such essentials as iodine. This was a most serious situation as we had no facilities at all for a while to treat urgent cases.

(**Above**) Private M. Allen RAMC, R Patrol medical orderly. He also had to serve as a gunner and recorded an overview of his time with the patrol.

(**Opposite, above**) A medical orderly administers first aid along the side of *Rotoehu* R8.

(**Opposite, below**) Though a poor image, it does reflect the atmosphere as per the original photo caption, 'a pre-dawn cup of tea before breakfast.'

Trooper Bill Hammond enjoys a bath in a 44-gallon drum. Note the 2-gallon water tins.

Trooper Sam Lucas filling tins of water from a well spring.

R Patrol celebrating Christmas with a rum at Siwa, 1941. Private Mick Allen holds the rum jar.

A variety of wartime tobacco products. Smoking was common among the troops.

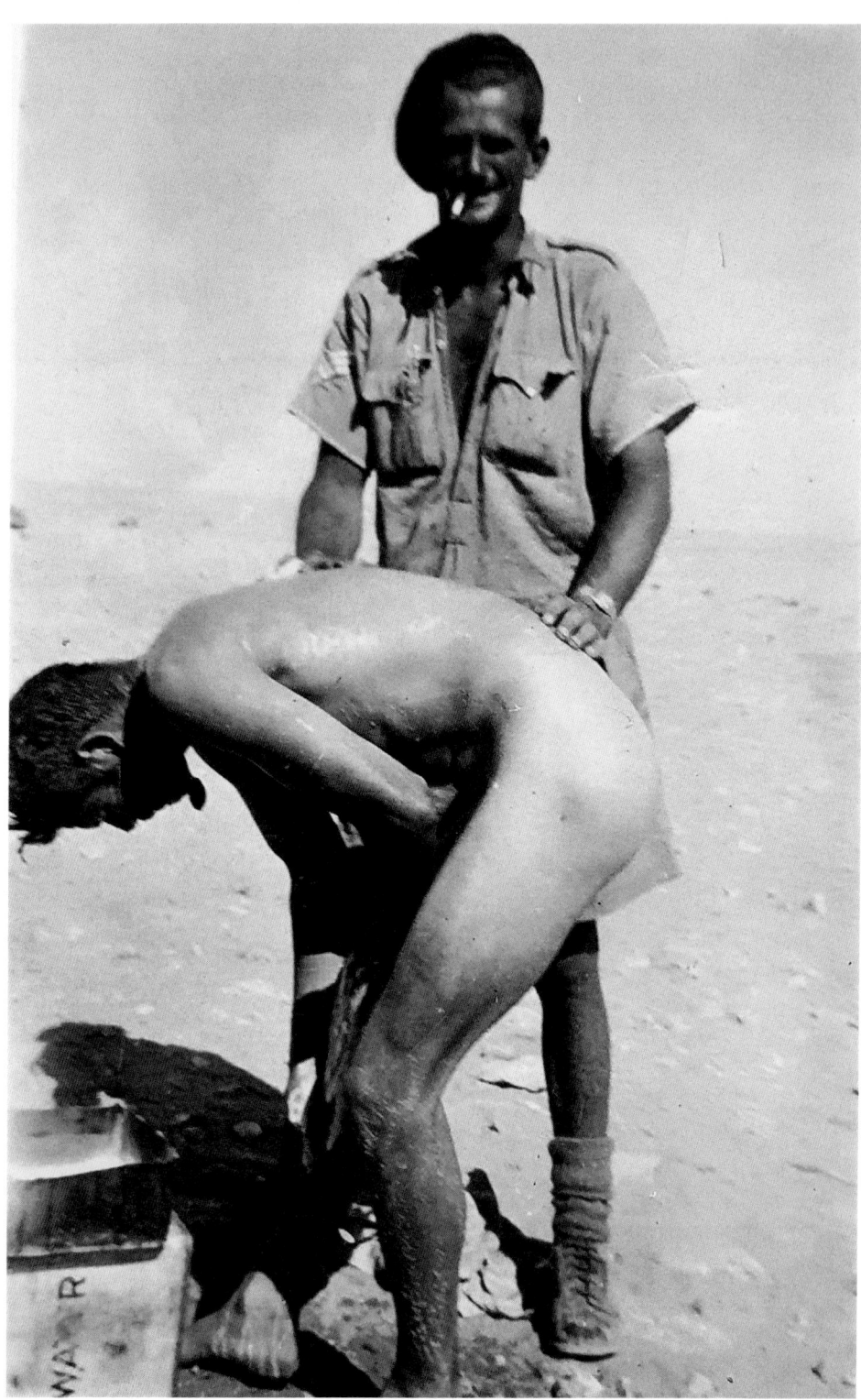
Sergeant Jim Kidd assists Trooper Alf Saunders with a desert body wash.

A trooper rests in the shadow of his truck while sewing a button on his greatcoat.

Trooper J.L.P. Macassey astride a camel carrying water-filled 'camel tanks'. The metal containers were sometimes also carried on the trucks as a bulk water supply.

(**Above**) Sergeant W.H. Rail showing off a side of bacon during a meal break.

(**Opposite, above**) R Patrol members after two months behind the lines. One Cairo newspaper said that they looked like 'Bearded Brigands'. From top left: Tpr. E.J. Dobson, Tpr. A. Boys. Middle: Tpr. A.R. Renwick, Tpr. L.T. Campbell, Tpr. L.A. Ellis, Tpr. J.B. Magee, Sgt. R.J. Landon-Lane, Tpr. H.L. Mallet (KIA, Levitha, 24 October 1943.) Front: Pte. J.E. Gill, Pte. R.R. Williams, Tpr. F.D. Rhodes, Tpr. A.M.D. Stewart.

(**Opposite, below**) Trooper L.A. Willcox and Private M. Allen RAMC, the R Patrol medical orderly. They have just returned to base from a nine-week patrol looking weary but cheerful in their dishevelled overalls.

R Patrol men shelter by their scrim-camouflaged truck parked up next to a cliff in 1940. They are dressed very warmly against the cold, wind and sand. The photo was taken during a lull in a series of sandstorms experienced by the patrol at the time. Left: Corporal C.G. Ball; third left: Private E. Harcourt. Standing back right: Private M. Allen. Extreme right: Trooper L.A. Willcox. The others are unidentified.

Chapter Fourteen

Buster Gibb Remembers

In the late 1990s the author interviewed and corresponded with Buster Gibb, an LRDG veteran who joined on the unit's foundation with W Patrol. When that was disbanded, he joined R Patrol and remained with the Group until leaving as a sergeant in 1942 to continue the war serving in the regular army. As an NCO he was also a driver for Captains Steele and Easonsmith on different occasions.

Alfred Duncan 'Buster' Gibb was born on 20 September 1916 and since the day after he was born, he was known as Buster. Before the war he was a trooper with the Marlborough Mounted Rifles, Service Number 1373, and when the call came he was posted overseas with the New Zealand Divisional Cavalry. While in Egypt in July 1940, he volunteered to serve with the Long Range Patrol Unit and joined W Patrol with the rank of corporal. Buster recalled his first impressions of the vast desert expanse:

> While on our first trip we stopped on an escarpment, and the view in front of us was magnificent desert that extended as far as the eye could see. I experienced a prickling in the scalp that was hard to describe. It wasn't fear, it was excitement at the start of an adventure that was to test our Kiwi ingenuity and lead to lifelong friendships.

W Patrol was commanded by Captain E.C. Mitford of the Royal Tank Regiment. At first the relationship between the Englishman and the New Zealanders was poor and confrontational, to such an extent that some of the men wanted to do him in; it was Buster's intervention that prevented that happening. W Patrol's first encounter with the enemy was when they captured two Italian supply trucks full of stores including Chianti and mail bags containing valuable information. It coincided with Buster's birthday, so he sought permission from Mitford to have a double celebration and was granted an extra rum issue. Unfortunately, some of the men added the captured Chianti to their rum, producing a very potent brew. Most of them, including Buster, got very intoxicated and played up that night. They were severely hung over the next morning, and some for several days more. Consequently Mitford was not amused, and Buster was faced with a court martial when they eventually returned to base.

Later on that same trip W Patrol attacked the Italian position at Ain Dua, where Lieutenant Jim Sutherland and Trooper Bill Willcox won the Military Cross and Military Medal respectively. At the end of the patrol just before they left the Sand Sea, they decided to ensure that they did not return to base with any rum. So they tipped it all into a 4-gallon tin, topped it up with lime juice and had a party. By this time Mitford had mellowed, as despite his initial impression that the men were ill-disciplined, when it came to combat, he had seen that the Kiwis had proven themselves to be tough and capable soldiers, and Buster had his court martial rescinded.

W Patrol was disbanded in December 1940 when a British Guards patrol was formed. Following that the unit became known as the Long Range Desert Group. Buster was promoted to sergeant and transferred to R Patrol. Later in 1942 he was offered promotion to warrant officer, but turned it down as it would have meant he would have to stay at base and would not have gone out on patrol. He left the LRDG and re-joined his original unit the NZ Divisional Calvary and fought in the desert campaigns. He was later commissioned and was invited to re-join the Group but declined. Buster received a Mention in Despatches (MID) for distinguished service, published in the *London Gazette* on 24 June 1943.

Buster and his wife Dee were regular attendees of LRDG reunions and brought much amusement and life to the gatherings. He passed away on 31 May 2002. Buster was a wonderful storyteller and shared with the author a great legacy of LRDG desert life tales, some of which are told as follows, in his own words and in no particular order:

Early Camouflage

In the early patrols each truck was issued with eight lengths of hessian scrim, 1.8 metres wide and 9.1 metres long. The idea was to drape them over the vehicle as camouflage and make it appear like a mound of sand or a large boulder. One day I was given the opportunity to view the effect from the air. I found that the scrim was obvious and stood out like a boil on a baby's bum. A complete failure. Before too long it was replaced by camouflaged netting, also less of a fire hazard. I know of two occasions where the scrim accidently caught on fire.

The scrim was obvious and where footprints were swept out, the change in the colour of the sand surface was dramatic. The sand surface having been burnt by the sun for hundreds possibly thousands of years took on an overall sunburnt colour. Disturb the surface and underneath it was a totally different colour. The change was obvious from any height or distance. Needless to say, the scrim was never again used for camouflage purposes.

It became an ideal medium for packing between the loads in the trucks to prevent vibration in the load especially among the tins of water or petrol. We found that tins vibrating against the side of the wooden cases soon wore the tins through and loss of petrol or water was a problem.

Tyres

All our original vehicles had Firestone tyres. It was estimated we did 1,500,000 truck miles on these tyres, with only one puncture. Suddenly just before our next trip, we were ordered to remove all Firestones and replace them with Dunlops. With Firestones each vehicle carried one spare with an extra one on every second vehicle. When traversing the Sand Sea, the tyre pressures had to be lowered to give a broader tyre base on the sand which reduced the breaking of the surface crust. We had no trouble with the Firestones. With Dunlops each vehicle carried two spares, with two more on each second vehicle. It was obviously considered that we might have trouble with Dunlops. I accused the bosses who prevailed at the time of accepting a bribe to put on Dunlops and demanded a cut for the patrol members. They in turn threatened me with a court martial. But the charge was eventually dropped. To this day I'm still convinced I was right. At the end of the trip, we had one spare between the eleven vehicles. We were ordered to remove all Dunlops and replace them with the original Firestones.

The Bomb

While on a trip from Kufra to Siwa we stopped for lunch, so I took the opportunity to test my guns. As the rest of the patrol took off, I was delayed cleaning my weapons. I followed on and eventually saw them lined up on a ridge. It was then that I spotted a bomb ahead of me. Evidently the patrol had given it a wide berth and the formation on the ridge told its tale.

Having a curious nature, I decided to have a closer look, so I left the vehicle at a reasonable distance and approached the bomb on foot. It turned out to be a parachute flare. The tail plate had lifted off and silk material was peeping out. Realizing what it was, I rushed in and hauled out the parachute and carefully cut the linen ropes, then bundled the silk into the truck. When I re-joined the rest of the patrol I was well and truly in the 'dogbox'. They thought it was a bomb and were waiting for me to clear the area as they were going to blast it to hell with their machine guns. Nobody likes to be made to look foolish.

The sequel to this story is that I carefully unplucked the linen bands holding the ropes to the silk. I then posted it home to my fiancée. Three years later I returned to New Zealand on furlough, and we were married. The wedding dress was made from the silk of the parachute flare that had been recovered from the middle of nowhere.

The Grease Gun

The French had taken Kufra, and a party of our blokes were going in, mostly medical cases. They would be the first. Bluey Grimsey purported to be writing a book at the time and wanted to be in the initial group. So I suppose the ideal way was to pretend to be crook [sick]. He claimed to be constipated and made a great song and dance about it. Nothing would move him, and nobody was convinced. The medical orderly suggested an enema, but we had no proper equipment, so I suggested a grease gun. Unfortunately, ours had a square nozzle on the end of a flexible tube. Bluey's desire to be one of the first prompted him to agree to this being used, so we bound it with soft cloth and greased it with Vaseline. We filled the gun with soapy water and stuffed it up his backside and pumped the liquid in. He was very determined and didn't complain about the indignity. Needless to say, it didn't achieve any result. We also gave him the No. 9 pills for constipation, but he said they didn't work either. He publicly dug holes all round the perimeter of the camp, saying if he had to suddenly go out into the night there would be no problem finding a hole. I believed he was having us on and sneaking out at night to relieve himself. I got sick of the whole performance and after discussion with the skipper I informed Bluey that constipation is not bad enough to get a bloke a trip into Kufra. That night, to great fanfare, he announced that things were working again.

Pistol-Shooting

I had a .38 revolver, preferring it to a .45. I became quite good in the use of it and decided to try the old cowboy quick draw. The holster was tied down and I practised for days with an unloaded gun, drawing and firing. After a time, I considered I was becoming very proficient, so I decided to have a go with the gun loaded. I tried the quick draw and came within half an inch of blowing off my foot because I was pulling on the trigger while still drawing. Needless to say, I gave that pastime away.

Snakes and Scorpions

One chap was enjoying a piddle into a camel thorn bush, when suddenly he noticed a snake wriggling about three inches away from his penis. Cutting short his relief, the trooper quickly withdrew in case the serpent had intentions of mating or worse!

I carried in my truck an Italian wire wove bed which I managed to fit in just behind the gun mount. When we stopped somewhere for the night, I would take it out and place it on four benzine boxes to make a comfortable bed. While based at Siwa I had the locals make me a palm hut where I set up my bed and used other boxes for beer and books etc. One night we had a party to celebrate my birthday and we were able to obtain a supply of Australian beer.

When I woke up in the morning Clarke Waetford came into the hut looking through the empty discarded bottles hoping to find an overlooked full one. He was successful and sat there enjoying a beer for breakfast. Then suddenly he changed hands and reached down beside him, grabbed a large knife, and threw it right next to me, giving me a hell of a fright. He said a snake had just come out from under my pillow. Soon again after giving his knife back he did it again, as another snake appeared. I was more frightened of the knife than the snakes. Then finally a third snake wriggled out. That night I had shared my bed with three snakes!

On another occasion Corporal Tony Browne was bitten twice on his back by a snake that had settled in his bed roll. Fortunately, it was not poisonous and with medical assistance Tony recovered after six hours of agony. Bluey Grimsey was stung three times by a scorpion. Though he recuperated overnight, the scorpion died. His mates wondered what Bluey had coursing through his veins that enabled him to recover so soon, but would kill a scorpion. Normally a sting could incapacitate a person for up to 36 hours or more, as the poison worked its way through the system. From then on at that camp, the men felt safer sleeping in their trucks rather than on the ground.

Grimsey seemed to have a lot to do with scorpions: not only did he design the LRDG cap badge based on the one that stung him, but also on one occasion saved his commander from much suffering. While operating with W Patrol, Captain Mitford was stung in the foot by a scorpion, whereupon Bluey quickly cut the affected area with a razor blade and sucked out as much of the poison as he could. Though the sting had given Mitford severe pain, Bluey's quick effort prevented the condition from worsening.

Edward Mitford later wrote of this incident in an issue of the LRDG Association annual newsletter:

I would like to record that Bluey Grimsey was the means of saving me a good deal of unpleasantness when, during one of my patrol journeys, I was stung on the foot by a scorpion. Bluey cut my foot with a razor blade and sucked out as much of the poison as he was able. It still hurt a great deal, but I thank Bluey for his great effort. But for him I might have been in a much worse state.

Sandstorms

There were sandstorms that drew blood from exposed skin, burnished the paint of the sides of vehicles and created static electricity in the trucks powerful enough to knock you over. Also, some that only blew sand about 8 feet above ground level. During such a storm it was possible at times, if you stood on top of a loaded truck, to eat your meal in clean air.

Bob Rawson hated snakes. Though he feared them, he would attack them vigorously and with much profanity. The episode in question happened one day when we had a sandstorm. Bob had left his woollen blankets on the ground where he had slept the night before. Evening came, and Bob decided to rescue them from the sand which had now covered them and shake them clear. When he reached down to grasp the blankets, he heard a loud hissing. But he didn't see what I saw: blue sparks from his fingertips from static electricity. He just heard the hiss. Jumping back with much profanity, including the word snakes, he rushed to the truck to grab a shovel and started to beat the hell out of his blankets.

After a long period of bashing and rolling the blankets about, Bob reckoned no snake would survive that performance. Reaching down once more, he again got the loud hissing and so repeated the pantomime. When he had finished the second time, Bob saw that I was bottling up laughter so much that tears were streaming down my legs. Naturally I came into much abuse. Static electricity from the encroaching sandstorm had built up in the wool and when it was touched, it shorted. He didn't see the resulting sparks, but one heard the hissing. I had already had a shock from the vehicle.

On one occasion when we had a sandstorm, our radio operator went to use his set and he put his hand on the truck and it flattened him, knocked him unconscious. That was static electricity in the truck.

The *keffiyeh* or Arab headdress was good in a sand or dust storm. Ours were a yellowy khaki colour to blend in with the desert. You could wrap it around your face and with your goggles it gave good protection. In hot weather it protected you from the sun and even in cold weather you could wrap it around like a scarf.

Rations

One of my tasks in the early days as an NCO was under the guidance of Dr. Edmundson to draw bulk rations and break them into daily lots. The doctor, along with Bagnold, had worked out a diet suitable for the conditions we would be working under. Separate rations for breakfast, lunch and dinner had to be compiled. For the 28 members of the patrol, one day's rations fitted compactly into a Benzine case. Some rations considered hospital comforts were carried separately, such as tinned Irish potatoes, red beet, fruit, etc. Everyone also received a daily ration of a small cake of chocolate.

From the army supply stores, I had to draw 68 gallons (308 litres) of rum. Each man was entitled to a gill measure a day (about 140mls). For a start, I had difficulty attempting to draw this issue. I was 'palmed off' from a sergeant to a lieutenant, to captain, then colonel, via a major. The colonel set me on the grade down, and when I got back to the captain, I asked to use the phone. I rang Colonel Bagnold at LRDG HQ and explained the situation. After he had finished with them, I could have collected anything I required, even without a chit!

When we were at Abbassia, I remember there was a railway line nearby and a goods train had parked there. Part of their cargo was potatoes and an enterprising LRP forager was able to feed the patrols for quite a while!

For fresh meat in the desert, we occasionally came across gazelle. We would chase them and run them down. We were told that gazelle tasted better after being hung for a while, like hares. We tried eating them fresh and eating them hung. But I would rather eat them fresh than have them stinking in the back of the truck.

A problem developed during one trip, where the rations included tins of herrings in tomato sauce. Unfortunately the fish, when canned, still had the roe in them. Half the blokes wouldn't eat what they described as 'pregnant' herrings and wanted something else. I wasn't too popular when I refused to broach next day's rations. This would have meant that we would have finished up only with herrings. As it was, we ended up with a surplus of this ration.

When we were based in an oasis, we used to barter tea with the natives for eggs. We saved the tea leaves we used ourselves and dried them out in the sun. We would use them to trade for eggs with. We had also captured a lot of

Italian tea; it was green tea, and we didn't like it. We tried to barter this for eggs too, but the natives didn't like it either.

When a patrol camped at night, where we could, we would park two trucks close together. We had a great big tarpaulin that we lay on the ground and ran the back wheels over the edge of the tarpaulin and then pulled it up over the trucks and had a bivvy tent inside. We would place our metal sand tray like a tent pole in the centre of the covering. We had our Primuses and comforts set up underneath. We would sit in there and drink our gill measure of rum and tell our stories or lies! Some would take the rum straight; others would take it with an egg if we had some. On the last night of the patrol after three or four weeks out, we would put all our rum together and have a big booze-up. We dare not take it back to base again or we would get less the next time.

The Weather Conditions

In the summertime it was so hot you dare not touch the vehicle because it burnt you. We had rubber mats on the seats, we would flip them over before we got in and we sat with our arms tucked in until you started moving. Once you were underway, the metal started to cool a bit. The man who said until the deserts grow cold never had a clue! Because in the winter months the desert grew very cold. It was so cold that dregs of water left in food dixies after washing froze to ice in a few minutes. The vehicles were open and when travelling it was like an icy blast in a freezer. So, you sat there with your woollen underwear and thick shirts on, covered with a jersey and your battledress under your greatcoat, and some wore balaclavas too. You looked like you were dressed for an Arctic expedition. We had also been issued with these great big woolly sheepskin coats. But they were rough and hadn't even trimmed the dags off them, and they stunk like hell. Nonetheless, some of the blokes wore them; I used mine as a mattress. I would lay it on the ground and sleep on it, but I never wore it.

Health and Wellness

Flies abounded in the inhabited areas, so we moved our camps into the desert and dug our own well. We carried a cast-iron hand pump to extract our water where we could. Our diet must have been good as we had very little stomach trouble. Included in our daily ration was a prescribed issue of lime juice. This was to combat scurvy or desert sores etc. There was a small incidence of desert sores to start with and we found the accepted method prescribed for dealing with them not very successful. In my youth I had a serious run of boils and the resulting sores I dealt with by bathing them with an Epsom salt solution and leaving them uncovered to dry and form a scab. Unwrapping them seemed to cause the sore to spread and form proud flesh. The dry method proved successful, and the sores healed quite quickly. I personally didn't experience any. Members who were more susceptible were issued with more lime juice and later we had ascorbic tablets.

In my experience we had only one bad case of heatstroke. Rex Beech was really knocked out. We considered cold water or ice were the only method to reduce the heat. Neither were available. We could chill small quantities of water by evaporation, but not in sufficient amount or in the time needed. Once again Kiwi know-how came to the fore. We had a supply of methylated spirits for starting our burners. Some meths was tried and it worked. Quick evaporation of the meths caused a chill factor and I was happy to say the patient recovered.

One of our patrols was stationed in Siwa and had a high incidence of malaria and we were dispatched from Kufra to take over. On the way a few days out from Siwa we had to start taking quinine tablets. One a day. I took the first one, and the next morning I had a real hangover. The following morning after the second tablet I was even worse. I concluded it was the tablets. So I refrained from taking the next couple. When I eventually took another tablet, the same condition reappeared. I then refused to take any more. On arrival in Siwa I discussed the problem with a doctor who was stationed there. He told me not on any account to take any quinine tablets as I had a bad allergy to it. He said he had seen men go blind and others so ill they had to be shipped out to hospital in Cairo. One patient eventually died, he informed me. The orders in Siwa were to don long-sleeved shirts and trousers and sleep under mosquito nets. There was a permanent gang spending their days hunting mosquitoes to identify carriers.

Our water issue was two pints a day. At Ain Dalla there was a 6-inch pipe with water continuously running out of it. We got all these empty 4-gallon tins and filled them with this fresh water. We sealed the caps with a soldering iron to prevent them coming loose and losing water on the trip. If you were preparing tins for a concealed storage dump you could not overfill them as when buried in the sand heat expansion could burst the seams. Sometimes false dumps were placed with empty tins and cases to confuse the enemy.

If you were at an oasis you could swim to have a wash, but not in the desert though Bagnold showed us how to have a bath by rubbing dry sand over you. We all grew beards to save water from shaving. I always felt sorry for those who couldn't grow a beard. There were always one or two that couldn't grow a beard, that never grew a hair on their face, or if they grew hair there was only one or two isolated hairs.

Celebration

In the early patrols things could get a little piratical with our raids on Italian convoys. Often, we would then drink the captured wine and brandy. However, when this was combined with our rum, it made for a very potent combination. My birthday had coincided with the day we captured the Italian 'Truckees'. I asked the skipper as it is our first capture, could we have an extra issue of rum. He agreed, but some said they didn't want the extra rum and gave it to others; in the end there were five of us who were still enjoying the additional rum. The rest of the patrol had had enough and gone to bed. Ray Gorringe said the rum jar was empty, but we had the taste; I said there was plenty more and to get another. We had also had six bottles of Chianti from the Italians in the big wicker-covered bottles and long necks, so we had that too. I remember sitting on the truck running board with one of those bottles in one hand and a gallon jar in the other. I would have a swig of rum followed by a Chianti chaser. But before too long my whole world tipped upside down and I flaked out. In the meantime, during the night Tony Dodunski had got rip-roaring drunk and threatened to do the Italian prisoners in with what he reckoned was a hand grenade, but fortunately it was only a box of matches. Apparently, four men had to hold him down and it was several hours before he had finally settled. It took him four days to recover from his hangover and for a while we thought he was going to die. The skipper was pretty upset about the whole thing, especially being woken up with Tony's screaming, wanting to blow up the prisoners, who must have been terrified!

When I woke up in the morning there were three rum jars on the ground and six empty Chianti bottles. One rum jar was about a third full and the other two were empty. By my calculations the five of us drank over a gallon and a half of this over-proof rum and six bottles of Chianti. We all had terrible hangovers of a varying degree including me.

Veteran Ray Gorringe recalled in a letter to the author about the occasion. He said it was the worst hangover he had ever had in his life, which he understated as 'an overdose of issue rum'!

Two others were carrying an RAF observer Tommy Farr in their truck; he was looking out to plot emergency landing grounds. But his LRDG crew were so far gone with their hangovers that they had to get Farr to drive the truck. It took a day and a half before they came right.

I got the blame for it all, though I slept through it, as I had issued the rum and wine and as an NCO should have been in control. And rightly so. I was told I would be court-martialled when we returned to Cairo.

Also, when I had awoken feeling very unwell, I found Gordon Parkes on his hands and knees telling the duty cook to put the primus out and wait till morning, but it was morning. I knew there would be trouble looming, so I decided to get Gordon out of the way and shut him up before the Skipper found him. I considered all options and the only one which was feasible was to roll him up in one of the lengths of scrim we used as a camouflage net. I managed to do this, but he rolled himself out again. I rolled him up again, but this time I used a sail needle and string and sewed him up. When we moved off, we threw Gordon in the back of the truck with the spare tyre behind the gun mount.

At the midday stop I let him out and without a sound he rolled under the truck in the shade. After a time, I prodded him and enquired if he would like some grub. Suddenly he stood up and hit his head on the chassis with such force you could almost see the truck rise. With an outstretched arm and pointing a finger he yelled, 'Look at them, look at them, big yellow buggers with long black tails!' We managed to get some liquid into him, and he recovered the next day.

With all this going on the skipper never came near. He just sent one of his minions to say I would be up for court-martial. He never knew it, but I saved his life. The boys were 'pissed off' with him and they were devising ways to do him in. Fortunately, as the patrol continued and we saw some more action, mutual respect developed as he learnt to understand the Kiwi.

We had learnt our lesson and while I was there, we never had another session mixing our drinks like we did on that occasion. For most of the time we were self-disciplined troops who served well as a unit, respected our officers and got on with the job. We had heard that the Guards patrol used to have to do PT in the morning and rifle drill in the afternoon; we didn't need that sort of discipline while serving in the desert. T Patrol was invited to join them on one occasion, but declined, considering it a waste of time and energy in the hot sun.

The Siwa Pools

An experience in Siwa was not a humorous one and could have had tragic consequences for me. It was an oasis steeped in history going back thousands of years. It was said it was the playground of Cleopatra. Siwa is some 200 miles from the coast and is 80 feet below sea level. It had literally hundreds of artesian wells. Some as large as a standard swimming pool and some of varying shapes. One is a perfect figure of eight. A large number of these wells are walled and have trap doors set at various heights. By closing the bottom doors, they can raise the level of the water and by opening the top doors they can irrigate the higher levels of land.

There were two identical round pools near our campsite which we used to patronize. The two pools were 40 or 50 feet apart. One day while sitting on the rim of a pool while the boys were sunning themselves and getting the Arabs to fetch choice dates down from the palms, I saw an Arab dive under the opposite pool and thought nothing of it until I saw him enter the pool I was dangling my feet in. He told me where he had come from, so I investigated and found that a tunnel connected the two pools.

The entrance was about 8 feet down and it was stone-walled with an arched ceiling. Having been good at underwater swimming before the war I thought if an Arab could do it, I could too. Rising to the surface again, I did a few breathing exercises and without telling anyone went down to swim through this tunnel.

Halfway through, my natural buoyancy took me up to the ceiling and there I was stuck. I started to panic, and this would have been my downfall if

I let it continue. I relaxed and considered a plan of action. I needed to get off the ceiling and the only way to do this was to try and turn over. The curved ceiling made this difficult but with the loss of a little skin which I discovered later, I managed to turn over. Then, with my feet and hands I pushed myself right down to the bottom, twisted over again and swam for the end. Things had got critical, and I didn't think I was going to make it. I just submitted to the urge to breathe when I finally got my mouth out of the water.

With a lot of coughing, I got rid of the water I had sucked in and then with great difficulty I climbed out of the pool. It was some time before I told the gang what I had done but didn't tell them how critical it had been. I went through that tunnel several times more afterwards and a few of the others achieved it also.

The date harvest in Siwa would put a man off dates for life. There was a brand that was large and luscious. They were known as the King's dates.

It was from Siwa that I left the patrols. We had another new 'Pommy' (British) officer and he and I couldn't see eye to eye. The morale was low, and all the blokes wanted to return to their units. One day after a hate session I was asked to get a list of everyone who wanted to return, and my name was to head the list. I knew it was going to come sooner or later because I refused promotion. This would mean I would be a Warrant Officer and remain at base and that was abhorrent to me. Anyway, a group of us left while at the same time as a group of new recruits arrived. After a few days' leave in Cairo with Len Mather who left at the same time as me, I reported to the Reinforcement Depot.

Lance Corporal A.D. 'Buster' Gibb on duty in Cairo before he joined the LRP. He wears a Military Police armband.

Buster Gibb (left) on leave photographed with shoeshine boys in Cairo.

Comrades, left: Corporal Rex Beech, killed in action at Jebel Sherif on 31 January 1941, and Sergeant Buster Gibb. Both are armed with .38 revolvers. Gibb was a close friend of Beech and was greatly saddened by his loss.

Sheepskin coats issued to the LRDG to help protect them from the extreme winter weather. Left: Trooper M.E. Hammond, Private E. Harcourt and Private M. Allen. Note the scrim camouflage over the truck. This was ineffective and later replaced with camouflage netting.

The parachute flare 'bomb' found by Buster Gibb.

R Patrol troops wearing multiple layers of clothing to protect them from the cold. Centre: Corporal R.O. Spotswood; the others are unidentified. They stand in front of their heavily-loaded F30 truck.

A trooper wears his wrapped *keffiyeh* and goggles as he would in a sandstorm or travelling in heavy dust conditions.

The R Patrol cookhouse, Siwa.

An Arab elder who traded with the LRDG.

Troopers filling their 2-gallon water cans from a spring. Note the 'W' on the can.

R Patrol men pumping ground water at Tazerbo. Their Ford F30 truck R3 is at the back.

A Fiat 508 *Militare* convoy escort vehicle. The large cognac barrel would have impeded the effective use of its defensive machine gun. This indicated that they were not seriously anticipating enemy action. Buster Gibb tried to bring one of these back to Cairo as a personal vehicle, but without success.

A handy souvenir pocket map of Cyrenaica 1942. It was designed to send home to family for the buyer to illustrate where they had travelled.

Trooper Gordon Parkes (left) and Sergeant Buster Gibb looking very staunch in his pose. Parkes got very intoxicated and hung over for two days after a desert birthday celebration drinking rum and Italian wine with Gibb and others.

A military manual on the *Field General Courts-Martial*. This copy belonged to Major R.B. McQueen who served in the LRP as a lieutenant.

R Patrol group pose in front of a truck. They were en route to Kufra oasis in October 1940. Left back: Trooper J.W. Eyles; fourth from left: Lieutenant C.A. Holliman, Private J.H. Williamson, Private E. Harcourt; third from right: Trooper A.F. Dodunski. Corporal A.D. Gibb sits front left. Others unidentified.

Men enjoying a swim in Cleopatra's pool at Siwa. Buster Gibb almost drowned in this pool.

"R" Patrol.

Captain D.G. Steele.			O.C.
Lieut. J.H. Sutherland M.C.			2nd. 1/c.
1373	Sgt.	Gibb A.D.	
594	Bdr.	Respinger A.E.	
7483	Pte.	Tinker R.H.	
7423	L/C.	Ball C.G.	
1189	L/C.	Butler W.G.	
7082	L/C.	Hamilton W.J.	
1290	Tpr.	Willcox L.A., M.M.	
8753	Pte.	Brown F.R.	
7881	"	Campbell K.	
7364	"	Emslie J.	
7748	"	Spotswood R.O.	
1104	Tpr.	Hammond M.E.	
1250	"	Mather A.F.	
7427	Pte.	Nelson G.H.	
8809	"	Rawson R.	
7381	"	Russell E.T.	
8825	"	Sadgrove A.D.	
1329	Tpr.	Saunders A.N.	
551	Gnr.	Grimsey C.O.	
1204	Tpr.	Dodunski A.F.	
1100	"	Eyles J.W.	
1211	"	Gorringe R.O.	
7834	"	Gorringe E.F.	
1292	"	Landon-Lane R.J.	
3420	"	Waetford C.	
1383	"	Parkes G.C.	
29657	Pte.	Gill J.E.	Fitter

Copy of the original of R Patrol Nominal Roll of 31 March 1941.

Chapter Fifteen

The Aftermath

The Eighth Army entered Tripoli on 23 January 1943. The rapid advance of 2,250km in three months had made it necessary for the LRDG to move its base from Kufra 965km north-westwards to Zella and later another 240km to Hon. These moves from one place to the next were successfully completed with the aid of the trucks of the Heavy Section in a single journey.

One of the last significant desert actions of the Group was supporting the Eighth Army advance into Tunisia. In preparation for this, it was required to reconnoitre and map the country's southern approaches through which a column would have to pass, outflanking the Axis-held Mareth Line. In January and February 1943, the LRDG and Indian Long Range Squadron explored the territory, undertaking topographical work to the south and the west of the range of hills extending southwards from Matmata. As they progressed the patrols signalled HQ daily, reporting the 'going', obstacles, cover, water supply and sites for landing grounds. On their return the commanders conferred with LRDG Intelligence Officer Captain L.H. Browne at the NZ Division HQ, where a model was made to demonstrate possible lines of advance.

On 12 January 1942, T1 Patrol under Captain N.P. Wilder crossed the frontier and became the first troops of the Eighth Army to enter Tunisia. They found an uncharted pass south through the Matmata Hills, which became known as Wilder's Gap. It was by this route two months later that the NZ Division executed its 'left hook' round the fortified Mareth Line. Other patrols explored the country further to the west. T2 operated in the area to the south of Djebel Tebaga between Matmata and Chott el Djerid, which was a high salt marsh, while G2 explored in the area between the Chott and the Grand Erg Oriental, which was an impassable sand sea extending into southern Algeria.

The final task assigned to the LRDG by the Eighth Army was the navigation of the New Zealand Corps during the outflanking of the Mareth Line in March 1943. Appropriately the work was performed by New Zealanders, Captain R.A. Tinker with three men from T2 Patrol in two jeeps, who would be acting as guides. The New Zealand Corps passed through Wilder's Gap and remained at an assembly area, while the route was plotted to the north-west. A wadi with steep, rocky escarpments presented a very difficult obstacle but Tinker, accompanied by New Zealand Engineers, found a place where tracks could be constructed with road-making machinery to get heavy transport across.

The following day, the Eighth Army launched its frontal attack on the Mareth Line. From there they moved forward to Tebaga along the route reconnoitred by the Group and engaged the enemy on 21 March. Eventually the Axis forces were driven back to a corner of Tunisia, ending with their final surrender in North Africa on 13 May 1943. There being no further scope for the LRDG, they were released from the Eighth Army and returned to Alexandria in Egypt to rest and reorganize.

In a letter dated 2 April 1943, General Bernard Montgomery wrote to the LRDG commander, Colonel G.L. Prendergast, of his appreciation of the work of the Group:

> I would like you to know how much I appreciate the excellent work done by your patrols and by the SAS in reconnoitring the country up to the Gabes Gap. Without your careful and reliable reports, the launching of the 'left hook' by the NZ Division would have been a leap in the dark: with the information they provided, the operations could be planned with some certainty, and as you know, went off without a hitch.

An overall appreciation of the LRDG came on 13 May 1943, the day the Axis forces surrendered in North Africa when, as part of a message sent by General Alexander to Winston Churchill, the following was stated:

> The victory has taken three years, many battles, and much sacrifice; of the formations engaged, the desert raiders of the LRDG and SAS formed numerically a minute part. But it is true to say that without their efforts victory would have come later at a far greater cost. Their role in the history of warfare remains unique.

Much reorganization was undertaken at Alexandria before the two squadrons eventually moved on to their new training ground in Lebanon. With the three-year desert war finally over, many long-serving veterans returned home on furlough or re-joined their parent units. This meant further recruitment and re-establishment of the squadrons. Nevertheless, they were never short of volunteers. By this time, the reputation of the LRDG as an elite force had been well recognized and was desired to join by those looking for something distinct from the constraints of the regular army.

On 1 April 1943, the LRDG received a directive that required the unit to be able to operate by jeep or on foot in mountainous country with the object of liaison with patriot forces. Thus it became necessary for the Group to readjust its thinking and arrange a comprehensive training programme. The second-in-command, Major J.R. Easonsmith, travelled to Syria to find a suitable training ground. He was fortunate to be able to arrange to take over the Cedars Hotel, which was a peacetime ski resort in the Lebanon mountains previously used as the Middle East Ski School.

From May 1943, the LRDG A and B Squadrons spent almost three and a half months training at the picturesque Cedars of Lebanon. The patrols were reorganized into small self-contained units varying from four to eight men depending on their task. They had to be capable of maintaining communications over distances of 160km while operating covertly behind enemy lines on foot. This was a radical departure from almost three years of relying on transport to now having to walk to complete their mission. The stamina and fitness level required was of an exceptional standard, so some desert veterans who were unable to make the transition had to return to their original units.

Following the Italian armistice in September 1943, British forces began to occupy the Dodecanese Islands in the Aegean Sea between Greece and Turkey. Britain's Prime Minister Winston Churchill saw it as an opportunity to open a new front in the eastern Mediterranean. He thought such a strategy could only add more pressure on Hitler's stretched military forces, already fighting on many fronts. It might also provide encouragement for Turkey to join the Allies. However, the Americans did not support the proposal as they were already heavily committed with the invasions in Sicily and Italy and had no ships to spare.

Nonetheless undeterred, Churchill went ahead on 9 September and approved the plan, code-named Operation ACCOLADE. He cabled Middle East Command with the words 'This is a time to play high. Improvise and dare.' Churchill concluded that the island of Rhodes with its vital airfields offered the key to the command of the Aegean and ultimately Turkey's decision to enter the war. However, the Germans also had plans to occupy the islands, and so the race began.

The day after Italy capitulated on 6 September, the Germans began to occupy all the main Italian-held islands. By 13 September, the Germans had taken Rhodes and its vital airbases. This immediately put Churchill's plan in jeopardy because it left only Kos, with its small airfield, as the sole RAF fighter cover for operations in the Dodecanese. However, in early October that was also taken by the enemy. The Luftwaffe dominance meant that throughout the islands most British destroyers and smaller vessels were only able to re-supply and transport troops under the cover of darkness.

The LRDG became part of the Raiding Forces, Middle East, which was made up of around 200 LRDG, 150 men of the SBS and No. 30 Commando. Colonel G.L. Prendergast was appointed second-in-command of the Raiding Forces and now Lieutenant Colonel J.R. Easonsmith was promoted to Officer Commanding, LRDG. The New Zealand (A) Squadron was commanded by Major A.J. Guild and B Squadron, the British and Rhodesians, were led by Major D.L. Lloyd Owen. They were to be used to support 3,000 regular British troops of 234 Brigade holding the islands, under the command of Major General F.G.R. Brittorous, as Leros Fortress Commander, later replaced by Brigadier R.A.G. Tilney.

The island outposts were manned by detachments of the SBS and the LRDG. The Group had set up watches on the islands of Astypalaia (Stampalia), Kos, Kythnos, Mykonos, Naxos, Gyaros, Serifos and Symi. They acted as observers in the outlying islands astride the sea and air routes to the Dodecanese to report the movements of enemy shipping and aircraft. Many of these islands were occupied by the Germans, so the patrols had to keep well concealed and often had to withdraw with some narrow escapes when discovered. This important coast watch role of reporting all observations was a job like the famous Road Watch employed in the North African campaign. Between September and November 1943, the gathering and transmitting of this vital intelligence of sea and air activity was one of the primary tasks of the LRDG Aegean operations.

The full story of the R Patrol and LRDG operations in the Dodecanese operations is told in the author's book *The Long Range Desert Group in the Aegean* (Pen & Sword, 2020). Thereby, under the leadership of Lieutenant D.J. (Jack) Aitken, R1 Patrol, and Lieutenant R.F. (Frank) White, R2 Patrol, the R Patrol story continues to be told in detail in that work.

The LRDG suffered their greatest loss in one action with the assault on the island of Levitha on 23 October. This ill-conceived operation lasted almost two days and cost the Group five killed or missing and thirty-seven taken prisoner with only seven escaping the island. Of that number, nineteen captured and four killed or missing were New Zealanders. The patrols were ordered by the brigade commander to embark on an infantry assault mission to take the small island occupied by the enemy. It was thought to be defended in low numbers. Yet despite protest from the LRDG commanders, an initial reconnaissance was not permitted to confirm this. Furthermore, the men did not normally operate as infantrymen as they were specifically trained as specialists, skilled in intelligence-gathering and covert operations. Nonetheless, they undertook the mission and landed under cover of darkness. At first a steady advance was made, taking enemy positions and a good fight was mounted, capturing many prisoners. Eventually they were worn down and had to surrender to an overwhelming force, which attacked from both the ground and air. It was a big setback for the LRDG as almost a third of its members had become casualties or were taken prisoner; a tragic waste of specialist troops, more so when several thousand British servicemen were still based on Leros. A brigade infantry assault would have been better suited to the task.

The losses caused an immediate flurry within the New Zealand government because it was revealed that their troops had been consigned to the Aegean without official approval. The government required that it had to be consulted first before its soldiers were committed to a new theatre of war. Further discussions with the British government concluded that the New Zealanders would be permanently withdrawn from the LRDG. It was agreed, therefore, that the A (NZ) Squadron LRDG would be pulled out as soon as the tactical situation allowed, although they remained in Leros until its capitulation on 16 November.

The regular air-raids and final assault on Leros lasted for more than fifty days and nights from 23 September to 16 November. The actual invasion on 12 November led to five exhausting days of fighting as both sides lost and retook ground in a series of seesaw actions. It was a very violent clash with much close-quarter fighting along with extensive bombing resulting in significant casualties. In this conflict, the LRDG were also one of the few military units where majors and colonels led patrols into combat and fought alongside their men. They equally shared all the privations and hardships, and some were killed in action including their commander Lieutenant Colonel J.R. Easonsmith DSO, MC and S Patrol commander Major A.G. Redfern MBE.

On the night of 16 November 1943, Easonsmith was ordered by Brigadier Tilney to undertake a reconnaissance into Leros town. Accompanied by several men, he reconnoitred the area to evaluate the situation around the approaches to Fortress HQ at Meraviglia. At first there were no enemy sightings, but he returned later before midnight to make a second inspection. By that time the Germans had established themselves in the town and while Easonsmith, who typically always led from the front, rounded a bend in the road he was ambushed and hit by sub-machine gun fire at close range. The rest of the men dived for cover and then withdrew. Just prior to that, Corporal Roy Duncalfe, who had been behind Easonsmith, recalled him saying, 'Roy, always keep your grenade handy.' A few minutes later as they walked towards the village, Easonsmith was killed. This badly upset Duncalfe as he and his commander had served closely together for a long time. They had both been decorated the year before for their gallant roles in the famous Barce Raid in Libya in September 1942. On hearing the tragic news, Colonel Prendergast reassumed command of the LRDG.

The *LRDG Operations in Aegean: War Diary* recorded the following about Easonsmith's death:

> The death of such an outstanding officer, whose ability and cheerfulness in all conditions was an inspiration to the unit, is a blow that has taken so much from us all. He was a magnificent leader, who had done such grand work in the desert as patrol and squadron commander, and whose experience and kindness made him the perfect commanding officer. The news seriously deranged the LRDG and Colonel Prendergast reassumed command pending appointment of a new CO.

W.B. Kennedy Shaw also described Easonsmith in his book *Long Range Desert Group*: 'He was brave, wise, with an uprightness that shamed lesser men; he was, I think, the finest man we had in the LRDG.'

Five LRDG patrols were assigned to the Italian gun battery positions, employing the heights as coastal observation points, but also to stiffen the morale of their new allies, ensuring the guns and their crews performed effectively. Initially the coastal defences gave good service but were eventually knocked out by regular Luftwaffe dive-bombing attacks. The patrols that were not employed at observation points and/or overseeing the coastal gun batteries were formed into independent reconnaissance and fighting units, patrolling by day and night. Essentially they were in an anti-paratrooper role, moving between combat zones more quickly than the regular troops were able, supplying information and providing support as required.

The British troops were especially worn down. Their ammunition was running low and many suffered from thirst and fatigue. Battle conditions often caused the failure of essential supplies and ammunition in reaching the front lines or caused them to become erratic in receipt. After five days of sustained fighting, on the evening of 16 November, the Brigade HQ at Meraviglia was taken and the Fortress Commander Brigadier Tilney was forced to surrender. The Germans had total unopposed dominance of the air, which was the main factor in their victory over Leros. According to German records, on Kos and Leros combined almost 4,600 British service personnel were taken prisoner, along with another 357 troops killed. The Italians suffered the worst, with approximately 8,500 captured and an unknown number killed.

During their three months on the islands the LRDG had twelve of their number killed in action, including its commander and two missing, presumed dead. Another later died in England due to serious injuries from a jeep accident on Leros. In addition, about 115 patrolmen were captured and one later died while a prisoner. In all, almost two-thirds of the LRDG committed to the Dodecanese operations were lost, although many did manage to escape the enemy by employing their specialist evasion skills.

The Dodecanese operations proved to be the last action A (NZ) Squadron was to undertake with the LRDG. After that debacle, the Group transferred to a new base at Azzib, north of Haifa in Palestine, to rest and reorganize. On orders from the New Zealand government, due to the losses the squadron was to disband on 31 December 1943. However, prior to this, the Christmas celebrations were somewhat prolonged. There was a party almost every night as memories were shared and farewells exchanged with their British and Rhodesian comrades.

The final break-up dinner was on the night of Friday, 14 January 1944. The next day in Cairo the squadron was officially wound up. Most of its members, if they did not go home on furlough, spent time training in Egypt. From there they were posted as reinforcements to the Divisional Cavalry with the 2nd New Zealand Division in Italy.

In Chapter 14 of the *LRDG War Diary 1/12/43 to 1/4/44*, the following extract noted the disbandment of the New Zealand squadron:

> On 29 December A (NZ) Squadron were withdrawn from the LRDG and full reorganisation could then be completed. This was a sad day for the LRDG, for not only had NZ personnel formed the original Long Range Patrols in June 1940, but there was a unique spirit among them that gave the LRDG a tone of which we were all proud. The New Zealand officers and men had always been of the highest standing and their success on operations was always assured. Their departure was a bad blow for the unit and came at a time which was already difficult as a result of our losses in the Aegean.

By December 1943, the Group under the command of Lieutenant Colonel D.L. Lloyd Owen DSO, MC was reorganized into two squadrons, each of eight patrols consisting of one officer and ten men. To replace the New Zealanders, a new A (Rhodesian) Squadron was formed under the command of Captain K.H. Lazarus MBE. He had earned much credit as a surveyor in mapping the Libyan sands and later as a patrol commander. The British B Squadron was commanded by Captain M.P. Stormonth Darling.

To ensure that the LRDG did not lose its high level of expertise, Lieutenant General Freyberg allowed Lloyd Owen to retain several long-serving New Zealand members. Initially they were Captain L.H. Browne MC, DCM who was made the Group's Intelligence Officer; Captain R.A. Tinker MC, MM became second-in-command of B Squadron; Captain C.H.B. Croucher MID was appointed Officer Commanding, Boats; Captain D.J. Aitken, Patrol Commander, X1 Patrol; and Captain R.J. Landon-Lane, Patrol Commander, X2 Patrol. Also Private L.J. Hawkins was retained as a fitter employed in the workshops. Later, Captain K.F. McLauchlan and Sergeant M.H. Craw MM also re-joined.

Two new bases were established at Bari and Rodi in southern Italy. Bari was the main operational HQ till the end of the war, and it was from there that most of the missions were planned and directed. Rodi, although a long way from Bari, was a good site for base communications and a quiet place for the men to rest after operations. By May 1944, after months of diverse and specialized training which included the handling of pack mules and small boats, parachuting, mountain warfare, skiing and how to operate in snowy conditions, they were ready for the first of many intrusions into enemy-occupied territory. Their initial actions were behind the lines in Italy, and from then on until the end of the war, patrols operated in Yugoslavia, Albania, Greece, the Dalmatian Islands, Istria and Croatia.

The Group maintained its intelligence-gathering and reconnaissance role, but also operated with local partisans in many sabotage and hit-and-run actions. The LRDG set up coast watches to report on enemy shipping as targets for Allied naval and air commands. In addition, they planned, often in conjunction with the SBS, small-scale raids against enemy shipping in harbours and island garrisons. Objectives were reached either by parachute or by sea. By the middle of September 1944, there were a total of eighteen different parties on various tasks stretching from the north-east corner of Italy through Yugoslavia and Albania to Greece.

For operations around the Dalmatian islands the LRDG could not always rely on the Royal Navy for assistance at short notice, so they created their own shipping fleet of two motor fishing vessels: the MFV *La Palma* and the MFV *Kufra*. Both were armed and had a good carrying capacity for communication systems, men, stores and equipment. These robust vessels with their LRDG crews performed much valuable work. A Waco liaison aircraft was still in service and flown by New Zealander Captain R.F.T. Barker. Along with the Group's vessels, it was probably one of the few Special Forces units in the Second World War that could boast its own Air Force and navy!

The MFV *Kufra* was skippered by ex-R Patrol commander Captain C.H.B. Croucher, a most suitable appointment given his pre-war experience in the Merchant Marine working for both the P&O Shipping and Union Steamship companies. He had also served as an Intelligence officer. The *Kufra* was an 80-ton deep-sea fishing trawler converted into a mobile headquarters with a crew of eight. It was armed and equipped with a sophisticated communication system capable of keeping in touch with the LRDG bases of Bari and Rodi. It was also used as a signal HQ keeping in contact with all the patrols, the RAF and navy. Along with the MFV *La Palma* under Captain Alan Denniff, both vessels undertook much valuable work.

By the time the war had ended in Europe, the Group had completed more than 100 successful operations. Allied Force HQ recommended that the LRDG should continue its role in the Far East. The response for volunteers had been impressive. At one time more than 300 members of the unit were prepared to go, with half that number volunteering to defer their release from the army to do so. Consequently, in June 1945 they were ordered as a unit back to England to regroup. However, instead Lloyd Owen received a War Office signal stating that the LRDG was to be disbanded.

On 1 August, five years and fourteen days after its formation in Cairo, what began as Ralph Bagnold's small reconnaissance force ceased to exist. During those years the LRDG achieved a great measure of success, making a significant contribution in their diverse areas of operations. This was out of all proportion to the size of the unit and the number of casualties they suffered. A few who had joined the unit as Other Ranks in June 1940 still remained in June 1945. All were New Zealanders, and interestingly all original R Patrol members apart from one. They were Captain L.H. Browne MC, DCM; Captain R. Tinker MC, MM; Captain R.J. Landon-Lane; Captain C.H.B. Croucher MID; and Private L. Hawkins (originally T Patrol).

The patrols had operated in Egypt, Cyrenaica, Tripolitania and Tunisia before going to Europe where they were deployed in the Aegean, Greece, Albania, Yugoslavia and Italy. They had marked their place in Special Forces' history, true to their motto 'Not by strength, by guile.'

In the postwar years, like most veterans many would gather for reunions. The first one took place in New Zealand on 14 July 1946. It was held in Wellington, with Major C.S. (Bing) Morris being appointed president. Interestingly, three of the four members of the committee were R Patrol veterans: Joe Eyles, Bluey Grimsey and Ron Landon-Lane. Eighty-five members attended, many travelling from all around the country to do so. Bing Morris wrote in the summary of his reunion notes his observation of their first gathering:

> It was good to see our chaps together again and to watch their expressions and their faces as they talked and to hear almost forgotten moments brought to mind again. It would be hard to count the number of 'stunts' fought again that night! In my opinion this, our first reunion, was a 'good show' and that is the best that can be said.

There was always a great sense of camaraderie among those who served sharing common bonds and memories, but for others, the idea of going to a reunion brought back painful memories they would rather remain forgotten. For them it was not until much later in life, as older men, that they finally felt more at peace in attending these gatherings. In September 1950 the LRDG Association introduced a tie with the design being small gold scorpions on a dark blue background. The Association also produced a tie or lapel pin.

In 1980 a 30cwt Chevrolet WA *Waikaha* was found in the Egyptian Sand Sea. It was later recovered and returned to Britian. The vehicle is now on display at the Imperial War Museum, London. It is the only surviving LRP/LRDG Chevrolet WA and provides a good example of what an early patrol 'warhorse' looked like. Many R Patrol members served in the short-lived W Patrol, so the vehicle was a rare find and a tribute to those special men.

In 2023, an ex-Royal Marine Simon Willis, who served as a mechanic for 45 Commando and the Special Boat Service (SBS), took five months to construct in metal a magnificent and detailed model of the *Waikaha* as it is displayed in the Imperial War Museum. The model is 460mm long, 200mm wide and 170mm tall, and it weighs 6 kilograms; a great one-off museum-quality tribute to an iconic LRDG vehicle.

Finally, the special bond between veterans, even though they may have not seen each other since the war, still held strong throughout their lifetimes. This is reflected in one example as told to the author by Heather Dodunski whose father-in-law was Tony Dodunski of R Patrol. She recalled a family story about two veterans meeting in the 1980s:

> In the eighties my husband Tony and I purchased a fish and chip shop near Mt. Maunganui Returned Services' Club. One day a man asked Tony if his father (also called Tony) was in the LRDG. The gentleman's name was Norm Gedye. So, Tony arranged for his father to come over from Morrinsville to meet him. I remember vividly Tony telling me that they sat over a few beers and talked for hours about their experiences in the desert, and both were crying as they spoke! Even Tony came back to the shop crying as he said it was so emotional.

Norm Gedye was the last surviving New Zealand LRDG member and died aged 98 on 21 December 2018.

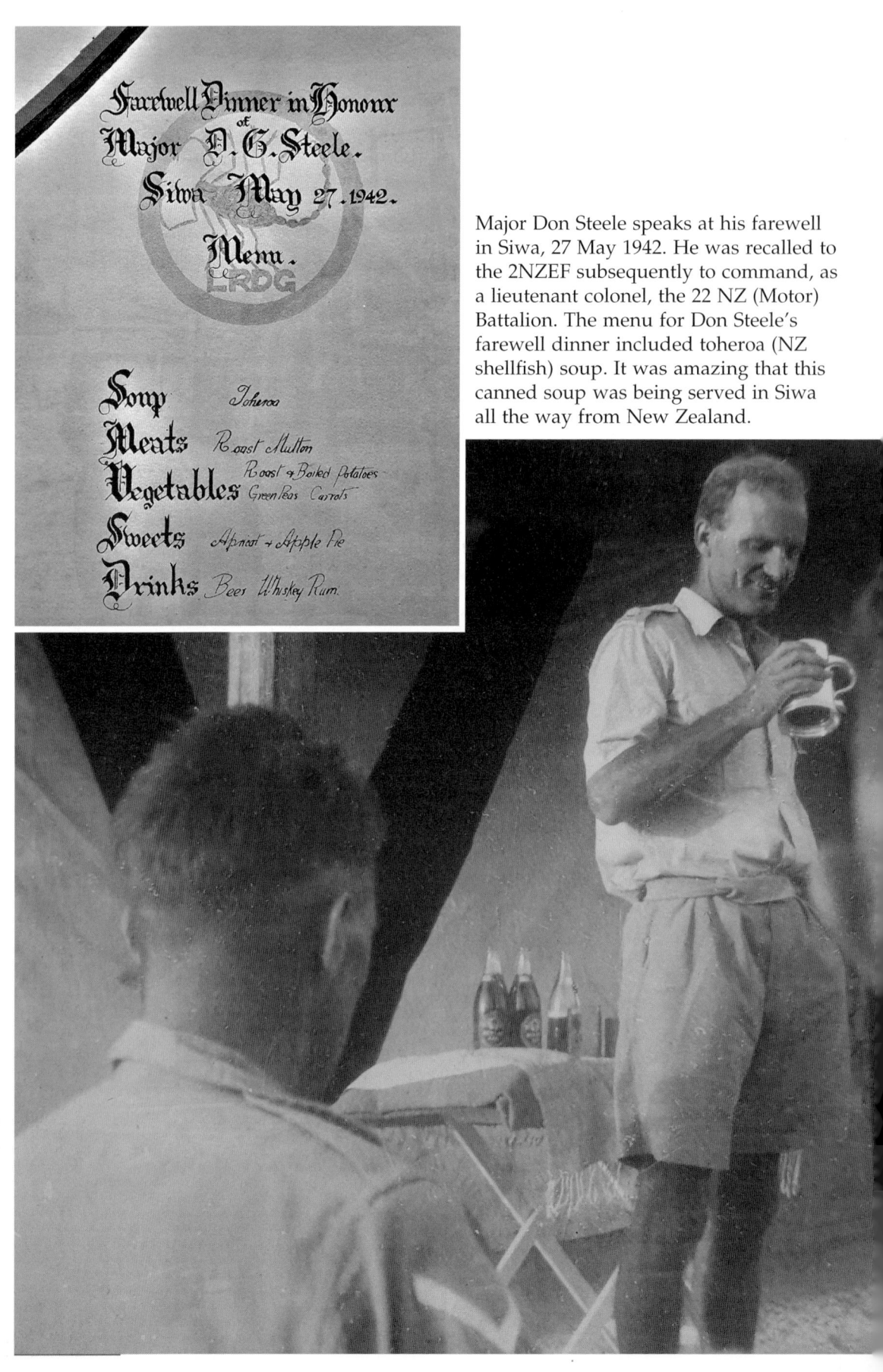

Major Don Steele speaks at his farewell in Siwa, 27 May 1942. He was recalled to the 2NZEF subsequently to command, as a lieutenant colonel, the 22 NZ (Motor) Battalion. The menu for Don Steele's farewell dinner included toheroa (NZ shellfish) soup. It was amazing that this canned soup was being served in Siwa all the way from New Zealand.

Colonel David Lloyd Owen, Y Patrol commander, who took part in a number of operations including the SAS raid on Tobruk in August/September 1942. This earned him the Military Cross. He was wounded in an air-raid at Kufra in October 1942 and almost lost an arm. Lloyd Owen rejoined the LRDG in February 1943, when they underwent training in Lebanon before being sent to the Aegean. He took command of the LRDG at the end of 1943 after the death of his predecessor Jake Easonsmith during the Battle of Leros.

Tripoli was taken on 23 January 1943. A statue of Mussolini on a horse is still in place. An Italian Fiat 626 truck is parked in the foreground.

(**Left**) A cartoon drawing of an 'LRDG Kiwi'. This was drawn for Bluey Grimsey by a fellow prisoner 'Nicholson' in 1944 at Stalag VIIIB in Germany.

(**Opposite, above**) Left: Bill Kennedy Shaw wrote the first book about the unit titled *Long Range Desert Group* published by Collins Ltd in 1945. It was republished many times, including this paperback version by Four Square Books in 1959. Right: The NZ wartime magazine *Korero* included an article on the LRDG which they described as 'Kiwi Bedouin'.

(**Opposite, below**) Buster Gibb, right, with General B.C. Freyberg VC greeting First World War veterans in the early 1950s.

FOUR SQUARE BOOKS
Long Range Desert Group
'If you have a taste for piracy . . . the L.R.D.G. is the unit to join'—ALAN MOOREHEAD, A Year of Battle
W. B. KENNEDY SHAW
2/6
Illustrated

KORERO
KIWI BEDOUIN page 3
AEWS BACKGROUND BULLETIN VOL 2 NO 20

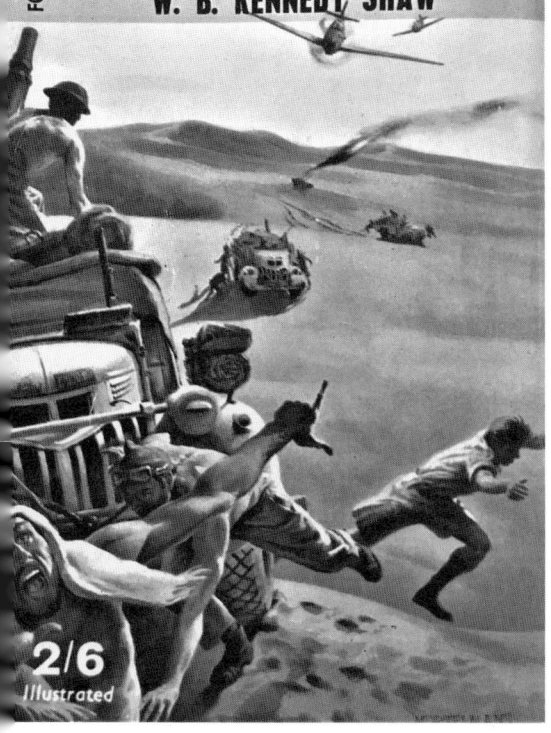

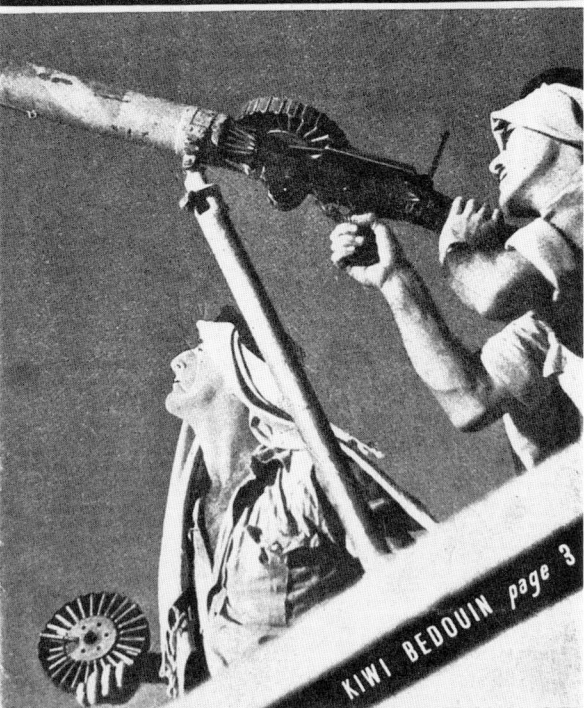

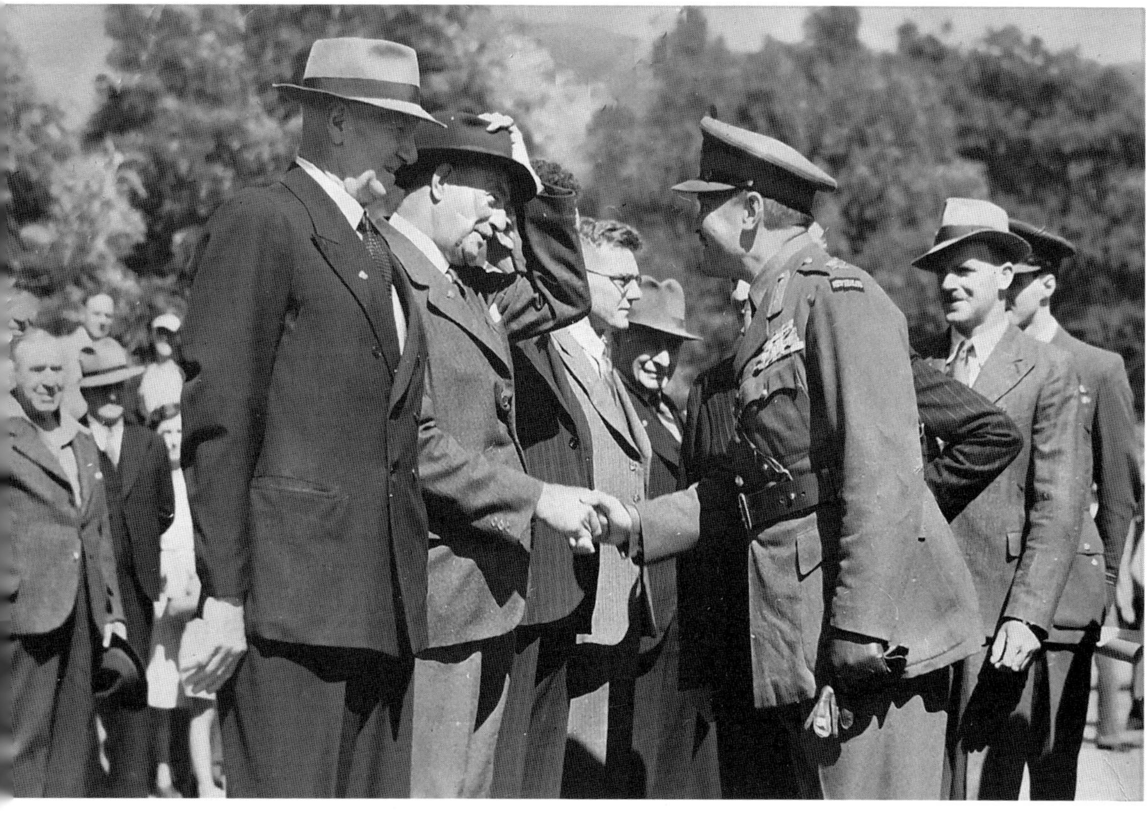

Post-war reunions of the LRDG (NZ) Association were well attended by veterans. Left: Paddy Mackay, Bill Willcox, Tony Dodunski, Cliff Collett and Keith Tippett.

On 5 November 1959, LRDG veterans attending the New Zealand release of the British-made LRDG film *The Sea of Sand*. Back left: Ron Davies, Ron Landon-Lane, Joe Eyles, Buster Gibb and Athol Hood. Front left: Bruce Dobson, Sam Lucas and Bill Hammond.

UNIT ASSOCIATIONS

Of the many Unit Associations which have sprung up since both World Wars, perhaps none has flourished to such an extent as the Long Range Desert Group Association.

Formed by a small band of enthusiasts, headed by Major C. S. Morris (M.C.) in 1947, the Association has grown from strength to strength until to-day there are over two hundred former members of the Unit paying regular subscriptions to make the Association perhaps the most solvent of all Unit bodies formed since 1939. With £400 in the bank, the Committee has every reason to be satisfied with its financial position.

The most important task of the Committee, is to keep members in touch with each other, and this is done by holding Annual Re-unions in Christchurch, Wellington and Hamilton in successive years. In addition to these re-unions, there have been two issues of a membership booklet showing the name and address of every known member, and newsletters are sent out to every member twice each year.

The Unit has its own tie, gold scorpions superimposed on a royal blue background, and Unit badges are in course of manufacture.

Marlborough had more than her fair share of members in the original Long Range Patrol, and of the thirty-two men who formed the first experimental patrol, no less than nine came from Marlborough. These comprised Joe Eyles, Ian Ferguson, Bill Hammond, Buster Gibb, Joe Zimmerman, Athel Hood, Ron Landon-Lane, Rex Beech (killed in action with the Patrol), and Clarrie Roderick (killed while leading Partisan troops in Italy). On the formation of the Desert Group, Marlborough supplied a further four members in Sam Lucas, Keith Yealands, Ron Davies and Jack Taylor. Local men are also well to the fore in the administration of the Association. Ron Lane is a Vice-President, Bill Hammond is Honorary Auditor, and Athel Hood is Honorary Secretary.

The relief of hardship amongst members is not overlooked by their cobbers and as a result of an appeal for assistance to one member who had suffered in health as a result of his service in the Unit, a sum of over £100 was raised and handed over.

As long as this spirit exists the Association must continue to flourish.

W. A. HOOD.

Thanks Athel, now what we'd like is a series of articles on incidents humorous or otherwise of this select band. Here are three extracts from "Popski's Private Army" by Lt. Col. Vladimir Peniakoff.

1. "The New Zealanders are all brothers and sisters and cousins, for they have all known each other from childhood and they are gentle, playful and earnest, like serious children who don't break their toys!"

2. Of the L.R.D.G. he said, "I graded their squadrons, drawn from various parts of the Empire, on a scale of human excellence, which ranged from the New Zealanders high on top, through the Rhodesians and British Yeomanry down to, etc.—"

3. "Though I was not strictly entitled to it, I was admitted to the New Zealand hospital along with my companions, and I felt I was receiving a great favour."

Later he says: "New Zealanders are New Zealanders and there is no one like them."

—Editor.

Paid your £10 to the Building Fund yet? Do it Now!

J. L. ANDREWS - Charles St. - Always Deliver the Goods - Ring 1348

An LRDG (NZ) Association newsletter page, early 1950s. It describes the association and quotes from Vladimir Peniakoff's (Popski's) book *Private Army* on how he saw the New Zealanders.

(**Above**) LRDG reunion, 1960s. Back left: Clarke Waetford, Alf Saunders, Dave Burnnand, Walter Ellingham, Tom McLelland. Front: Ron Moore, Bluey Grimsey, Alf Ferguson, Wink Adams and Doug McDonald.

(**Opposite, above**) NZ LRDG Association reunion in 1970. Left: Ray Gorringe, Alf Saunders, unidentified, Ralph McQueen and Len Hawkins. Sitting: Don Steele wearing his LRDG-issue *keffiyeh* and *agal*. He was the patron of the association at the time.

(**Opposite, below**) Buster Gibb (left) and Alf Saunders at a reunion at Picton, NZ in 2001. Alf wears his LRP badge on his tie.

LRDG Association artifacts. Rear: a mounted association vehicle plaque. Model of Ford V8 command car. Left: LRDG (NZ) Association rolls, 1960s. W.B. Kennedy Shaw's book on the LRDG published in 1945. LRDG Preservation Society woven badges.

A rare image of *Waikaha* taken at Abbassia barracks in Cairo, 1940.

The Chevrolet WA truck *Waikaha* recovered from the Egyptian Sand Sea in 1980. It is now displayed in the Imperial War Museum, London.

A magnificent *Waikaha* model crafted in metal by artisan Simon Willis, an ex-Royal Marine mechanic. This one-off museum-quality model is 460mm long and was a five-month build.

LRDG reenactors in Cambridge, New Zealand, 2017. Top left: Myles Gedye, who reconstructed the Chevrolet 1533x2 truck in the background, T4 *Tainui*. His father Norm Gedye, seated middle front, was the last remaining New Zealand LRDG veteran. He passed away on 21 December 2018 aged 98 and *Tainui* served as his funeral hearse. Second back: Phil Hobbs, Mike Jenner, Sean Rickard and Brendan O'Carroll (author). Sitting front left: Mike Hughes.

Appendix I

The LRP Lament

By Gunner C.O. 'Bluey' Grimsey, December 1940. LRP W & R Patrols.

It was written at the Citadel in Cairo when the LRP became the LRDG with the introduction of the Guards Patrol. It was his response to the news coming through that some New Zealand members had to return to their original units with the disbandment of W Patrol:

> They wanted soldiers stout and strong to cross the arid lands,
> To pioneer the rolling dunes across the Libyan sands,
> Where never camels trod, nor wog, nor Sudanese,
> Where never brush nor grass can grow upon the great sand seas.
>
> They wanted men who could, when wished, go short of food and drink.
> Be left unshaven and unwashed, yet not so much as stink!
> To stand up to the furnace blast of scorching sand and heat,
> Which drives into your eyes and mouth, and blisters face and feet.
>
> Now where to find these men made GHQ to wonder,
> Till Major Bagnold came along and stole away their thunder.
> I-N-N know where to find these men, he cried.
> If you just give me time, they come from one New Zealand,
> A land of sunny clime.
>
> And so it was they got us, tho' Freyberg, much annoyed,
> Said, 'Why should bloody Pommies send "my" men into the void?'
> However, now we'd started this we meant to see it through,
> And soon convinced the older hands we'd thrive out in the blue.
>
> No sooner had we shown them, than it was thought quite fit,
> To let the Tommies have a go and leave us in the shit.
> To go back to our units was all they told us now,
> If you don't, there would be one holy bloody row!
>
> So we'll go back to our units and fight in Greece or Spain,
> Or any God Damn country, for preference where there's rain.
> But don't forget when you read of scraps up on the border,
> New Zealanders have blazed the trail, we've carried out an order.

Appendix II

R Patrol Truck Names and Officers

Truck Names

The name and numerical panels on R Patrol vehicles were of white letters on black. The Tiki image displayed on the truck bonnet was green with a red tongue and red rings around its eyes. Photographic evidence shows that the Tiki could be placed on either the right or left side of the bonnet. Please note that the list of truck names shown below may not be complete.

Rotoairo	*Rotokakahi*	*Rotomanu*	*Rotowaro*
Rotoehu	*Rotokawa*	*Rotoroa*	*Rotowhero*
Rotoiti	*Rotoma*	*Rotorua*	*Rotowhio*
Rotokaki	*Rotomahana*	*Rotowai*	

List of Officers

LRP R Patrol
Capt. D.G. Steele
Lieut. C.A. Holliman
Lieut. J.H. Sutherland

R1 Patrol
Capt. J.R. Easonsmith
Capt. A.I. Guild
Capt. L.H. Browne
Lieut. K.F. McLauchlan

R2 Patrol
Lieut. C.H. Croucher
Lieut. J.R. Talbot
Capt. K.H. Lazarus
Lieut. J.M. Sutherland

Appendix III

A Selection of Images from Trooper Frank McKeown's Photo Album

Album introductory page. Trooper F.J. McKeown.

Men gather on a Ford F30 truck on the way to swim in the Siwa pools.

Well-stowed F30 trucks.

Supplies being sorted and loaded.

A dead buzzard spread out on the front a F30 truck.

Major D.G. Steele at the wheel of a Ford F8 15cwt. A 20mm Solothurn S18-1000 anti-tank rifle is mounted in the rear.

Trooper J.T. Bowler. Was later recorded as missing, presumed killed, 24 October 1943, on the island of Levitha in the Aegean.

Trooper F.J. McKeown in front of his truck *Rotowaro*.

Chevrolet 1533x2 30cwt radio truck, R9. The driver is Trooper M.E. Hammond.

Right, Captain C.H.B. Croucher, next to Major V. Peniakoff (Popski). They await the return of agents previously dropped off.

Trooper C. Kidd driving in Chevrolet R6, *Rotoehu*.

Left, Trooper J.A. Franks on a Dingo Mk 1A scout car of the King's Dragoon Guards.

A pair of heavily-loaded Chevrolets R3 and R5. The guns are covered against dust.

Trooper F.J. McKeown, unshaved after a four-month patrol, stands next to the truck *Rotowai*.

Radio truck R9 transmitting.

LRDG truck alongside a Bristol Bombay transport/bomber.

Trooper F.J. McKeown dressed for going on leave in Cairo.

A Chevrolet navigates a steep wadi.

Resting up for the night. The officer checks his charts.

Lance Corporal R.J. Landon Lane (left) and Private J.H. Jones about to go on a foot reconnaissance. Jones secures his equipment.

RAF crew picked up in the desert by R Patrol.

Trooper J.A. Franks poses against his Chev.

Bibliography

Primary Sources

Lance Corporal Mick Allen, LRDG Gunner/Medical Orderly. Interviewed by WO2 R.L. Kay, NZ Official Archives at HQ LRDG on 3 May 1943.
Dick Croucher, *LRDG Association Annual Newsletter. Trip to Zouar with R2 in December 1941* (1986)
Merle Fogden, LRDG R Patrol veteran. Personal interviews and letters, 1998–2000.
Buster Gibb, LRDG W and R Patrol veteran. Personal interviews and letters, 1998–2000.
Gunner C.O. Grimsey, R Patrol LRDG. Extracts from his diary 17 October 1940 to 10 February 1942.
Claude 'Bluey' Grimsey, written recollections regarding the creation of the LRP/LRDG badge, 16 June 1949.
Eric Harcourt, R Patrol veteran, *War Anecdotes* (1988).
Kennedy Shaw, W.B., *Long Range Desert Group* (London, Collins, 1945).
Ron Landon-Lane, LRDG R Patrol veteran. Personal interviews and letters, 1998–2000.
Lloyd Owen, Major General D.L., *Providence Their Guide* (Harrap, London, 1980).
Moynet, Paul, Le Capitaine, *Les Campagnes du Fezzan* (Publications de la France Combattante No. 54, London, 1944).
O'Carroll, Brendan, *Kiwi Scorpions: The Story of the New Zealanders in the Long Range Desert Group* (Honiton, Devon, Token Publishing, 2000).
Alf Saunders, W and R Patrol veteran. Personal interviews and letters, 1998–2000.
Don Steele, R Patrol veteran, recollection letters to Mr L.K. Kay, New Zealand War History Branch, Dept of Internal Affairs, Wellington, 12 June 1949.

The National Archives, Kew

All below relate to Ref. No. TNA: WO 201/815 268890:

LRDG Operation Report No. 17 by Captain J.R. Easonsmith, 1 April 1942.
LRDG Operation Report No. 44 by Lieutenant J.R. Talbot, R2 Patrol, 23 September 1942.
Appendix to LRDG Operation Report No. 44 by Sergeant L.A. Willcox, R2 Patrol, 23 September 1942.
LRDG Operation Report No. 48 by Lieutenant J.R. Talbot, 22 November 1942.
LRDG Operation Report No. 49 by Captain L.H. Browne, 2 December 1942.
LRDG Operation Report No. 52 by Lieutenant J.R. Talbot, 26 December 1942.
LRDG Operation Report No. 53 by Captain L.H. Browne, 4 December 1942.
LRDG Operation Report No. 56 by Sergeant C. Waetford, R2 Patrol, 21 January 1943.
LRDG Operation Report No. 59 by Lieutenant J.R. Talbot, 18 February 1943.
LRDG Operation Report No. 62 by Lieutenant J.M. Sutherland, 10 April 1943.
LRDG Operation Report No. 65 by Second Lieutenant K.F. McLauchlan, 27 December 1942.

Other Sources

General Notes of a Road Watch 17 March to 29 March 1942 by Captain J.R. Easonsmith, R1 Patrol.
Notes on the Long Range Desert Patrols by Lieutenant Colonel Ralph Bagnold, 11 February 1941.
Special Forces in the Desert War 1940–1943, Public Record Office War Histories, Kew, 2001.
LRDG/Nav/4: *Rapid Determination of Latitude and Longitude, Grimsey Method & Graphic Method* by Gunner C.O. Grimsey.

Index

Abbassia, 3–4, 9, 20–1, 39, 58, 238, 273
Adams, Wink, 270
Agedabia, 90, 105, 107–8, 185
Agheila, El, 108, 141, 146, 185
Ain Dalla, 35–6, 42, 240
Ain Dua, 233
Ain el Gazala, 77, 89
Aitken, Lt. D.J., 258, 261
Alexander, Capt. W.G., 186–7
Allen, L/Cpl. E.M., 19, 48, 58, 81, 146, 216, 221–4, 227, 230, 232, 246
Antelat, 107
Atkins, Sgm. R., 168–9
Augila, 166–7, 193

Bagnold, Col. R.A., 1–4, 7–9, 22–3, 55, 57, 61, 71, 83, 207, 221, 238, 240, 262, 277
Ball, L/Cpl. C.G., 20, 30, 42, 69, 81, 126, 214, 232
Ballantyne, Lt. L.B., 2–3, 9, 56
Baltet ez Zalagh, 94–5
Barce, 106–7, 259
Bardai, 119, 122–4, 126
Barker, Capt. R.F.T., 261
Barrett, Capt. D., 30, 70
Beale, Pte. D.O., 117
Beech, Cpl. F.R., 210, 240, 245
Benghazi, 73–4, 105, 107–8, 122, 141
Bir El Communia, 190
Bir Hacheim, 92, 107, 122
Bir Tala, 170, 172
Bir Tengeder, 90–2, 122
Blamey, Gen. T.A., 1
Bowler, Tpr. J.T., 146
Boys, Tpr. A., 230
Brown, Pte. F.R., 30, 42, 81, 98, 146, 216
Browne, Capt. L.H., 78, 92–3, 105, 108, 170–3, 183, 185–6, 194, 236, 255, 261–2, 278
Bruce, Lt. B., 190–1
Buck, Capt. H.C., 94–5
Burnnand, Dave, 270

Campbell, Pte. L.T., 126, 230
Chott el Djerid, 255

Churchill, Winston, 256–7
Clayton, Maj. P.A., 2, 4–5
Cleaver, Tpr. H.H., 177
Collett, Cliff, 268
Connelly, Tpr. A., 178
Cramond, Lt. A.R., 65
Craw, Cpl. M.H., 261
Crichton-Stuart, Capt. M.D.D., 7, 55
Croucher, Capt. C.H.B., 4, 7, 10, 58, 66, 91, 94, 119, 122, 126, 130, 261–2

Davis, Tpr. J.L.D., 58
Davies, Ron, 268
Denniff, Capt. A., 262
Derna, 95, 126
Dobson, Bruce, 268
Dobson, Tpr. E.J., 230
Dodd, Lt. R., 77, 94
Dodecanese Islands, 257–8, 260
Dodunski, Tpr. A.F., 69, 81, 126, 136, 167, 169, 175, 214, 241, 253, 263, 268
Dodunski, Heather, 263
Duncalfe, Cpl. R., 259

Easonsmith, Maj. J.R., 56, 73–8, 83–5, 90–1, 96, 100–1, 108, 122, 142, 146, 150–1, 154, 233, 256–7, 259, 265
Edmundson, Lt. F.B., 2–4, 30, 39, 57, 238
Ellingham, Walter, 270
Ellis, Tpr. E., 169, 195
Ellis, Tpr. L.A., 230
Emslie, Pte. J., 214
Evans, Sgm. T., 178, 187
Eyles, Tpr. J.W., 19, 62, 69, 91, 210, 253, 262, 268

Farr, Pilot Officer T., 39, 241
Ferguson, Alf, 270
Fisher, Tpr. C.L., 169
Fogden, Pte. M.F., 172–3, 178, 180–2
Franks, Tpr. J.A., 81, 85, 146, 160
Fraser, Lt. W., 90–1, 93
Freyberg, Lt./Gen. B.C., 7, 55, 62, 185, 194, 261, 266

Garet Khod, 72
Garet Tecasis, 74
Gazala, 90, 92, 122
Gedye, Norm, 263, 276
Gedye, Myles, 276
Giarabub, 40–1, 46, 48, 50–1, 72, 91, 93, 108, 121, 192–3
Gibb, Sgt. A.D 'Buster', 6–7, 30, 40, 51, 60, 81, 165, 207–8, 210, 233–46, 250–1, 253, 266, 268, 270
Gibb, Dee, 233
Gill, Pte. J.E., 126, 170, 175, 214, 230
Gorringe, Sgt. E.F., 185, 216
Gorringe, Tpr. R.O., 146, 192, 241, 270
Grand Erg Oriental, 255
Grimsey, Cpl. C.O., 21, 25–6, 31, 35, 48, 55, 57–8, 62, 81, 91, 95, 98, 122, 126, 133, 137–9, 159, 187, 197–8, 214, 223, 235–7, 262, 266, 270
Gueret el Halib, 92–3
Guild, Maj. A.I., 94–5, 100, 146, 172, 178, 257

Hammond, Tpr. M.E., 7, 19, 30, 48, 62, 64, 100–1, 126, 134, 149, 153, 177, 214, 219, 226, 246, 268
Harcourt Pte. E., 7, 17, 19, 30, 48, 61, 81, 232, 246, 253
Haselden, Col. J., 74, 83
Hatema, 147–8
Hawkins, Pte. L.J., 261–2, 270
Hayes, Tpr. R.D., 187
Hobbs, Phil, 276
Holliman, Lt. C.A., 2, 55, 93–4, 101, 253
Hood, Athol, 268
Hon, 190, 192, 223, 255
Hughes, Mike, 276
Hunter, Capt. A.D., 100, 171

Ineson, Pte. K.C.J., 187

Jalo, 9, 70–1, 108, 121, 165–9, 176, 192–3
Jebel Akhdar, 56, 73, 76, 107
Jenner, Mike, 276
Jones, L/Cpl. J.H., 173, 216
Jordain, Lt. A., 94–5

Kalansho Sand Sea, 72
Kay, WO2 R.L., 221
Kayugi, 119, 122, 126
Kennedy Shaw, Capt. W.B., 2, 4, 7, 70, 77, 100, 108, 126, 259, 266, 272
Kendall, Tpr. F., 221
Kinsman, Lt. A.H., 189, 191

Kitney, Tpr. E.W.R., 78
Kufra, 58, 62, 71–2, 77, 79, 121, 125, 147–8, 165–8, 170–3, 188, 192–3, 222, 224, 235–6, 240, 253, 255, 265

Landon-Lane, Lt. R.J., 30, 98, 130, 141, 172–3, 178, 216, 230, 261–2, 268
Lawson, Capt. R.P., 116
Lazarus, Lt. K.H., 260
Le Roex, Capt. F.E., 185
Lloyd Owen, Capt. D., 76, 100, 257, 260–2, 265
Low, Sgt. K.T., 106–7
Lucas, Pte. J.C., 100, 214, 217, 226, 268

Macassey, Tpr. J.L.P., 229
Mackay, Paddy, 268
Magee, Tpr. J.B., 230
Mahomet, Sgm. S.J.E., 126, 214
Mallet, Tpr. H.L., 126, 230
Marble Arch, 141–2, 147–8, 159, 192
Mareth Line, 184, 255
Mather, Tpr. L.F., 81, 243
Matmata, 255
Mayne, Lt. R.B., 90, 94, 99
McCraith, Capt. P.J.D., 55
McCulloch, Tpr. I.G., 94
McDonald, Doug, 270
McGregor, Sgt. P., 35, 51
McInnes, Tpr. I.H., 32, 214
McIntyre, Capt. P., 199–200, 210, 219
McKeown, Tpr. F.J.W., 84, 146, 216
McLauchlan, Lt. K.F., 186–7, 194, 261
McLelland, Tom, 270
McLeod, Sgt. A.F., 6
McQueen, Lt. R.B., 3, 56, 252, 270
McRea, Lt. D., 173
Mechili, 74–6, 92, 105, 122
Middlebrook, Pte. L.J., 178
Misurata, 172, 186
Mitford, Capt. E.C., 2, 4–5, 39, 56, 141, 233–4, 237
Montgomery, Gen. B., 185, 194, 256
Moore, Ron, 270
Murdoch, Pte. A.A., 214
Murzuk, 32, 78, 214

Nelson, Pte. G.H., 42, 62, 126, 214
Nofilia, 185–7, 197
Norton, L/Cpl. H., 187

O'Carroll, Brendan, 276
Olivey, Lt. J.R., 105–6, 108

O'Malley, L/Cpl. N., 171–3, 178, 180
Ormond, L/Sgt. A.R., 221

Parkes, Tpr. G.C., 146, 241–2, 251
Peniakoff (Popski), Lt. Col. V., 269
Pilkington, Capt. M., 170–3, 178, 180
Prendergast, Col. G.L., 83, 91, 187, 256–7, 259
Pressick, L/Cpl. A., 27, 78
Puttick, Brig. E., 1

Rail, Sgt. W., 230
Rawson, Tpr. R., 146, 178, 237
Redfern, Maj. A.G., 259
Reid, Tpr. P.G., 108, 178
Renwick, Tpr. A.R., 230
Rhodes, Tpr. F.D., 230
Richardson, L/Cpl. M.D., 173, 178, 181
Rickard, Sean, 276
Ritchie, Pte. T.E., 184
Rommel, Gen. E., 107–8, 114, 141
Russell, Pte. E.T., 26

Sadgrove, L/Cpl. A.D., 167, 169, 214
Sanders, Gnr. E., 165
Saunders, Tpr. A.M., 39–40, 42, 46, 48, 58, 81, 208–9, 217, 228, 270
Sceleidima, 107
Schaab, L/Cpl. J.L., 42
Sciuref, 190–2
Sebha, 187–8
Sirte, 93, 141
Siwa, 6, 9, 47, 56, 58–9, 69, 71–5, 77, 79–81, 83, 89–91, 93–5, 105–6, 116, 121–2, 124, 141–2, 175, 222, 227, 235–6, 240, 242–3, 248, 253, 264
Sollum, 73, 105, 180, 192
Special Air Service (SAS), 9, 89–91, 93–100, 103, 208, 256, 265
Spicer, Lt. E.F., 147, 192
Spotswood, Cpl. R.O., 6, 61, 75, 81, 146, 150, 216, 247
Steele, Maj. D.G., 2, 6–7, 9, 17–18, 30, 34–5, 37–8, 40, 44, 48, 55, 59, 61, 71, 73, 78, 89, 91, 93, 101, 103, 141, 189, 207, 233, 264, 270

Stewart, Tpr. A.M.D., 230
Stirling, Maj. D., 89–93, 95–6, 103, 190–1, 208
Stormonth Darling, Capt. M.P., 260
Sudan Defence Force (SDF), 165, 167–8, 176, 182
Sutherland, Lt. J.H., 2–3, 39–40, 56, 233
Sutherland, Lt. J.M., 192–3

Talbot, Lt. R.J., 147–8, 161–6, 168–70, 176, 187–9, 191, 199
Tazerbo, 58, 79, 125, 171–2, 188, 222–4, 250
Tinker, Lt. R.A., 30, 91, 107, 113, 130, 146, 192, 216, 255, 261
Timimi, 90, 92, 126
Tippett, Tpr. K.E., 268
Tripoli, 141, 173, 255, 266

Uweinat, 36, 38

Waco aircraft, 57, 61, 83, 116, 261
Wadi Farigh, 166–8
Wadi Hatema, 147–8
Wadi Tamet, 171–3, 185–6
Wadi Zem Zem, 185, 190
Waetford, Sgt. C., 2, 69, 106–7, 111, 119, 121, 125, 136, 166–7, 190, 193, 214, 236, 270
Waetford, Pte. E.B., 119, 121, 126, 214
Wavell, Gen. Sir A., 1, 5
Whitaker, Pte. F.J., 178
White, Lt. R.F., 258
Wilder, Capt. N.P., 255
Willcox, Tpr. L.A., 42, 48, 51, 81, 98, 107, 166–70, 175, 177, 230, 232–3, 268
Willams, Sgm. B., 208
Williams, Pte. R.R., 126, 146, 152, 200, 230
Williamson, Pte. J.H., 253
Willis, Simon, 263, 274
Wilson, Gen. H.M., 1

Zella, 172, 187, 189–90, 255
Zighen, 147, 167–8
Zouar, 7, 119–26, 128–9, 130–1, 133–4, 136, 214

Dear Reader,

We hope you have enjoyed this book, but why not share your views on social media? You can also follow our pages to see more about our other products: facebook.com/penandswordbooks or follow us on Twitter @penswordbooks

You can also view our products at www.pen-and-sword.co.uk (UK and ROW) or www.penandswordbooks.com (North America).

To keep up to date with our latest releases and online catalogues, please sign up to our newsletter at: www.pen-and-sword.co.uk/newsletter

If you would like a printed catalogue with our latest books, then please email: enquiries@pen-and-sword.co.uk or telephone: 01226 734555 (UK and ROW) or email: Uspen-and-sword@casematepublishers.com or telephone: (610) 853-9131 (North America).

We respect your privacy and we will only use personal information to send you information about our products.

Thank you!